ELUSIVE DAWN
FAIZ AHMED FAIZ - A PEOPLE'S POET
Centenary Publication

Edited by
Mohsin Zulfiqar & Fabbeh Husein

Supported by
ARTS COUNCIL ENGLAND

'Faiz Ahmed Faiz is a people's poet unparalleled in his quest for harmony, love and peace. In celebration of his centenary Kala Sangam is exceptionally honoured to offer this centenary publication'.

Dr. Geetha Upadhyaya, CEO of Kala Sangam

FIRST UK EDITION 2010
REVISED SECOND UK EDITION 2011

ISBN 978-0-9535373-4-1

Visit our website at www.kalasangam.org

Printed in the United Kingdom by Kudu Products, Leeds.
Published and distributed in the United Kingdom by
Kala Sangam, Bradford and Faiz National Organising Committee UK
Kala Sangam, St Peters House, 1 Forster Square,
Bradford BD1 4TY
info@kalasangam.org

Dedication

In the name of this day
And
In the name of this day's sorrow:
Sorrow that stands, disdaining the blossoming
garden of Life,
Like a forest of dying leaves
A forest of dying leaves that is my country
An assembly of pain that is my country
In the name of the sad lives of clerks,
In the name of the worm-eaten hearts and the
worm-eaten tongues
In the name of the postmen
In the name of the coachmen
In the name of the railway workers
In the name of the workers in the factories
In the name of him who is Emperor of the Universe,
Lord of All Things

The farmer,
Representative of God on Earth,
Whose livestock has been stolen by tyrants,
Whose daughter has been abducted by bandits
Who has lost, from his hand's breadth of land,
One finger to the record keeper
And another to the government as tax,
And whose very feet have been trampled to shreds
Under the footsteps of the powerful.
In the name of those sad mothers
Whose children cry out in the night
And will not be silenced by the defeated arms
of sleep,
Who will not say what saddens them
Or be consoled by tears or entreaties.
In the name of those beauties
The flowers of whose eyes
Blossomed from every curtain and balcony
And withered away in waiting.
In the name of those wives
Whose unloved bodies
Have grown tired of the treachery of beds
In the name of the widows
In the name of neighbourhoods
Whose scattered garbage the moon
Blesses every night,
And from whose shadows cries out
The fragrance of veils
The tinkling of bangles
The scent of loosened hair
The smell of passionate bodies burning in their
own sweat.

In the name of students
who went to the masters of drums and banners
Prostrating themselves on doorsteps
With their books and pens
Praying, with open arms, to be heard,
But never returned.
Those innocents, who, in their naiveté
Took their tiny lamps,
Their candle flames of hope, to where
The shadows of endless nights were being
given out.
In the name of those prisoners
In whose breasts the shining gem of the future
Burns, polished by the noise of the jailer's night,
To a star like radiance.
In the name of those harbingers of the days
to come
Who, like the flower with its scent,
Have become enamoured of their own message.

Faiz Ahmed Faiz

i

Contents

Remembering Faiz Ahmed Faiz

'He was a highly endearing person in addition to being a poet par excellence. I remain among his greatest admirers.'
Inder Kumar Gujral - Former President of India

'Faiz Ahmed Faiz was a socially committed genius and dedicated Communist poet. A particular lesson that every one of us who inspires for and works towards revolution must learn to commit the passion of commitment with creativity. He became powerful symbol of fight against oppression, defence of democratic rights and love for humanity'.
Sitaram Yechury - Editor Peoples Democracy and parliamentary leader Left Front India

'His moving and flowing metaphors have the fragrance of flowers of our land. His thoughts reflect the brightness of truth and of democratic aims which has illuminated the hearts of overwhelming majority of our people.'

Sajjad Zaheer (1905-1973) - Eminent Urdu writer and Marxist thinker *'Faiz Ahmed Faiz is the voice of wretched of the earth in the contemporary era. This voice is a song as well as a battle cry. It has the certainty of truth also the pain of the world; it has the thunder of resistance and of revolution as well as the lyrics of beauty and love.'*
Sibte Hasan (1916-1986) - Leading Pakistani radical writer, historian and active Marxist.

'Millions of people hear and sing his verses throughout Pakistan, India and Bangladesh as his imageries are drawn from our common history, aesthetic traditions, epics, religious symbols, and literary allusions. Above all, Faiz writes and protests the post-colonial conditions – of continued poverty and the neglect of the poor, inequalities and injustices, hunger and oppression – which afflict all of South Asia.'
Eqbal Ahmad (1934-1999) – Renowned political commentator and writer.

'It was not solely the excellence of his poetry that won him this position, but his poetry is nonetheless his most important legacy to us and demands our main attention.'
Ralph Russell (1918-2008) - British scholar of Urdu literature and a Communist

'Faiz was always the poet and a citizen. He, with realistic sense, was getting in touch with groups of workingmen, and would spend evenings teaching them reading and writing and the ABC of politics'.
Professor Victor Gordon Kiernan (1913-2009) - British Marxist historian and translator of Faiz Ahmed Faiz

'Faiz Ahmed Faiz symbolised for millions in the subcontinent and elsewhere the struggle of the people of the Third World to regain their self-respect and put an end to the tyranny of colonialism and its 'post independence' political and intellectual variants.'
Khalid Hasan (1934-2009) – Writer, journalist and translator of Faiz Ahmed Faiz's poetry

'Faiz's poetry articulates the aspiration, anguish, pain and suffering of not only the people of Pakistan but the whole world'.
Progressive Writers Association, Pakistan

'Have you ever seen someone raising voice against oppression and tyranny with all the gentleness at one's command? See Faiz Ahmad Faiz.'
Raza Ali Abidi - Renowned Urdu writer and veteran broadcaster

'Faiz was not only a great Urdu Poet but the 'Voice' of the voiceless multitude and of the suffering humanity. It found its expression in his immortal verses that were a balm for the pain of the suffering humanity. He says, 'Kisi ka dard ho, kartey hein apney nam raqam'. He

empathised with the wretched of the Earth but also taught them to resist and never to lose hope. Resisting the oppression and exploitation and keeping faith in ourselves is his legacy for us.'
Rahat Saeed - Joint Secretary of Progressive Writers Association, Pakistan

'Faiz was the 'Socialist Humanist'. It is no wonder that the silken softness, dewy translucence and soothing allure of Faiz's poetry have sustained revolutionaries and ordinary people.'
Amin Mughal - Leading Pakistani journalist and political activist

'Faiz greatness lies in his commitment for social change, for the establishment of an exploitation free society and for the emancipation of the downtrodden. He uses his creative skill for the cause of social justice excellently.'
Abid Hasan Minto, President of Workers Party Pakistan

'Faiz has come to symbolize the quest for freedom and equality, fraternity with the Third World, opposition to oppression and a thirst for peace. Moreover, Faiz is seen as the poet who felt that the pursuit of freedom was incomplete despite the end of British rule. It was he who wrote: Cha'lai cha'lo keh voh munzil aabhi nahin ay' ee (keep going, the destiny is still far away).'
Lisette B. Poole - American academic and journalist

'Neither jail nor exile could still the lifelong creativity and revolutionary commitment of Faiz Ahmed Faiz.
His words "So long as these hands are alive, so long as there is warmth in this blood, so long as there is sincerity in this heart, so long as there is strength in this mind" encapsulate the inexhaustible compulsion to struggle for peace and socialism of every true communist.'
John Haylett - Political Editor, daily Morning Star London

'Faiz Ahmed Faiz is a powerful ideological symbol of fight against oppression, defence of democratic rights, emancipation of oppressed people from all forms of exploitation internationalism and love for humanity.'
Dyal Singh Bhagri - President of Indian Workers Association (Britain)

'Faiz was a great a poet. Has influenced whole generation of poets and bestowed new trends to contemporary Urdu poetry. But Faiz as a person was greater than the poet. No poet can be a brilliant artist without being a better human being. To understand Faiz this is the best litmus test.'
Hameed Akhtar – Famous Pakistani intellectual and columnist

'Faiz Ahmed Faiz combined in him the finest traditions of the eastern people – their scholarship, their culture, and their humanism and he had derived full benefit from progressive western thought. He was the voice of his age and also the author of an alternative vision of life not only for his people but also for the whole humankind. This latter quality is making Faiz increasingly relevant with the passage of time. As the powerful nations of the world develop new weapons to enslave, oppress and exploit the weak and the poor, and as Pakistan faces increasing challenges from a new breed of blood-thirsty morons, more and more people are finding in Faiz's life and work the will and the strength to build a better future'.
I. A. Rehman – Writer, journalist and chairperson of Human Rights Commission, Pakistan

'Faiz was the first great writer I ever met, and through his oeuvre and his conversation he provided me with a description of the writer's job that I accepted fully. Faiz was an exceptional lyric poet, and his many ghazals (love poems), set to music, earned him literally millions of admirers.'
Salman Rushdie – Leading novelist and essayist

'Faiz Ahmed Faiz stands in the tradition of the great communists poets who celebrate humanity at its finest, expressing its triumphs and tribulations, while also challenging every manifestation of inhumanity. He devoted his life to the noblest cause in the world – even at the cost of his own personal freedom. People will recite his words long after the name of every petty oppressor has been forgotten'.
Robert Griffiths – General Secretary, Communist Party of Britain

Acknowledgements

Faiz Ghar has been very supportive to this project by allowing the use of poems as well as photographs. Salima Hashmi, while in Britain, encouraged the editors to work on the publication. We are extremely grateful for all the help received from all the people who are linked with Faiz Ghar, a Lahore-based organisation, committed to preserving the documentation related to Faiz Ahmed Faiz. In appreciation of this support, It has been decided that a contibution of the proceeds from this publication will go towards the Faiz Ghar, Lahore, Pakistan.

Dr. Geetha Upadhyaya, the Artistic Director and Chief Executive Officer of Kala Sangam –
Bradford-based South Asian cultural organisation – was the one who first suggested the idea of a centenary publication to honour Faiz Ahmed Faiz. Dr. Upadhyaya and Ajit Singh, Head of Progammes and Business Development of the organisation, worked closely with the editors and provided all the necessary support and financial resources to turn an idea into a concrete reality.

The patrons and officials of the Faiz Centenary National Organising Committee (UK) have been very helpful with ideas and suggestions. Pervez Fateh, the secretary of the Committee, despite his busy schedule, always made himself available to meet our demands for information about Faiz Ahmed Faiz. Editors are indebted to Nazir Tabbasum - a patron of the national committee - for typesetting the Urdu section of the publication.

Rahat Saeed, Joint Secretary of Progressive Writers Association Pakistan, provided us the photographs and other resources for inclusion in this centenary publication. Our thanks to Karachi-based artist, Hasan Mehdi, who managed to produce several paintings of Faiz in record time to be included here.

Editors are particularly thankful to two of Faiz's friends, Syed Badar Uddin Beider from England and Georges Fischer from France, for accessing valuable material, including photographs and letters from Faiz Ahmed Faiz, Alys Faiz, Salima Hashmi and Moneeza Hashmi. Our thanks to young documentary-maker, Leila Sen, for typing manuscripts and helping to decide the best translation of poems.

Credit for producing an attractive publication goes to Richard Beverly of Kudu Products and Stuart Mooney who had the patience and enthusiasm to work with us. Finally, we wish to register our gratitude to all the authors of articles and translators of Faiz's poems. We are particularly thankful to British-based writer Mahmood Jamal and Sian Sucha from Sweden for their invaluable support.

Mohsin Zulfiqar and Fabbeh Husein

Faiz Ahmed Faiz reciting at mushairara Delhi, 1955

Preface – Remembering Faiz Ahmed Faiz

FABBEH HUSEIN AND MOHSIN ZULFIQAR

Every now and then a person is born through whom greatness is lived. Faiz was one of these blessed humans. 2011 is his centenary year. This publication not only honors his greatness but also marks the end of centenary celebrations both in UK and the rest of the world.

The background to this publication begins in 2010 when a series of meetings were held across UK to organize the celebration of 75th Anniversary of Progressive Writers Association (PWA). These meetings were organised by the South Asian Peoples Forum (SAPF) in conjunction with Indian Workers Association (Britain) and other progressive organisations in Britain. The Bradford Declaration issued by SAPF noted that: 'The PWA, since its inception, became a major vehicle for national liberation, anti-imperialist and anti-fascist struggle in India. It also provided an important cultural platform for social transformation and against backward reactionary and feudal values. The PWA reflected the aspiration of Indian masses through the medium of culture. The movement attracted numerous artists across India and the PWA became one of the most powerful cultural movements in the world.

This powerful movement confronted communalism, caste exploitation and sexism, racial and religious antagonism. It openly espoused the cause of equality, social justice and socialism. It maintained that anti-imperialist struggle cannot succeed without supporting the establishment of a democratic and socialist system in India.

The movement attracted the support of giants of Indian literature, such as, Rabindranath Tagore, Munshi Prem Chand and Moulana Hasart Mohani. The PWA dominated the literary and cultural landscape for almost four decades. The literature produced in this period is unparalleled in terms of its impact on Indian masses and became an integral part of the arsenal of our struggle against imperialism and colonialism.

PWA has its following in the Indian, Pakistani and Bangladeshi diaspora in United Kingdom besides other locations in the world. As indicated above PWA meetings were held in Birmingham, Bradford, Leicester, London, Newcastle and other cities. They were well attended by progressive South Asian communities as well as local progressive people.

It was during this time, in 2010, that the idea of celebrating Faiz's Centenary surfaced with much gusto. As such these meetings in 2010 became a vehicle for organizing events across UK.

The declaration of PWA set the mission statement and the process to celebrate Faiz.

As a result Faiz National Organizing Committee UK (FNOCUK) was launched in early 2011 in an inaugural meeting in Manchester that outlined the programme for the centenary year.

The centenary programme involved over 20 political, artistic and cultural events that were staged in United Kingdom under the aegises of FNOCUK. These took place in Barnsley, Birmingham, Blackburn, Bradford, Harrogate, Leeds, London, Manchester, Newcastle, and Oldham. The events had contributions from distinguished

intellectuals, writers, poets, trade unionists, filmmakers, actors, singers, and competent lay people with admiration for Faiz and surviving daughters of Faiz Ahmed Faiz. Noteworthy comrades contributed to the programmes across UK. Some of these included Tariq Ali, Abid Hasan Minto, Raza Ali Abdi, A. R. Rehman, Salima Hashmi, Saqi Farooqi, Choudhry Mohammed Fateh amongst others. Early in the year, a website was launched which also became the official website of the Faiz Centennial Committee of Progressive Writers Association, Pakistan.

Simultaneously, in 2011, the idea of this publication came from Dr Geetha Upadhyaya, CEO of Kala Sangam, who saw it as a major commemoration to honour Faiz. The editors have facilitated the collaboration between Faiz Ghar, Faiz Centenary National Organization Committee and Kala Sangam to realize this book. Since the inception of the idea from Dr Geetha Upadhyaya, the editors have worked closely with Salima Hashmi especially during the time when she was involved in events in Bradford and Leeds. In recognition of this support and in agreement with Kala Sangam and with Salima Hashmi a contribution from the proceeds from this publication will be donated to Faiz Ghar.

This book has been compiled with the help of a range of resources. Internet searches, correspondence, telephone conversations with and visits to some of the contributors' have enabled us to collect and collate a lot of published and unpublished material. We have used articles, poems and translations from well-known contributors including Aga Shahid Ali, Shiv K Kumar, Dawood Kamal, Khalid Hasan, Victor Krienen, Sia Sucha, Rehman Qayyum, Hamid Rehman Sheikh and Mehmood Jamal. We have also included new material especially written for this publication such as that from Jane Holloway, Syed Badar Uddin Beider and George Fischer.

The book is divided into six sections. **Section One** consists of published and unpublished articles that give the reader an insight into the greatmans craft, life and the social, political and economic context of his contributions and his humanity. It examines Faiz as a poet and a person. **Section Two**, on the other hand, is very much Faiz on Faiz and we include selected autobiographical material from the great man. **Section Three** adds a European dimension to understanding him in his 'self-exile' times. **Section Four** offers the reader some of the greatest poems of Faiz in Urdu and in English translations. **Section Five** is a very helpful chronology in seeing Faiz's life at a glance. Finally, **Section Six** indicates a fulsome bibliography to enable the reader to undertake further inquiry into Faiz and his contributions to humanity.

In Section One and Chapter 1, we begin with a statement from PWA that was co-founded by Faiz in the 1930s. In setting the aims for the centenary year PWA declare their expectation as to how the centenary could act as a vehicle to promote 'peace and harmony amongst people of all races and nationalities to transcend religious, ethnic and linguistic differences'. In doing so PWA asserts the universality of Faiz in time and space.

This theme is further explored by Helen Goodway, in Chapter 2, where she looks back at the cultural forces and the historical context that defined Faiz's birth in 1911 and his death in 1984. In such a reflection she perceives Faiz as 'a man for all seasons'. However, she laments that Faiz is 'nowhere as well known and appreciated as he deserves to be in the English-speaking world'. Is it that or is it that the public relations machinery available to writers and poets in the late twentieth and twenty-first century were not deployed enough

or is it that his message did not sit well in the colonial and post-colonial world where English was and is still lingua franca?

Javed Ahmed Lone, in Chapter 3, also looks back into the social, political and economic rhythms of mid twentieth century. He focuses on the early history of PWA and its socialist ideals and how Faiz's and others crafted such values in their writing. Lone fondly celebrates these times. At the same time he recognizes that PWA voice may have only given partial independence when 'gora sahibs were replaced with apna sahibo' and when socialist writing was increasingly being replaced with modernist and de-contextualized writing leading to the 'here and now' of unfinished business towards a socialist revolution in the sub-continent.

The crafting of socialist values into writing without being obvious requires some technical ability. In admiration of such a skill and sensibility Gaugher Raza, in Chapter 4, explains how Faiz was able to blur boundaries of love poetry and revolutionary poetry. In particular, Raza admires the subversive craft entailed in Hum Dekhenge (We will see) where anti-dictatorship, anti-imperialist and anti-fascist sentiments are obvious to the discerning. This sophistication and distinction rendered him the ability to be subversive and transcend ideological boundaries and perhaps did not make him into an easy target like other freedom fighters such as Ashfaqullah, Ram Prasad Bismil and Shaheed Bhagat Singh who were easily identified, judged and killed by the British.

The craft of blundering of boundaries can seemingly give rise to perceived contradictions and enigma. Afsan Chowdury, in Chapter 5, examines these themes critically in Faiz's life with particular reference to emergence of Bangladesh in 1971. In doing so, Afsan questions the problematic relationship between being a poet and a Marxist and how Faiz was both until he was jailed in 1950 as a result of the famous Rawalpindi Conspiracy. With reference to Faiz, Afsan adds that 'people who dream of a better world are often condemned to become what history demands of them'. However, Afsan regrets that Pakistan, the country, reduced Faiz to just being a poet rather than a Marxist revolutionary poet. Perhaps that says a lot about the peculiarity of Pakistan in the context of its history of long and frequent waves of suppression and oppression.

Ikramul Haq, in Chapter 6, recognises this role in history for revolutionary poets like Faiz Ahmed Faiz and Pablo Neruda. In celebrating the commonalities of their lives, Haq highlights their contribution to poetry and solidarity against oppression and suggests how Faiz's and Pablo's lives were meant to serve the agenda of cultural revolution for all oppressed peoples of the world. In asserting that point of view Haq refers to the late Edward Said who emphasized the need of poets like Faiz and Neruda to expose the tyranny of the ruling elite and to encourage the ordinary to fight against them through solidarity at national and international levels.

It was no accident that Faiz Ahmed Faiz evolved into an international Marxist poet. He was not just shaped by the prevailing historical forces alone. He made conscious decisions which were expressed in his humanist, Marxist and internationalist sentiments. Mir et al, in Chapter 7, verify this by indicating that Faiz was an internationalist not only out of circumstances but also by inclination. In examining the poem: Come Africa, Mir et al inquire whether Faiz too was influenced by the then international racial stereotypes in his writing. This intimation is soon undermined when Mir et al concede that Faiz deployed his poetic aesthetic that he learnt from African-Caribbean poet like Aime Cesare who was one of the pioneers in addressing

racism and oppression in English and French literature. In this concession, Mir et al see Faiz as being an anti-racist, anti-oppressive man whether he was at home or abroad.

This moral continuity and consistency at home and abroad is also evident in Faiz's craft of writing. Narang, in Chapter 8, chooses one of his poems entitled *Dast-e Teh-e Sang* to appreciate how Faiz transcended from the personal to the social and from the micro to the macro. According to Narang, Faiz does this by appropriate choice of words, intentions in the silences between the both the present and absent meaning. Narang attempts to steer the reader into 'how not to or how to' configure Faiz's writing and offers useful direction. For example, Faiz's use of 'displeased atmosphere' is a metaphorical reference to 'tyrannical environment'; breeze that hurts 'becomes unjust order and its oppression'; 'fellow drinkers' is metaphor for fellows with social consciousness. In doing so, Narang powerfully argues that Faiz's writing is grounded in 'metaphorical edifices' of the oriental tradition where in an Althuserian way ideology, art and literature are intertwined.

Narang's observation on Faiz's gift in Urdu poetry and craft does not seem to mirror itself in his prose writing in English. Rakshanda Jalil, in Chapter 9, explores with some trepidation, this limitation. She focuses on Faiz writing in English when he was the editor of The Pakistan Times between 1947 and 1951. She critically examines the content, context and the actual craft involved in Faiz's prose writing in English. In doing she draws tributary attention to his most trenchant commentary entitled *What Price Liberty*, April 1948, where he deplores the inappropriate use of the infamous Public Safety Act by emerging Pakistan. She seems equally moved by his famous editorial in March 23, 1949 entitled *Progress of a Dream* and simultaneously expresses dismay at Faiz's glowing tribute to Jinnah on September 13, 1948 in the editorial entitled *To God We Return*. In evaluating Faiz's craft in English prose writing, Jalil concludes that the use of the English medium renders him 'trifle ponderous' and 'long-winded' and points to the understandable idea that Faiz was a better Urdu poet than a writer of English prose.

Jalil's celebration of Faiz marks the end of Section 1. We hope that we have done justice to the kaleidoscopic celebration and representation of Faiz by noteworthy authors.

No book is authentic in celebrating Faiz if it does not use some of his own writing to celebrate him, understand him and remember him from his own reflections. In this vein, in Section 2, we offer the reader Faiz on Faiz in three chapters – 10, 11, and 12.

We felt it was important to include Faiz's autobiographical notes in Chapter 10, if only to hear from the horse's mouth. Here, we get a sense that one is sitting in his study and he is literally reminiscencing in his usual gentle and shy manner directly to one about his father, family, childhood and how he began to write poetry. In doing so, Faiz gives us insights into his enthralling life before he became a household name and achieved the Lenin Peace Prize in 1962.

In his acceptance speech for the Lenin Peace Prize, in Chapter 11, Faiz illuminates his vision for world peace and informs us how only the 'foundation of love' between the peoples of the world will yield that dream. In the context of Asia and Pakistan Faiz saw that dream could come true through effective and responsible cultural planning.

In Chapter 12, Faiz explains why there is need for cultural planning. He does not only demonstrate the damage done by colonial period

but also illuminates, like Franz Fanon and Aime Cesar amongst others, the damage the colonized had done to themselves. In addressing that 'two way damage', he proposes a post-colonial blue print of a policy of social, cultural and economic planning for Asia and Pakistan that many a reader would feel is as relevant and needed as it was in Faiz's times.

This publication and understanding of Faiz cannot be complete without reference to Faiz's time in Europe. In Section 3, we set the scene in Chapter 13 and highlight how it came to be that he was in Europe on an on-and-off basis. We note that most of these frequent visits to Europe coincided with the anti-progressive situation in Pakistan besides the fact that he was invited to attend many a mushairas and public speaking engagements as a dignitary in Europe. We get further insight to how he spent his time in Europe through his very close friends and comrades.

One of his closest friends in Britain was Syed Badaruddin Beider. Syed Badruddin Beider, in Chapter 14, reflects upon a memorable lifelong friendship since they met each other in 1949. Beider admired Faiz as a great human being and suggests that no matter how one looks at Faiz ' you always look at his right side'. For Beider, Faiz 'wore a deeply human and intensely mellow message of love and good friendship'. Beider reflects upon the forces that informed Faiz poetry. Beider acknowledges that Islamic culture shaped the aesthetic of Faiz's poetry as evident in the 'ever-present fund of religious' references in his poetry but points out that did not make him into an Islamic poet.

George Fischer was another of his life long friends and admirers who saw Faiz as more of a literary and practical activist in his trade union activities. Fischer, in Chapter 15, charts the oppression of the trade unions and brutal treatment of its leadership and members through the life of Pakistan as a state. In doing so, Fischer highlights some of Faiz's encounters with the state as an active advocate of collectivism; reviews the timeless paper Faiz wrote on ' Problems of Cultural Planning in Asia and Pakistan', as in Chapter 12. Fischer points to the difficulties Pakistan experiences towards becoming an inclusive prosperous society. Fischers remembers Faiz as a loyal, courageous and serene man who was a ' crusader of the rights of the wretched'.

Faiz was not just a great intellectual and visionary but an ordinary man with child-like curiosity and immensely good humoured person who was an excellent guest. This is partly evident in Askari's account in Chapter 16 when Faiz stayed in Paris for a while.

In Section Four, we present the reader with a collection of 100 famous poems by Faiz and corresponding translations by the many. We hope that in reading these poems the reader will not only admire his craft but also recognize that 'personal is political' and that he was more an international Marxist than a celebrated romantic poet. This contention is well argued by many of the contributors in Section One. We are using his poems to reinforce that understanding.

We accept that selection of poem in an anthology is a subjective process. However, one of the primary objectives of this volume is to introduce Faiz to a new generation of people. Hence we have included many of the poems addressing international issues familiar to a non-Urdu audience. Faiz's poetry is still relevant to contemporary readers as the themes transcend boundaries and time.

It is interesting to note that the total poetic output of Faiz Ahmed Faiz is relatively small. Though Faiz started writing poetry at the age

of nineteen; his first poetry volume: 'Naqsh-e Farayaadi' (Sorrowful Imprints) was published in 1941 when he was thirty. In addition to the seven volumes of poetry, the last 'Ghubbar-e Ayyaam' (Dust of Days) was published after his death in 1987. Over fifty years Faiz wrote nearly 300 poems. It included 27 quatrains and a number of translations. It means that on average Faiz wrote six poems per year.

So what are the reasons for the popularity of his poetry?

Firstly, Faiz masterfully employed established Urdu similes and metaphors but provided new interpretations by addressing contemporary issues. His unwavering commitments to socialism and equality engendered fresh dimensions to traditional themes. He continued to follow the style and metaphors employed by the giants of Urdu poetry, i.e. the eighteenth century poet, Mir Taqi Mir (1723-1810) and the nineteenth century master craftsman, Mirza Assadullah Khan Ghalib (1797-1869). Faiz, like Mir and Ghalib, has penned poems in a lyrical style.

Secondly, despite being part of the communist movement, Faiz refused to apply the principles of social realism in mechanistic fashion. Despite addressing the contemporary issues in his poems - the division of India; the killing of Iranian students who were fighting against foreign intervention; the awakening of freedom movements in Africa; the military dictatorships in Pakistan or the haunting poems about the genocide in Bangladesh – have achieved an iconic status. This quality has alleviated Faiz to a galaxy of luminous twentieth century poets including Pablo Neruda (Chile), Cesar Vallejo (Peru) and Ernesto Cardenal Martínez (Nicaragua), Nazim Hikmet (Turkey), Mahmoud Darwish (Palestine) and Yannis Ristos (Greece).

Thirdly, the popularity of Faiz, apart from its political messages, has been the lyrical quality of his poems. South Asian classical music is one of the most complex and fascinating music systems in the world and according to its theory, different types of melodies should express different moods. Classical and contemporary South Asian singers generally employ well-established ragas and the poetry (ghazals, nazm or folk) provides the basis for conveying layered emotions by entwining music and words.

Mirza Ghalib still remains the favourite for ghazal singers in India and Pakistan. Ghalib's universality and the freshness of his language attract many singers. Similarly, the poetry of Faiz also enjoys widespread support among the singers from Bangladesh, India and Pakistan. After Ghalib, Faiz is the most popular poet among ghazal and contemporary singers. Both the political and love poems of Faiz are the essential repertoire of countless singers. The most heartening aspect of present-day struggle in Pakistan is the employment of Faiz's poetry and songs as an integral part of arsenal to mobilise and energise the population.

The universality of Faiz's poetry spurred a number of excellent translations. His poems have been translated by many individuals. The first major translation was under taken by his friend and fellow communist, Victor Kiernan, in 1962. Now we have access to many other excellent translations in English by Agha Shahid Ali, Ikram Azim, Estelle Dryland, Khalid Hasan, Mahbub-ul-Haq, Mahmood Jamal, Daud Kamal, Shiv K. Kumar, Noami Lazard, M. N. Menai, Riz Rahim, Sarvat Rahman, Sian Sucha, M. Yaqub and Muhammad Zakir.

Faiz poems have been included in several anthologies, too numerous to mention here. In addition to English, Faiz's work has been translated in many other languages including Arabic, Baluchi, Bengali,

Chinese, Czech, Farsi, French, German, Hindi, Italian, Japanese, Kazakh, Nepali, Russian, Polish, Punjabi, Sindhi, Singhalese, Turkmen, Swahili and Uzbek. Recently some of his poems have been translated in Danish.

In this centenary publication, we have included 100 poems. The internet has provided us the possibility of including less known translations – many by young people throughout the world. We are grateful to Faiz Ghar and the translators for their contribution.

At the end, in Section Five, we have also included a detailed chronology relating to life of Faiz Ahmed Faiz as well as an extensive bibliography, in Section Six, for readers to access other publications on Faiz.

In summary, we hope that this publication enables us all to re-assess and re-evaluate Faiz in the present political milieu in order to mainstream his vision. He is as relevant today as he was in the past. We appreciate that many left intellectuals in the world, including Faiz, looked in the 1930s and 1940s toward the Soviet Union as a source of human progress, virtue, and human rights. The demise of Soviet Union in the 1990s has been a great setback and many became disillusioned with the idea of Communism. What has not ended is the economic exploitation of vast masses of humanity. Therefore the struggle against oppression is bound to continue and Faiz will live through the engagement of others now and beyond. As such we need to continue to humanize rather than deify Faiz to enroll the ordinary. We need to see Faiz paradoxically as both an ordinary and a great human being to anthemise his vision for freedom, equality, solidarity and justice. We say long live the struggle and memory of Faiz.

Reference

[1]Bradford Declaration - Progressive Writers Conference 2010, http://pwa75.sapfonline.org/

Mohsin Zulfiqar and Fabbeh Husein, originally from Pakistan, are well known human rights activists and educationists. They have taught in schools, colleges, universities and in community settings. They have participated in social and educational campaigns locally, nationally and internationally. Both have been involved in Faiz Centenary National Organising Committe (UK). They are authors of several articles and books on education, anti-racism and the history of minority communities in Britain.

Section One
Faiz Ahmed Faiz
Poet and the person

Chapter I

On the Centenary of Faiz Ahmed Faiz
Statement of Progressive Writers Association

Faiz Ahmad Faiz was one of the most prominent poets of the Indian sub-continent who won unparalleled global acclaim. He symbolised all that is humane, dignified, refined, brave and challenging in Pakistani society. His poetry written in Urdu and Punjabi reflects his intellectual resentment and resistance against an unjust and archaic social order which he rejects on rational grounds as anti human; yet it has no bitterness. He remains loving and loveable, respected and respectful.

Faiz's poetry articulates the aspirations, anguish, pain and suffering of not only the people of Pakistan but that of the whole world, as well as their unremitting resolve to create a better and just society. His was the voice of sanity, for he sought peace in a troubled world.

Faiz lived in the times of literary giants like Josh Malihabadi, Sardar Jafri, Kaifi Azmi, Majaz Lakhnawi, Majrooh Sultanpuri, Pablo Neruda, Nazim Hikmet and many others.

Faiz was their equal, and can rightfully claim a place in this galaxy of world-renowned poets.

Faiz is recognised and respected by the literati of the world. His works have been translated in many languages including translations in almost all the languages of the erstwhile Soviet Union. The year 2011 will be the 100th birth anniversary of Faiz. This will be celebrated throughout the world by admirers of this great poet of the twentieth century.

Mission

The mission of the Progressive Writers Association (PWA) of Pakistan is to hold Faiz centenary celebrations throughout the year 2011, both in the country and abroad. The PWA Pakistan invites all institutions, organisations, groups and individuals from Pakistan and around the world to come forward and join hands in an endeavour to celebrate the 100th birth anniversary of this most prominent son of the nation in a befitting manner that will aptly project his ideals and the central concerns of his poetical work.

In Pakistan, at least one event will be organised every fortnight in one of the cities of the country. Efforts will be made to celebrate the event in as many foreign countries as possible, especially in those places where there is a significant presence of the Pakistani and South Asian Diaspora. We aim to enlist the participation of the indigenous intelligentsia, literati, artists, media persons and other segments of the civil society.

We are aiming to focus on the following foreign cites/countries where events to celebrate the Faiz Centenary will be organised:

India (Amritsar, Chandigarh, Delhi, Aligarh, Luckhnow, Allahbad, Bhopal, Hyderabad, Mumbai, Kolkata and any other cities where this might be possible); Bangladesh (Dhaka); Nepal (Kathmandu); U.K. (London, Oxford, Cambridge, Bradford/Leeds, Birmingham and Manchester); U.S.A. (New York, Chicago, Washington D.C., Houston, Los Angeles and San Francisco); Canada (Toronto, Calgary and Montreal); Germany (Berlin); Holland (Amsterdam); Sweden (Stockholm); France (Paris); Italy (Rome); Russia (Moscow); Gulf (Dubai/Abu Dhabi and Muscat).

If found practicable, events will also be organised in Cuba (Havana), Japan (Tokyo/Osaka), Australia (Sydney), Turkey (Istanbul), China (Beijing), Iran (Tehran), and South Africa.

Main Objective

In Pakistan: To promote peace and harmony amongst people of all races and nationalities, transcending religious, ethnic and linguistic differences.

Globally: To present Faiz as the ambassador of the soul and feelings of the people of Pakistan by projecting his poetry and other literary works, as well as his struggle for world peace and prosperity.

Central Theme of the Faiz Centenary

Aaiyey hath uthaein hum bhi
Baraey amn-e-alam aur insani khushhali

Come, we too should raise our hands (in supplication) For world peace, and for the prosperity of its people

Process

The aim is to spark peoples' interest in his person as a poet of the people and in his poetry as an inspiration to work for a better world and to gather all sections of society in the collective celebration of Faiz's Centenary—an amorphous yet synchronous event that would be democratic, inclusive and universal in its approach.

We would be working to create an umbrella association of individuals, informal groups and organizations that have an interest in Faiz and can act as 'nodes' in their part of the world. While the central theme of the celebrations – *Aaiye haath uthaaen hum bhi* for world peace and for the prosperity of its people (appropriately representative of Faiz's oeuvre) — would remain the defining sentiment, organisers would be free to opt for any idea or expression inspired by Faiz's life and work.

The celebrations will be a combination of online and on-ground activities. Online, because we can and will use our

2

existing network and overcome the physical limitations of geographical boundaries. On-ground activities will include academic conferences, seminars and lectures in addition to music and dance performances, theatre, films, mushaeras, and exhibitions of paintings, books and photographs where possible. All this, and what ever else can possibly be done. If Faiz has been re-imagined or his work has been rendered in song, on canvas or in a theatrical performance, and if Faiz has been translated, then our effort must be to make that piece of work widely accessible.

Faiz in London, 1968

Faiz when he was Editor-in-chief of The Pakistan Times, Lahore, 1948

Chapter 2

Life of Faiz – A Historical Context

HELEN GOODWAY

The Delhi Durbar of December 12th 1911, displayed all the pomp and splendour of an imperial triumph. Ostensibly, it was held to formalize the transfer of the capital of imperial India from Calcutta to Delhi. In fact, it served to placate many interests and groups which had agitated in widespread, mainly urban, areas of this vast and heterogeneous country in the wake of the partition of Bengal in 1905. The decision so to divide Bengal had been made in a despotic manner by Lord Curzon, Viceroy to the Crown. As well as bestowing flattering titles and honours on the elite of princely rulers, many of whom had enjoyed a measure of protection and status in return for their collaboration with empire, also, under the cloak of royal largesse, significant political and constitutional concessions were made. The Morley-Minto reforms, mooted in 1909, were implemented. As a result, limited provincial electorates and assemblies with similarly limited powers were established.

Their implementation was a crucial development. It fostered the increasing involvement of 'the new generation of Indian politicians'[1] in constitutional political activity. The new generation had emerged from the tumultuous and sometimes contradictory events of the era. The Indian National Congress, initiated in 1885, had already been very active in pressing for reforms that would benefit and include Indians within the imperial system of rule. After 1905, Congress became a regular focus for resistance to the Bengal partition proposal, a resistance that took many forms. The strong and widespread Swadeshi movement, encouraging the purchase of indigenously produced goods and the boycott of foreign ones, made a big impact. 1906 saw the founding of the All-India Muslim League, which supported Bengali partition for communal reasons, and which was, like Congress, to play a decisive role in the Independence movement and the eventual partition of the Subcontinent. In many ways, including the institutionalization of communal identities as public and political entities contained in the Morley-Minto reforms, the internal forces which would propel Britain, finally, into relinquishing its rule over the Subcontinent in 1947, and would create the nation states of Pakistan and India, were formed and active on a national scale already.

Different threads of nationalist sentiment were expressed contemporaneously in literary and intellectual terms. The economic nationalism of the Swadeshi movement was inspired by the writings of Dadabhai Naoroji and R.C.Dutt[2]. The great Urdu poet, Iqbal (d. 1938), who also wrote in English and Persian, wrote his 'Trana e Hindi' (Indian Anthem) around this

time, expressing in it 'feelings of national pride and a desire to assert national rights'[3]. The ironic poetry of Akbar Ilahabadi (1846-1921) consistently attacked collaboration with British rule, viewing this behaviour as a kind of prostitution:

> 'They give us learning – just enough to sell our services
> And understanding – just enough for government purposes[4].'

The early stories of Prem Chand, who wrote in Urdu and Hindi, written before the decade of the First World War, display him as a 'naïve nationalist', at this stage[5].

It was into this paradoxical world of India – the Delhi Durbar on one hand, constitutional concessions on the other; nationalist and communal stirrings leading to direct action and beginning to undermine the foundations of an empire apparently at its zenith – that Faiz Ahmed Khan[6] was born on February 13th, 1911, at Kala Qadir, Sialkot, in the Punjab. With his wife, Fatima Khan, Faiz's father, Chowdhry Sultan Mohammed Khan had settled there after spending time in the service of an Afghanistani ruler, it is thought. Faiz was born into relatively comfortable circumstances and at a time when families such as his were becoming politicized. Like the vast majority of Indians, his family lived in the shadows of, and, metaphorically, on the periphery of empire. The British were adept at maintaining an uncrossable divide between themselves and the imperial subjects[7].

The world of Pakistan, the location from which Faiz Ahmed Faiz departed this life on Tuesday, 20th November, 1984, aged 73, at the Meo Hospital in Lahore, was one unimaginable to the inhabitants, both subjects and imperial rulers, of the world of India in 1911. Pakistan, in the early 1980s, was in the throes of the 'state-sponsored process of Islamisation'[8] , which exacerbated tensions between different strands of Islam within the state, leading, for example, to serious Sunni-Shia conflicts in Karachi and confrontations between Deobandis and Barelvis in Lahore.[9] Complex language issues complicated such clashes. Human rights abuses were common, provoking protests from the Pakistan Human Rights Society as well as Amnesty International[10]. The martial law government of General Mohammed Zia ul-Haq, however, remained firmly in the driving seat, the regime buttressed economically by large receipts sent home by migrant workers and by vast support, military as well as economic, from the U.S.A., which saw Pakistan as being on the front line of the Cold War since the Soviet Union's invasion of Afghanistan in December, 1979. For Faiz, who said, 'What matters is the world outside and the people in it and what happens to them. What is important is the larger human equation of pain and pleasure'[11], this scenario must have been depressing.

Faiz, long established as an outstanding exponent of Urdu poetry and one of Pakistan's foremost poets, had entered into self-imposed exile in response to Zia's seizure of power in the autumn of 1977. He had returned to Lahore only in 1982. But, such was Faiz's popularity, the government felt compelled to order three days of national mourning in his honour when he died. The remarkable action of Zia's government testifies to the fact that, 'As a poet whom his countrymen are proud of, and at the same time a target of frequent attacks, Faiz's situation has been a contradictory one, reflecting the contradictory moods of a nation still – as Iqbal said of all the East – in search of a soul.[12]'

Nearly thirty years on, Pakistan is still a young nation and, until recently, was, not for the first time, governed by a form of martial law. Faiz's popularity remains undiminished to this day. During the month of November, events to celebrate his life and work are held annually in Pakistan and around the world wherever the Urdu-speaking diaspora has settled. And, of course, here we are, in the year of the anniversary of his birth, participating in a wide-ranging celebration of his life in his country of origin; and celebrations and events in his honour are being held worldwide.

Faiz Ahmed Faiz lived for seventy-three years: not an overly long span for modern times. But, the years in which he lived, 1911-1984, straddle the great majority of the seminal historical events of the twentieth century. He experienced directly the yoke of British imperialism in India and was, intellectually, at the heart of the struggle for independence, becoming a member and proponent of the Progressive Writers' Association in India soon after its inception in the mid-1930s. He participated in the Second World War as a Lieutenant-Colonel in the British army, working in Public Relations, viewing this involvement as part of the wider struggle to defeat fascism[13].

Faiz undertook a variety of important roles in the newly formed state of Pakistan starting with his editorship of the English language Pakistan Times between 1947 and 1951 and, simultaneously, the Urdu Imroz. In spite of suffering two spells of imprisonment, 1951-55 and 1958-9, the first under the threat of the death sentence, he continued to serve his nation as Chairman of the national Council for the Arts (1962-1965), as Vice-President of the Pakistan Trades' Union Federation, twice representing it at International Labour Organization conferences, and as a teacher, becoming principal of the Haji Abdullah Haroon College in Karachi. Even in exile, in Beirut, he was active as editor of Lotus, the Afro-Asian Writers' Federation journal, a position he occupied until his death.[14] I'll return to the subject of this editorship a little further on as an illustration of the essential qualities of Faiz's life and work.

Although this summary is by no means exhaustive, its range gives a clear indication of Faiz's wholehearted commitment, a quality that he brought to bear on all the various, interconnected causes that he championed. The nature of this quality will constitute a recurring matter of consideration in the course of the proposed biography and may be seen as an important element of the reason why Faiz was so highly regarded in his lifetime and remains so, if not more so.

Faiz Ahmed Faiz produced eight volumes of poetry, all in Urdu, beginning, in 1941, at the age of thirty, with *Naqsh-e-Faradi*[15] and ending with *Ghubar-ey-Ayyam* (Dust of Days), published two years before his death. Faiz's opus also contains two collections of letters[16], Mizan, (1962), a book of literary criticism and Hamari Qaumi Sakafat, (1976), a cultural commentary.

For someone whose poetry 'is……his most important legacy to us', as Ralph Russell wrote in his *Pursuit of Urdu Literature*[17], this is not a vast output. It is striking that, on the basis of three volumes[18], Russell says, 'By the middle of the fifties, he was already recognized as the leading Urdu poet of Pakistan[19].' Furthermore, Faiz's popularity as a poet was not confined to an educated *elite*. It extended, and still does, to all strata of the vast Urdu-speaking world[20] within Pakistan, India and the worldwide diaspora.

Kiernan maintained that Faiz stood in 'the position of an unofficial poet laureate'[21] in Pakistan in his lifetime. This does not mean the fusty, rather remote figure that passes for a poet laureate in Britain! Rather, the opposite, for poetry, par excellence, still, is the quintessential form of Urdu literature, conveyed well beyond the literati and an informed readership through a deeply embedded oral tradition made even more widespread by the modern means of communication of radio, television and film, and the use of Urdu as the lingua franca of the Pakistani nation.

On a personal note, I cannot describe adequately the feeling of delight and relief that swept over me at the first mushaira that I attended and participated in. Here was a cultural milieu in which it felt perfectly normal to be a poet! – No self-consciousness or fayness of the kind you find at English poetry gatherings.

Why and how Faiz Ahmed Faiz arrived at, maintained and maintains a unique position in the pantheon of Urdu poets are the underlying questions to be examined in the story of his life. The nature and content of his poetry, the confluence of social, economic, political and personal circumstances that form the context of his writing and their relationship to it, the essential personality and intellect of Faiz that fed into and coloured his multifarious activities, are all matters that contributed to the making of a man of creative stature. Not for nothing was he nominated for two years running, in 1981 and 1982, for the Nobel Prize for Literature.

This nomination came bang in the middle of Faiz's editorship of *Lotus*. Victor Kiernan, the distinguished intellectual, a friend and confidante of Faiz, kindly lent me his sole copy of the journal, No. 47/48-1-2/81. Faiz visited Victor Kiernan, in Edinburgh, to discuss about Lotus prior to assuming its editorship. They both had a laugh at the fact that the name, *Lotus*, sounded distinctly unrevolutionary, contrariwise to the intentions of it! A discussion of this copy throws a bright light on the nature of Faiz as poet, intellectual and human being.

In its heyday, *Lotus* was undoubtedly a constituent of the 'Communist Front', much as Encounter, the pre-eminent contemporaneous journal, was for the 'Western Axis' (aka, US). Both journals, however, in spite of their glaringly obvious political agendas, contributed substantially to the world(s) of literature.

In the particular issue of *Lotus* under discussion, a third of it is dedicated to Mongolian literature in the form of a Special Section. I guess this is an almost unique occurrence. What we are presented with is what might be termed 'heroic realism', with works extolling the virtues of the patriotic young and the stoicism of the long-suffering older peasantry. Some of it reaches the heights, as in this beautiful and enigmatic poem by Luvsandambyn Khuushan (b.1929) and translated by D. Altangerel:

> I shall rein in my horse
> In the middle of the open field,
> And let him recover his breath
> Before the long journey.
> I shall throw myself on the ground
> To feel freedom.
> Suddenly, I am troubled
> By the sight of the blessed earth.
> Then I remember
> The sweet fragrance
> Of the old coat
> My mother used to wear
> When milking the cow.

There is much else besides: a long, scholarly article by Josif Braginsky about the universally recognized pioneer of medieval Science, Philosophy and Letters, Ibn Sina, better known to European audiences as Avicenna; and a similarly meaty study of the novelist Prem Chand and his relationship with the Indian village by Dr. P.C. Joshi. Under the categories Studies, Poems, Anniversaries, Short Story, Jubilees, Reportage, Lotus Prize Winners, From the Afro-Asian Library and Song, a massive swathe of cultures is portrayed. Altogether, the issue is a fascinating, wide-ranging read.

Its editorial is entitled, 'Towards a Planetary Culture'. Essentially, it explores the perceived possibilities of that era for the formation of 'A time when man, having accumulated in his consciousness the culture, the historical and spiritual

experience of all countries and peoples, will be able to live with the wealth of that whole which is its essence, the real core of the universal concept of culture.' It asks the question, 'Is it possible to conceptualize a universal culture which overrides and yet does not obliterate the specificities of the diverse cultures of different cultures and their peoples?'

In response to the question, the editorial analyses the forces at work that may promote the proffered ideal state of affairs; the replacement in some parts of the world of the cultural hegemonies of elite economic, social and political groups by the new configurations of class power; the effects of the then, relatively recent triumph of anti-colonialist movements; a greater unanimity of purpose towards a 'more just and humane world order based on common moral and cultural values.' And it analyses the forces ranged against harmony and creativity: in the cultural field, the efforts of elites to pervert the minds of people particularly 'in countries of the Third World, by a deluge of anti-cultural trash that extols crime, violence and profligacy.' The latter is an accurate summation of conditions in the present world, within and across cultures, describing US cultural, political and military hegemony and imperialism, assisted, to all our shame, principally by the UK State.

The editorial is unsigned, in the normal manner, but its respectful tone, its intellectual rigour combined with its great, humane optimism, contains the essence of Faiz Ahmed Faiz's life and work.

Clearly, the life and works of Faiz Ahmed Faiz were, and are known beyond the boundaries of the Urdu-speaking world. Not least because of his Marxist sympathies, Faiz was recognized as a figure of political, as well as literary, importance by the U.S.S.R. In 1962, he was awarded the Lenin International Peace Prize. Significantly, there has been a fairly recent publication of a biography of Faiz in Russian by the great expositor of Faiz's life and work, Dr. Ludmila Vassilyeva. His poetry has been translated into many different languages, notably into several languages of India, including Bengali, as well as German, Swedish and Russian. Selections of his poetic output have been translated into English[22]; though, as yet, there is no complete works extant in English. (I think I'm right in saying this, although I have not yet had a good look at Riz Rahim's translations that have come out in the US). This omission illustrates the point that Faiz is nowhere near as well known and appreciated as he deserves to be in the English-speaking world. The reasons for this lamentable state of affairs will be explored in the process of my extended work, including a thorough look at the cultural effects of the residual and negative legacy of imperialism and global post-imperial politics. The work will seek to address and redress the matter, a situation made all the more surprising in view of the fact of

10

the long-lasting marriage of Faiz with Alys George, a Scotswoman of remarkable qualities in her own right.

Whilst Faiz Ahmed Faiz has been claimed, informally, as Pakistan's national poet, as Rudolph Rocker says, 'Culture as such is never national, because it always extends beyond the political frame of the state structure and is confined by no national frontier[23].' With his expression in poetry of the universal themes of love, hope, despair and his use of them as powerful political metaphors whose relevance is just as fresh and resonant in the world's contemporary circumstances as those in which the poems were formed, Faiz's work and his life's work present us with the story of 'a man for all seasons'.

References

[1]David Ludden, India and South Asia: A Short History, Oneworld Publications, Oxon., England, 2002, p. 197.

[2]Ibid, p.193.

[3]Ralph Russell, The Pursuit of Urdu Literature, Zed Books Ltd., London and New Jersey, 1992, p.182.

[4]Ibid. p.133, III, 1402 of 'Kulliyat'. 1978; Mere Dil Mere Musafir (My Shadow, My Heart), 1981; Ghubar-e-Ayyam (Dust of Days), 1982.

[5]Ibid, p.197.

[6]He took the pen-name Faiz as a writer, becoming known universally as Faiz Ahmed Faiz.

[7]For an extensive and detailed portrayal of the nature of this divide, read, Narad C. Chaudhuri, Autobiography of an Unknown Indian, Macmillan, London, 1951.

[8]Ian Talbot, Pakistan, A Modern History, St. Martin's Press, N.Y., 1988, p.251.

[9]Ibid, p.251.

[10]Ibid, p.250.

[11]Faiz on Faiz, translated from Urdu by Khalid Hasan, and reprinted in Selected Poems of Faiz in English, rendered by Daud Kamal, Ahmed Bros., Karachi, 1984.

[12]Victor Kiernan, Poems of Faiz, Vanguard Books (PVT) ltd., 1971, p.27.

[13]Professor Fateh Mohammed Malik, Faiz, fascism and Mahatma Gandhi, in The Faiz, vol.1, Issue 1 and 2, July/August, 2004.

[14] Yaqub's Selection and Translation of Poems by Faiz Ahmed Faiz, Jacobs New Agents, Notts., England, 1987, A Biographical Note on Faiz Ahmed Faiz.

[15]The title consists of the first two words of Ghalib's first ghazal of his divan. Information from Ralph Russell, op. cit., p.275. In note 2 to Chapter 14, Russell says, 'The titles of Faiz's eight collections defy translations......Naqsh i Faryadin (sic)...carries something of the sense of an appeal against injustice...'

[16]Salibain Mere Darichey Main (Letters from Prison), 1976 and Ma-O-Saal-e-Aushanai (Letters to Friends), 1980.

[17]Ralph Russell, op. cit., p.229.

[18]Naqsh-e-Faradi, 1941; -- (Wayward Breeze), 1952; Zindan Nana (Reminiscences of Prison), 1956.

[19]Ralph Russell, op.cit., p.229.

[20]According to the latest U.N. statistics regarding numbers of speakers for given languages, Urdu speakers rank third in the world, after Chinese and Hindi and before English. (Precise source will be provided).

[21]Victor Kiernan, op. cit., p.26

[22]Victor Kiernan, op. cit.; The True Subject, Selected Poems of Faiz Ahmed Faiz; Naomi Lazard, transl., Princeton University Press, 1998; Yaqub, op. cit.; Daud Kamal, op. cit. Compendia of Urdu poetry not included.

[23]Rudolph Rocker, Nationalism and Culture, transl., Ray E. Chase, Rocker Publication Committee, Los Angeles, 1937.

Helen Goodway is a poet, performer and the editor of a literary magazine Tadeeb International. She has been engaged in promoting Young Writers Project involving young people in Lahore and Bradford. Currently she is writing a book on Faiz Ahmed Faiz. Her article is appearing for the first time in this publication.

Faiz Ahmed Faiz reiting at a Mushiara, Karachi, 1976

Chapter 3

Faiz and the lost Cause of the Last Generation: An Incomplete Revolution

JAVAID AHMAD LONE

It was not a new phenomenon to use art for procuring a specific social aim or using it as an instrument to gain individual purposes. Art, or so to speak literature, has always been seen as a proper medium to impart instruction along with its delights and amusements. According to Faiz Ahmad Faiz "Progressive Writers' Movement has always been there, since literature began....before the Movement, there were other progressives-men like Shiekh Saadi[1] and Iqbal".[2] There is not only a single reason behind the inception and creation of the Progressive Writers Association. The turbulent decade of 1930s was fraught with multiple historic episodes. Such a situation helped this movement to be launched on broader scale than any other literary movement before in south Asia.

It was the time when Ottoman Empire had ended with the rise of Turkish nationalism at the hands of Mustafa Kamal "Ata-Turk"[3]. Financial crises had begun in 1929 resulting in the shape of a depression which had never been felt before. The repercussions of such episodes were not region specific but they were felt globally. India was fighting a decisive battle for independence. The starting years of the 30s were the years of Non-cooperative Movement.

It was one of the evenings of those years when a small group of few Indian visionaries had got assembled in London's Nanking hotel on 24 November 1934, which include Jyotirmaya Gosh, Mulk Raj Anand, and Sajjad Zaheer, who were not only drawing a road-map for Indian literature but they were also weaving a dream of a socialist India. Russia was a success story and they wanted to follow the same path both in literal terms and at literary level. Those were the years when the concept Partiinost (party literature) had emerged of Russian literary scene, culminating in the creation of a single Union of Soviet Writers in 1934. Though the above act had been largely denigrated by majority of western critics as "propaganda Instrument", Sajjad Zaheer and his companions thought it fit for Indian environs where the literature had to be purposive in order to depict the actual reality and perform the function of public awakening. Thus on April 10, 1936 the first All-India Progressive Writers Association successfully took off at Luckhnow where Munshi Premchand urged Indian writers to change their standard of beauty. But at the same time the conference of the Progressive Writers Association indicated a potential snag in the texture of linguistic horizon of India. "Out of all twenty-five Uttar Pradesh delegates not one represented Hindi writers".[4]

Punjab was perhaps the most fertile land where the writers having Marxist bent of mind gave their full support to the movement. Faiz Ahmad Faiz, Ahmad Nadim Qasimi, Zahir Kashmiri, Sahir Ludhianvi, Krishan Chandar, Rajendra Singh Bedi, and Upendar Nath Ashk include the important ones.[5] The works of Russian writers, Chekov, Gogol, Turgenev, and Gorki had become popular among Indian writers. The middle class educated circle of Punjab was highly charged with the Marxist ideas. Some of the friends of Faiz "who had come back from Oxford, had become Marxists".[6] It is how Faiz got introduced to Marxism. Faiz himself narrates one of the episodes of his life:

"In 1935, when I started teaching at a college in Amritsar, the young teachers there used to discuss upon the same issues. One day my colleague (late) Sahibzada Mahmood-uz-Zaffar gave me a thin booklet and asked me to go through it... but he advised me to be cautious since it had been declared unlawful. I read it in a single sitting. Rather more than once".[7]

Thus, Faiz became an active member of Progressive Writers Association and participated in its conference in 1938 which took place at Allahabad.[8] The Progressive Writers Movement, according to Faiz "was not a Communist or Marxist as such" but only "a sort of realistic movement".[9] This sort of realism had already been started by Indian writers from the end of nineteenth century. One of the main reasons behind this development was the rise of nationalistic feelings among the common Indian masses. Being a part of this whole milieu, writers started giving vent to such feelings in a realistic or semi realistic manner.

"Consciously or unconsciously literary realism and freedom struggle were the essential elements of each other and this relationship between the two was very essential. Literary realism gave impetus to freedom struggle and freedom struggle helped our realism to achieve a discipline of its own".[10]

Progressive Writers Movement helped the writers to break free from the classical cliché, orthodox morality, and feudal imagery. It widened the horizon of Urdu poetry by introducing the contemporary realistic themes of social life. It liberated the writers not only from the cocoon of self but also from the sectarian and nationalistic bondages by exposing them to the revolutionary events taking place at a global level. It was the time when poets threw away the hackneyed content to adopt a new ideology and started revolutionizing their classical and tattered poetic form. It was the same time when Faiz wrote the poems like:

Mujh se pehli si muhabbat meri mehboob na mang...

Though he revolted against the use of classical content but he

14

kept on using classical diction in order to secure an aesthetic goal along with a new and realistic message. There is a resolution in Faiz. His compositions are packed with hope and optimism, strength and resilience. He raises a voice of revolt against tyranny, repression, and exploitation. While doing this he never forgets to abide by the rules of decency and respectability. Like other writers of the Movement, including Hasrat Mohani, Rasheed Jahan, Sshibzada Mahmood-uz-Zaffar, Asrar-ul-Haq Majaz, Makhdoom Mahi-ud-Din, Ali Sardar Jafri, Upendra Nath Ashk, Josh Malihabadi, N.M. Rashid, Firaq Gorakhpuri, Meeraji, Jannisar Akhtar, and Akhtar-ul-Eeman, he never takes to empty sloganeer-ism.[11]

Faiz expresses his realistic and progressive feelings in a unique style of his own and preserves the poetic qualities of language with a consummate ease. Faiz always preserves his individuality by not mingling into the trivialities of his age. He "kept himself aloof from the extreme-isms of progressivism. He was perhaps the only progressive poet whose progressivism helped poetry equally as his poetry helped progressivism. In others, either their poetry got injured by progressivism, or their poetry was not able to do any good to progressivism".[12] Whatever the standard or style of their writing, the majority of the writers involved with the Movement had a firm belief in Marxist ideology. The aim of their writings according to them was to resist the imperialism, capitalism, and fascism and their hegemonic order. They knew that the dawn of freedom was very near but mere independence was not their goal. They were under the complete and constant spell of the Russian Revolution and hoped for the same system of government for their own nation.

"Since most of the leadership and much of rank-and-file of the PWA was composed of the Leftist poets and writers; the goal of the anti-colonial struggle was seen as not merely independence, but the formation of a socialist society".[13]

Poets sung the songs of resistance in a tone of anticipation for a new and red dawn. Majaz wrote:

> Kohsaroonki taraf se surkh aandhi aayegi
> Jabaja aabadiyon main aag si lag jayegi
>
> A red storm is approaching from over the mountains
> Sparking a fire in settlements.[14]

And in the same vein Makhdoom Mahi-ud-Din composed his poetry to welcome the socialist dawn of independence.

> Lo surkh sawera aata hai, aazadi ka, aazadi ka
> Gulnar tarana gata hai, aazadi ka, aazadi ka
> Dekho parcham lehrata hai, aazdi ka, aazadi ka
>
> Behold the red dawn of independence arrives
> Singing the red anthem of liberty
> And look, the banner of freedom waves in the wind.[15]

Indeed the long awaited dawn of the independence arrived, but it was not the 'red dawn' of the dreams of those movementeers associated with the Progressive Writers Association. It too, had its redness, but this redness came from the blood of the victims of the partition.[16] There was none among the progressive writers who could be seen singing whole heartedly the songs of celebration. Indeed, they composed dirges to lament a faulty and incomplete revolution. Ahmad Faraz exhorted his countrymen to come out of the frenzy of celebration:

> *Ab kis ka jashn manate ho*
> *Us desh ka jo taqseem hua*
> *Us desh ka geet sunate ho*
> *Jo toot ke hi tasleem hua*
>
> *Now what do you celebrate?*
> *That country was torn into two*
> *Whose song do you sing*
> *Of the nation that came into being only upon being broken?[17]*

It was the Indian bourgeois society which replaced the foreign colonial authorities. The fruits' of revolution could not reach to the grass root level. The Progressive Writers tried to put the reality and the myth of independence before the common masses. They boldly expressed their feelings. As Sahir Ludhianvi said:

> *Ye jashn jashn-e-masarrat nahin tamasha nahin tamasha hai*
> *Naye libas main nikla hai rehzani ka jaloos*
>
> *This is not a celebration of joy, but a vulgar spectacle*
> *The same procession of robbers has emerged wearing new clothes.*

Faiz, in Pakistan, had the same feelings for all that. He also lamented for the loss of a 'clear dawn' of independence. His poem "Subhe Aazadi" (The Dawn of Freedom) is perhaps the masterpiece among this sort of poems.

> *Ye dag dag ujala, ye shab gazeedah sahar*
> *Ki intizar tha jis ka ye who sahar tou nahi*

After going through this traumatic disillusionment the movementeers urged themselves to go through pros and cons of the disappointing and ill fruition of their dreams. Sahir Ludhianvi wrote:

> *Aawo ki aaj gour karain is sawal par*
> *Dekhe the hum ne jo, who haseen khwab kya hue?*
>
> *Come and let us ponder on the question*
> *The beautiful dreams of ours, what became of them?[18]*

Independence and its aftermath was a great blow for the Progressive Writers Movement. It divided them into two parts like the subcontinent itself had got divided. But they had a great faith in their cause. They knew that this freedom was no 'freedom' at all, and they pledged to keep moving forward until the original goal is not achieved. This pledge can best be noticed in Faiz, who says:

Abhi giraniye shab main kami nahi aayii
Najate deeda wo dil ki ghadi nahin aayii
Chale chalo ki who manzil abhi nahi aayii.

The burden of the night still weigh us down
The eye and the heart are still not free
Move on, for our destination hasn't yet been arrived.[19]

The Progressive Writers Movement in Urdu had "thrived because it spoke to its time, its history and its politics".[20] But the wind of time and circumstances were now blowing against its direction. The poets and writers associated with the Progressive Writers Movement lost their earlier power and enthusiasm. As Wamiq Jonpuri rightly says:

Pabandiyon main the tou dikhate the moujze
Aazadyon mai shobdahgar ho ke reh gaye[21]

While in constrains we used to show miracles
Now being free, have become mere jugglers.

The conflict between Urdu and Hindi languages which was already there re-emerged in a new and communal shape. Urdu, which was earlier seen as an emblem of communal harmony, fell prey to communal forces. "Urdu" as a language in India "suffered a debilitating blow when it became identified as the language of Pakistan, and by specious extension, the language of Muslims..."[22]

Jin shehron main goonji thi Galib ki sada barson
Un shehron main aaj Urdu benam-o-nishan thehri
Aazadi-e-kamil ka ailan hua jis din
Maatuub zaban theri, gaddar zaban thehri

The same cities where once Ghalib's voice resounded
Have now disavowed Urdu, made it homeless
The day that announced the arrival of freedom
Also declared Urdu a cursed and treacherous language.[23]

The movement suffered due to various internal and external reasons. Progressive Writers Association had been from its very beginning a "group of committed socialists".[24] But it was not mandatory for anyone to have this type of ideology for becoming the member of this association. The majority of its members had no particular political ideology. The movement became a shaping force for Urdu writers for composing the songs of resistance and the narratives of revolt. The focus of the majority of writers who were directly or indirectly associated with The Progressive Writers Association was freedom of the country. Many of them dispersed and went to their respective ways when this goal was achieved. After directly confronting with communists, the non-communist members of Progressive Writers Association left and 'some of them' became 'the mouthpieces in return for benefits received directly or indirectly from the new Congress government'.[25] Others, who were ideologically motivated to follow a Socialist way, had their individual ideas about it. In this context Faiz says:

"Since there was agreement on...basic points, a movement

came into existence. It was a united movement. With independence, the first objective was met. However, it was soon evident that true independence had yet to be achieved. Everyone had his own formula. There were different views on how best to reach the goal. So, in that since, the Movement did suffer from schisms".[26]

As the graph of communal disharmony had been at its highest during the days of Independence, it too disturbed the unity of the Progressive Writers Association. Some of the communal elements had crept in or due to the unfavorable environment some of the members had got affected by the broader communal climate of those days, which also proved harmful for the organization of the Movement.

'In his book Tarraqi Passand Adab Ali Sardar Jafri...admits that by 1949, extremism and narrow-mindedness of a sort had entered the movement: 'The partition and the communal riots so impaired the conditions that some progressive writers moved away from progressivism, some became partisans of communalism and fell in the pit of decadence'.[27]

Some of the opponents of the Progressive Writers Association find faults even in the very idea of inception of the movement. "One of the reasons" according to Hansraj Rehbar, "was the distance of those young movementeers who started it in London with a lesser understanding of India's indigenous conventions of literature and politics".[28] Whatever be the actual reality, the movement was very successful in its heydays. Not only Urdu writers like Hasrat Mohani, Josh Malihabadi, and Firaq Gorakhpuri, but many literary giants of Indian literature like Rabindranath Tagore and Sarojini Naidu had also supported it. Some writers of other Indian languages who favoured the Progressive Writers Movement from the very beginning are 'the Telugu poet Sri Sri, the Gujrati poet Umashankar Joshi, the Punjabi writer Gurbaksh Sing and the Marathi writer Anna Bhasu Sathe'.

Other than the language issue in India, the division of the Communist Party of India (CPI) also proved to be very hazardous for the Association. Beginning with the 1962 Indo-China war, CPI has got divided several times while other people with 'their own leftist ideologies' set up their own political parties. It is very interesting (and a student of literature automatically gets reminded of all the types of drama as were enumerated by Shakespeare in his play Hamlet) when one goes through the catalogue of the leftist parties in different states of India. For example thee are parties like "CPI-Marxist-Leninist, Marxist Communist Party of India, Marxist Coordination Committee in Jharkhand, Janathipathiya Samrakshanva Samity, Communist Marxist Party and BTR-EMS-AKG Jabakeeya Vadi in Kerala, Party of Democratic Socialism in West Bengal, Janganotantrik Morcha in Tripura, the Ram

Pasla in Punjab, Orissa Communist Party in Orissa'[29] and Socialist Democratic Party in Jammu and Kashmir. While in earlier days Progressive Writers Association was directly or indirectly associated with the CPI, the division of the party and decline of Urdu from its prominence in India are responsible for the emergence of new literary associations that are associated with the New Leftist parties. Some of them are: Pregatisheel Lekhak Sangha (associated with the CPM and laid in 1982), Janvadi Lekhak Sangh (associated with CPM), and Jansanskriti Manch (associated with CPI-ML).[30]

In Pakistan, the Communist Party had yet to establish itself when, in 1951, the majority of its leadership was involved and arrested in notorious 'Rawalpindi Conspiracy Case' including Sajjad Zaheer, Major General Akbar Khan, and Faiz Ahmad Faiz.

"In 1954, the government in Pakistan banned the communist Party of Pakistan and Progressive Writers Association in order to woo the US leadership with which it had entered in military pacts in order to contain Communism'[31].

The property of Pakistan Papers Limited, under whose umbrella the weekly Lail-o Nahar, Pakistan Times, and Imroze (the mouthpieces of Communist Party of Pakistan and Progressive Writers Association) were published, was confiscated. Many of the writers 'prudently accepted new positions in semiprivate organizations supported by the government'[32] of Pakistan.

The new generation of Urdu poets got attracted by other literary trends like 'jadidyat' (modernism) and other 'art for art's sake' ideologies. Thus, they directly detached themselves from progressivism. Many of them distanced themselves from both of the trends. They expressed the 'sociopolitical concerns' of their age in an oblique and internalized diction. 'Thus, the poetry of Shahryar and Nida Fazli mostly speaks in understatements and undertones which denote a paradigm shift. It remained essentially 'progressive' in content, but form, texture and expression got transformed into the complexity of experience and the simplicity of language'.[33] In their poems there is less enthusiasm and no revolutionary zeal. Instead there is a loss of hope in their poetry and they seem to have taken refuge into the shell of their respective selves. They compose the poetry like:

> Ghar ki tamir tasawur main hi ho saktio hai
> Apne naqshe ke mutabiq ye zameen kuch kam hai
>
> House can be constructed only in my imagination
> There is less land for my proposed plan.

Some of the hopes of transformation were still alive in many well-wishers of the Progressive Writers Association until the break-up of the Soviet Union in 1991. It made tough progressives like Ali Sardar Jafri compose the elegies like:

Alvida, ay surkh parcham, alvida
Ay nishan-e-azm-e-mazlooman-e-aalam, alvida

Farewell, O Red flag, Red flag, farewell
Farewell, O symbol of the dynasty of the oppressed.[34]

Although, socialism no longer exists in Urdu poetry as it used to be, and socialism is not used as 'the frame of reference, [but] the progressive sentiment [still] infuses, informs, and some would say dominates a significant part of Urdu literary production even today'. There are many local progressive associations till existent, not only in India and Pakistan but across the globe. Recently, a conference of the 'Progressive Writers Association' took place in Bradford, UK. The first of its five point declaration reads to 'Support the struggle against imperialist cultural domination and fight against neo-colonialism and for social justice and democracy in South Asian countries'.[35]

Whether we need to revive progressivism in our literature or wind up the whole game, is an open question for our intellectuals and new writers. I would like to conclude my paper with couplet:

Aakhire shab ke hamsafar Faiz na jane kya hue
Reh gayi kis jagha saba, subha kidhar nikal gayi.
It was the final night Faiz

What happened to those who'd started out with you?
When did the morning breeze abandon you
and where on those last miles the dawn[36].

References

1 Abu-Mu_ammad Mu_lih al-Din bin Abdallah Shirazi (1207?-1291), better known as Sheikh Saadi was one of the major Persian poets of the medieval period. He is not only famous in Persian-speaking countries, but he has also been quoted in western sources. He is recognized for the quality of his writings, and for the depth of his social and moral thoughts.

2 Hafeez Malik, "The Marxist Literature in India and Pakistan", The Journal of Asian Studies 26.4 (1967): 650.

3 Mustafa Kamal Ataturk (1881-1938) was an Ottoman and Turkish army officer, revolutionary statesman, and the first President of Turkey.

4 Hafeez Malik, 652.

5 Sheema Majeed (Editor), Culture and Identity (Karachi, Oxford University Press, 2005) 9.

6 Shakeel-ur-Rehman, Faiz ki Jamaliat, 195.

7 Syed Siraj-ud-Din Ajmali, Taraqqi Pasand Tehrik aur Urdu Gazal (New Delhi, Azra Publications, 1996) 20.

8 Sheema Majeed, 9.

9 Hansraj Rehbar, Taraqqi Pasand Adab: ek Jayizah, (New Delhi, Aazad Kitabghar, Kalan Mahal, 1967) 10.

10 Dr.Syed Wasif Ahmad, Kashf-e-Faiz (Ptna, Book Emporium, 1990)161-62.

11 Nazeer Siddiqi, "Faiz Ahmad Faiz: Naqshe Faryadi se Zindan Nana tak", in Faiz Ahmad Faiz: Aks aur Jehtain, ed. Shahid Mahili, (New Delhi, Meyar Publications, 1987): 112.

12 Raza Mir and Ali Husain Mir, Anthems of Resistance (New Delhi , InkIndia Roli Books, 2006) 57.

13 Ibid, 55

14 Ibid, 57

15 Ibid, 11-12

16 Ibid, 62

17 Ibid, 67

18 Ibid, 64

19 Ibid, 10

20 Syed Siraj-ud-Din, 153 (translation mine)

21 Raza Mir and Ali Husain Mir, 12

22 Ibid, 12-13

23 Ibid, 8-9

24 "To All Progressive Writers: An Appeal", Desabhimani Study Circle, Social Scientist, Vol. 3, No. 3, (Oct., 1974): 64-71, http://www.jstor.org/stable/3516373, Accessed: 04/01/2011 10:1

25 Khalid Hasan O City of Lights: Faiz Ahmed Faiz, Selected Poetry and Biographical Notes (Karachi, Oxford University Press, 2006) 40

26 Raza Mir and Ali Husain Mir , 13

27 Syed Siraj-ud-Din Ajmali, 11

28 Raza Mir and Ali Husain Mir , pp. 7

29 Pramod Kumar Buravalli, Communism is on the Wane in India", Rediff News, April 29, 2010, www.news.rediff.com

30 Vijay Avant, "Irrelevant Writers Association", www.eng.chauthidunya.com

31 Shahid Husain, "Rememberin the Dreamer-Sibte Hasan" , www.progressivewriters.org, accessed on 4/1/2011

32 Hafeez Malik, 664

33 Manglesh Dabra, 'Of Lost Dreams', Frontline, 27. 22, (2010) ttp://www.frontline.in/fl2722/stories/20101105272209400.htm accessed on 05/01/2010

34 Raza Mir and Ali Husain Mir, 14

35http://www.groundreport.com/Business/Bradford-Decleration-Progressive-Wrters-Conference_1/2926614, accessed on: 05/01/2011

36 Agha Shahid Ali Faiz Ahmed Faiz: The Rebel's Silhouette (Delhi, Oxford University Press, 1992) 31

Javaid Ahmad Lone is a young researcher and a scholar in world literatures, literary theory and English literature. Currently, he's undertaking research on the Progressive Writers Association at Aligarh Muslim University (AMU). His article is appearing for the first time in this publication.

Faiz in Karachi, 1965

Chapter 4

Listening to Faiz is a subversive act, yes, even today...

GAUHER RAZA

Being unfamiliar with the name of Faiz Ahmad Faiz and what it signifies can make one extremely unwelcome in the literary circles of North India, Pakistan and Bangladesh, as well as most of the countries that boast a sizeable Southasian diaspora. In Punjab province, despite a positive dislike for Urdu among some sections, Faiz remains as popular as the Sufi saints, Bulleh Shah or Baba Farid. Faiz was a trade unionist, a Marxist, and lived and died a communist, yet even reactionaries hold the man in high esteem. In Pakistan, he was hounded by several successive governments, and yet no fundamentalist group has ever passed a fatwa against Faiz. How did this happen? How did this mild-mannered, soft-spoken Punjabi, who spoke Urdu in a heavy Punjabi accent and was master of an awful reciting style, manage to surpass all the stalwarts, his seniors and contemporaries, in popularity? Faiz is certainly the only poet after Ghalib to have been translated into almost all languages of the Subcontinent and many further afield.

Of the galaxy of south Asian heroes, pre-or post-Partition, it is difficult to find individuals whose greatness is acknowledged even by their enemies – perhaps Ashfaqullah, Ram Prasad Bismil and Shaheed Bhagat Singh would so qualify. Even those who disagreed with their methods and worked against their ideological positions saluted their commitment to the cause, and accepted them as heroes of the freedom movement. While Faiz has been able to garner similar respect, there is a marked difference with these other three. Ashfaqullah, Bismil and Bhagat Singh were killed while fighting against the British. During this period, Faiz was writing poetry – albeit revolutionary poetry.

Throughout, he remained a consistent votary against imperialism on almost all issues, particularly during the extremely polarised days of the Cold War. Yet, despite his publicly declared partisanship, how is it that many of those located on the other side of the ideological divide respected him? There seems to be only one answer: in his chosen field of poetry, Faiz simply stood tall – technically and, perhaps more important, morally. He chose poetry as his arena of revolutionary action, and he did this so well in the battle of ideas that he not only transcended the hitherto prescribed limits of expression, but also redefined the vocabulary of that expression. In doing so, Faiz successfully blurred the boundary between love poetry and revolutionary poetry to the extent that you cannot distinguish between the two.

With his felicity with languages and his brilliant academic record, Faiz could have had a bright career in nearly any field; but he chose a life of commitment, at great personal risk – to his freedom, citizenship and life – and at great cost to his family. Yet, it was this steadfastness in his ideals and the uncompromising manner in which he worked that compelled all those who chose to stick to a safe path to bow their heads before him and acknowledge his leading role.

That brings us to the next question – what makes Faiz universally popular, even decades after his death? Faiz was a committed dreamer, and he dreamt of a revolutionary movement that was humanist, self-sacrificing and egalitarian, but also firm and uncompromising. He dreamt of a future that many had dreamt of, but expressed his views in a convincing and gracious language. Indeed, this language did not alienate his ideological adversaries, but rather made them uncomfortable – shaking the foundation of the other side of the ideological fence, and therefore leaving them dumbfounded.

Faiz in Lahore, 1956

Sublime revolution

My own love affair with Faiz's poetry started when I was still in school. The love affairs of adolescence are intense. Yet, only some last. Of course, in retrospect it seems clear that I understood little of his poetry at that age. The true meaning of the poem 'Mere humdam mere dost' descended like a revelation upon me only when I was in the final year of my

24

masters programme in Delhi, when I recited it to a friend. The poem gently and beautifully says that revolution can be brought only by the working class; a poet can sing songs but cannot bring revolution – ie, though the middle class has an important role to play, the proletariat is the vanguard of any revolution. I must have recited this poem hundreds of times before then, but its import had somehow escaped me totally.

Still, during my school days it must have been the power and beauty of Faiz's language that attracted me. I memorised almost every verse from the anthologies of his works available at the time. Of course, much of this initial pull can be traced to my parents – my father a communist, both freedom fighters. They never asked their children to recite 'Twinkle, twinkle little star' or 'Goosy, goosy gander' before guests; instead, I was asked to recite the poetry of Mir, Ghalib, Iqbal (not one of my favourites), Faiz and Sahir Ludhianvi. During those years, *'Siyasi leader ke naam', 'Shishon ka masiha'* and the aforementioned *'Mere humdum mere dost'* were my favourites. The first of these was easy to understand, but the latter two are not. The soft, beautiful words might attract one to the beauty of poetry, but they depict extremely harsh realities of life.

Faiz realised quite early on that traditional Urdu poetry had immense potential to articulate modern revolutionary ideas, and that this medium was yet to be fully explored. Of course, the idioms, similes, metaphors and, above all, symbolism and structure of traditional Urdu poetry were already highly developed. So, Faiz was able to pick up words and expressions that were part of the traditional vocabulary of this form, and invest them either with new meanings or to actively create nuances within their traditional import. Words such as raqeeb (adversary), *laila, majnoon, qafas* (cage), *saba* (morning breeze), *naaseh* (sermoniser), *munsif* (judge), *hawas* (lust, greed), *muddaee* (complainant), etc, were each invested with new meanings. For example, in the poem 'Raqeeb se' (To the adversary), friends are addressed as adversaries in love (*raqeeb*). Calling a friend an adversary was a novel notion, tradition turned on its head. Such words had a long history of being used for love poetry, but Faiz was now appropriating them for a whole new context. He also borrowed the structure of love poetry from Mir Taqi Mir, the renowned poet of the early 19th century. Together, Faiz was able to use the traditional words and structure to symbolise capitalism and state oppression as enemies of harmony – lovers, hope, tranquillity and beauty symbolised revolutionaries and socialism for him.

Faiz's felicity with multiple languages, including English, Persian, Arabic and Punjabi, coupled with his understanding of their cultural and historical moorings, helped him to draw from diverse traditions to construct new metaphors in Urdu. His palette was large and he never hesitated to use words from

25

other languages, which had the effect of increasing his intensity of expression. For example, in his poem 'Intisab', he has used the word *clerkon* (clerks, English), *railbaanon* (railway driver, English), *katrion* (dwellings, Punjabi) and *wali-e-maasiwa fill arz dehqan ke naam* (dedicated to, the inheritor of destitution, god's proxy on the earth, farmer, Arabic).

Whenever Faiz deviated from traditional language, literary critics would feel increasingly uneasy, with many criticising him for not knowing proper Urdu. Once a famous Indian Urdu critic said, 'He does not know Urdu, and there are many linguistic mistakes in his poetry – after all, he is a Punjabi.' A journalist reported this to Faiz while he was on a visit to Delhi, and the poet, characteristically polite, said only, 'We will correct the mistakes.' His answer disarmed not only the reporter but also the critic, just as his poetry always has done with his opponents.

Faiz at his home in Model Town, Lahore, 1976.

Hum Dekhenge

As a poet Faiz is traditional in almost every sense. His choice of words, imagery and poetic structure are all traditional. What is not traditional was his content, and in this way he used traditions specifically to subvert worn-out conventions. This could be said about his entire corpus of poetry, but two poems in particular stand out: 'Dua' and 'Hum dekhenge'.

26

In Urdu and Hindi poetry, a collection of poems or even a prose book is supposed to start with a poem (or a chapter, in case of prose) in praise of god and other religious figures – this is referred to as the 'Dua'. Yet poets and writers associated with the Progressive Writers Association (PWA), most of them atheists, had given up this tradition – anti-god and anti-religion sentiments had become so strong that all such practices had become unacceptable. Faiz was the only one to realise that even this tradition could be used to subvert. The poem 'Dua' appears in the middle of his collection Sar-e Wadi-e Sina (Atop the Sinai Vlley), so the placement itself is the beginning of this subversion. Thereafter, the first couplet, hard-hitting as it is, sets the tone.

> Aiye haath uthaayen hum bhi Hum,
> jinhe rasm-e dua yaad nahin
> Hum, jinhe soz-e mohabbat ke siva
> Koi but, koi khuda yaad nahin.
>
> Let us raise our hands in prayer, we who remember not the tradition of prayer,
> We, who expect the pain of love, remember not any idol, any god.

The poet does not ask anything for himself, as is the case with all traditional duas. He prays for 'exchanging the toxic bitterness of the present with the sweetness of tomorrow', 'hope for the hopeless', 'vision for the visionless', 'courage for the timid', the 'ability to investigate for those who believe in lies and myths'. There are no harsh words, no ill feeling invoked; yet the content of each couplet is revolutionary, sharp, clear and loud.

The title 'Wa Yabqa Wajhe Rubbika' of the poem is taken from the Surah-e-rahman in the Quran. 'Hum dekhenge' draws its imagery from the description of qayamat, the Day of Reckoning, as 'revealed' in the Quran (Surah: Ziljal), and transforms it into to 'day of revolution'. The description of what will happen on that day is taken almost verbatim from the Quran, though with slight modifications. Instead of merely 'mountains', for instance, he writes 'jab zulm-o-sitam ke kohe giran' (when the heavy mountains of tyranny). Once again, Faiz is at his best in subverting traditional imagery that had been used over and over again. In this case, Islamic fundamentalism had been used by the authorities to reinforce religious ideas that General Zia ul-Haq was trying to instil for the consolidation of political and economic power. Gen Zia came to power in a coup, imposed martial law in Pakistan (1977), and soon unleashed fascistic terror in the name of Nizam-e-Mustafa (Islamic system). The poem was written in 1979, as Zia's tyranny touched its zenith. Faiz subversively uses the lines 'removal of idols from the Kaaba' and the 'reinstallation of outlaws' to symbolise the removal of General Zia and his political movement, and the restoration of democracy. Faiz made it amply clear that his reading of the Quran was quite different from General Zia's and the brand of 'Islam' that Zia

was trying to sell was not acceptable to him.

Iqbal Bano, the acclaimed ghazal singer, sang this poem in public during Zia's rule. Faiz was in jail. That night 50000 people, while listening to 'Hum Dekhenge', repeatedly chanted Inqilab Zindabad (Long live revolution). Shoaib Hashmi, Faiz's son-in-law, once narrated before a packed hall in Delhi how the recording was smuggled out, hurriedly edited with makeshift editing facilities, and a few copies quickly handed out to avoid confiscation. With these few audio cassettes, further copies were made. The number swelled in geometric progression and soon the copies crossed the border, and within weeks the cassette reached many individuals in Delhi.

Very often, I listen to a recording of this song at home and while travelling to work. Thunderous clapping and slogans of Inqilab Zindabad repeatedly interrupt the performance. A Telugu scientist friend who usually travels with me to the office had either given up hope that I will someday stop playing it – or had started enjoying 'Hum dekhenge'. I very often forced this song on him, told him stories about the context in which it was written and sung.

Recently, a Pakistani friend, a scholar of the history of science, told me that he had actually been at the programme when Iqbal Bano sang. Thereafter, a friend of his who worked in the Pakistani armed forces had rung him up late at night, warning him not to stay at home for the next two or three days. He took precautions and stayed away from his house. In the coming days, many of those present in the Lahore auditorium were hauled up and questioned, and some were detained. His home was also visited in the middle of the night by the military police, to enquire after his whereabouts.

One need not be surprised by this. Listening to Faiz's poetry, even when sung by the most celebrated musical diva of the country, was an inherently anti-imperialist, anti-dictatorship and anti-fascist act. It was highly subversive. We may not realise it, but tyrants always recognise the explosive potential of an apparently harmless piece of text. Perhaps it should be applied in translation or without to the tyrants that remain with us all over Southasia.

Ghauhar Raza is an Indian scientist, social activist, poet, documentary filmmaker and a leading Urdu poet. He has comes from a progressive liberal background. His parents were communists and were involved in India's struggle for freedom. He has worked, as a scientist, with India's National Institute of Science, Technology and Development Studies (NISTADS). The article in this publication has previously appeared in the on-line journal: Himal Southasia.

Faiz Ahmed Faiz with Rana Altaf

Faiz in Lahore, 1951

Chapter 5

Subsumed by History and Nation

AFSAN CHOWDHURY

Where does Faiz the poet and pan-Southasian Marxist end and Faiz the Pakistani begin? This is a question to which Bangladeshis, among others, still seek an answer.

Faiz Ahmed Faiz remains one of the great unsolved enigmas of Southasian literature. Where does Faiz the poet end and Faiz the politician begin? Where does the pan-Southasian Marxist end and the Pakistani begin? His engagement with these contradictory identities constitutes a painful puzzle for his admirers. This becomes all the more complex because Faiz never seemed to have belonged fully to any one land – the boundaries of his literary, political and cultural life are fluid, flowing and overlapping.

The issue becomes even more complex for a Bangladeshi admirer such as this writer, who was born in the 1950s and to whom Faiz offers a complex identity and a bonding to great ideals crossing all borders. He is one Pakistani whom Bangladeshis have looked upon with the greatest possible admiration and affection. Yet, what challenges this bond is how Faiz was during and immediately after 1971. During those terrible days, Bangladeshis who knew about or of him would ask each other, *What is Faiz saying about all this?* He had become the 'Good Pakistani' in the eyes of those in the East. Yet, was Faiz ever a person who represented more than Pakistan? Was it possible for him to escape being a Pakistani and have a wider identity encompassing all the admiring nations of South Asia and beyond?

During the late 1960s, Munir Chowdhury hosted a literary television show in East Pakistan, during which he would discuss various writers of Pakistan. He was a legendary speaker, and employed his dramatic skills to present literary luminaries to a devoted public. In one show he talked about Faiz, his friend and fellow-traveller. Chowdhury focused on the poem '*Mujhse pahli si muhabbat mere mehboob na maang*', presenting Faiz as a social revolutionary and a poet of the oppressed. This presentation suited Chowdhury, who had been a Communist Party member, jailed in 1952 for his activism during the Bengali-focused Language Movement, and a lifelong literary activist who had become an icon of Bengali nationalism. He had moved on from his firebrand days, however, to become more a writer than a politician, an unparalleled teacher and East Pakistan's leading dramatist.

Most importantly, Chowdhury's love for Faiz's poetry was real. His introduction was one of the memorable moments of my life, an introduction to a poet of passion and beauty whom I admire to this day. Though I understand little of the literary tradition that Faiz upholds or the magnificent language of his poetry, I appreciate it – somewhere, there is a deep bond that transcends poetic pursuits. Yet, my affection is also tinged with pain, as I see Faiz nationalised, regionalised, made language-specific. This is a tragedy for a poet who spoke to all of us once.

Defanging the revolutionary

During the 1940s, Faiz was certainly a Marxist. At that time he was in then-undivided India and had gone to war as an officer of the British Indian army, but returned home to become a journalist. He was married to Alys, a British sympathiser of the communists, whose sister was married to an Indian who taught in Aligarh. During this period, as the nation-states of Pakistan and India came into being, the Communist Party (CP) told its members to choose countries according to their religions. Thus, many communists in India and Pakistan emigrated across the new border obeying the party diktat. Many critics argue that the Communist Party went 'communal' even before that, when it asked cadres to join the Muslim League or Congress as per their respective religious identity. Harnessing India's political will proved to be quite beyond the capacity of the party, and the CP was relegated to a marginal role.

After partition, Faiz, who had earlier worked on both sides of the new border, chose to live in Pakistan. Was this because he believed in the political structure and state ideology of the new country, one that subsequently moved increasingly towards becoming what was obvious in its charter – a state for one faith alone? Faiz was never a Muslim Leaguer, nor even a 'Muslim', so why then would he choose Pakistan? Perhaps it was never more than a move to his homeland, which by all standards was much less open than India. It is difficult to pinpoint the exact reasons that attracted him to Pakistan, but the new country's ideals certainly would not have been guiding his decision – maybe, going home was all it was about.

In Pakistan, after 1947, Faiz was known for his views and activism, a man clearly a part of the left. He was involved with trade unionism, which even in those early days in Pakistan was considered an activity almost treasonous. In 1950-51, Faiz was arrested, along with Communist Party leader Sajjad Zahir and a few military officers led by General Akbar Khan, for planning a military takeover. There was a period of prolonged incarceration and a trial followed by a four-year sentence.

Faiz in London, 1962

What was Faiz trying to do? Gen Akbar, leader of what has since become known as the Rawalpindi conspiracy, was a rabid Pakistani nationalist. He wanted to take over Pakistan – not because he wanted a new form of the state, but because he was frustrated with the Pakistani leadership, considering it too moderate in dealing with India. How did Sajjad Zahir and Faiz get involved with such a person? Where was the common space? I have not come across any material on the motives of the participants, or of the deals that must have been made between these two completely disparate groups, the communists and the ultra-nationalists, to achieve this alliance.

Around the world, communist parties generally tend not to be pro-army when out of power. But there has always been a fatal attraction among communists towards the military, in the belief that a coup can deliver revolution in a quick stroke, rendering organisational work and resilience unnecessary. This has been tried in Africa with a marked lack of success, as in Ethiopia and Mozambique; and so too in Bangladesh, where a one-legged War of Liberation hero, Colonel Abu Taher, came to power for a few hours in November 1975. He led his Marxist activists in an anti-officer uprising, which was to deliver socialism. Along with many others, he was hanged. History has also shown that attempts by communists to use the military path to power usually end in failure.

There seems to be no satisfactory explanation for the left involvement in the 1950 Pakistan coup attempt. But Faiz was involved, or we assume he was, because no 'confession' exists. Soon after the imprisonment, his active political life also began to fade and, anyway, the CP was banned in 1954. In the public mind, Faiz gradually became many other things: one of the great poets of our time, a friend of the Sufis of Pakistan and, finally, the safest and most innocuous, an outspoken lover of alcohol. Faiz was transformed and fitted into the benign identity of a great poet who does not challenge the state. Yet the fact remains: he did challenge it, albeit unsuccessfully.

Poets as communists

The identities of poets and communists do not always go well together. Poets usually tend to be people of words and passion, moved to politics by the power of the heart, not ideology. Over time, the two identities can become contested, if not came in direct conflict. The Chilean poet Pablo Neruda was always a better poet than a Marxist revolutionary, but he did try to cultivate a mix of both identities. Bangladesh's national poet, Nazrul Islam, was jailed for sedition and was a fellow-traveller of the Communist Party; he even ran the party's official newspaper in Bengal but drifted away over time, as his poetry and songs began to take priority. Also his inter-faith devoutness, believing in the mystic constructs of Islam and Hinduism (hardly a Marxist attitude, whichever way you look at it) became increasingly important to him. Early senility robbed him of his faculties, when, barely past forty, and things

therefore never really reached a point where this conflict could grow larger.

Faiz had a better formal education than Nazrul, and also had a better knowledge of Marxist dogma and its application. He was also more middle-class and shareef (genteel). His poetry's roots and tools were the fine wine of Urdu and Persian literature; even his most famous poem '*Mujhse pehli si muhabbat*', was written in the language of a chosen few, a highly stylised articulate Persian-Urdu that would be meaningful only to the well-educated. He was in many ways far more representative of the CP leadership's class and cultural roots than was Nazrul, who came from a peasant background.

Yet, that only underlines the original question: Where could Faiz's politics find space in Pakistan? Unlike East Pakistan, where the communist tradition was deep and its politics itself spurred on by Marxist intellectuals and cultural activists, West Pakistan was almost completely bereft of such impulses, united in hatred for India but not much more. One could name Mian Iftikharuddin and Wali Khan, but these politicians were more Pashtun than Marxist, and much of the left nationalism was limited to NWFP and Balochistan. The Punjabis of Pakistan were not known for their leftist leanings. Was Faiz's much vaunted loneliness merely a poetic expression, or did it go deeper?

As children in Dhaka, we heard about Faiz's refusal to write a laudatory editorial in the *Pakistan Times* – the paper owned by Mian Iftikharuddin and edited by Faiz – about the martial law imposed by Gen Ayub Khan in 1958. Soon the paper was taken over by the government and Faiz had to leave. For some reason, the political Faiz went missing after that defiant stand, at least as far as pan-Pakistani politics was concerned – the kind of politics that could also resonate in East Pakistan. Faiz was from then on a poet, not a socialist poet.

Meanwhile, the Pakistan that Faiz wanted to transform in the image of his ideals ended in 1971. During the days after the crackdown on Dhaka on 25 March of that year, as people wondered how the people of the Western half felt about the bloody events in the East, they heard a chorus of approval, led by Zulfikar Ali Bhutto saying, '*Thank God! Pakistan is saved!*' This was a famously premature statement, of course, as all of Bhutto's machinations ran out of momentum in the end, with Pakistan collapsing in ignominy in December of that year. During those days, those who knew would ask, *What did Faiz say? Did he protest? Did he give a statement saying it was wrong?* In fact, we do not know what Faiz did. But we do know that this was one man many Bangladeshis expected to stand up for them. Of course, it was unfair to expect that Pakistanis who wished to express dissent could do so in a martial-law governed Pakistan. Very few could, and those who did went to

jail or paid an even higher price. But Bangladeshis were demanding all this from the person – poet and politician – they imagined Faiz to be, rather than a person of flesh and blood who lived in Pakistan. In a way, Faiz had become a prisoner of the history of Pakistan.

As the war reached a gory climax, Bengali supporters of Pakistan, particularly those belonging to the Jamaat-e-Islami, went around the curfewed city, picking up as many poets, academics and intellectuals as they could find. It was always their view that Bengali nationalism was produced by these people, the so-called Hindu-loving secularists and cultural activists. If the crackdown on 25 March 1971 was the beginning of the end, the day when most intellectuals were picked up, 14 December marked the explosive end of the carnage. Many bodies could be seen dumped in the swampy killing fields, but few could be identified due to the advanced state of decomposition. Corpses with arms tied behind their backs, bearing marks of torture and missing eyes, have become the visual memories of the torture and murder of 1971. Among the many who disappeared and were never found was Munir Chowdhury, the man who introduced me to Faiz.

Friends and strangers

Faiz did visit Bangladesh in 1974, as part of an official delegation as an advisor on culture. He met with his friends but the closest ones like Shahidullah Kaiser, Munir Chowdhury, Zahir Raihan, all writers and CP activists, had disappeared. Others were uneasy with Faiz as memories, unshared history and the reality of two distant states came between friends. He clearly missed the warmth of their friendship. In one of his most painful and beautiful poems, 'Hum ke thehre ajnabi' (We who have been rendered strangers), Faiz summed up his personal agony – and that of many Pakistanis and Bangladeshis whose friendship had been torn asunder by the war. The final lines are:

> Un se jo kehne gaye thhe Faiz, jaa sadqa kiye
> Ankahi hi reh gayi vo baat, sab baatoon ke baad

> Faiz, that one thing which I went there to say with
> all my heart
> That very thing was left unsaid, after so much had been spoken

Friendship is a much more complicated matter than one imagines, for in South Asia politics can burn friendship with the flames of conflict.

Faiz's politics died in Pakistan soon after he was jailed in 1950; only his poetry remained. With each day, though, his status as a poet soared, while admiration for him spread throughout the Subcontinent. Eventually, Faiz had become among the greatest legends of all. One could ask whether he left the building of his people – the somewhat fuzzy definition of 'people' which

south Asian socialism imagines existing beyond borders – as after 1947 his world was determined by the country in which he lived. His socialist imagination was encircled by Pakistan's politics, and the very politics he wished to change overcame his resolve.

Faiz's personality was much more than just that of a poet. Indeed, that is the root of my sorrow – an unreasonable feeling, I concede. We have also seen how people who are unable to change politics sometimes become depoliticised beings. Munir Chowdhury once lamented publicly that he was defeated by the temptations of life – he gave up the life of a party cadre to become a teacher. I am not sure what path Faiz followed, but I hope he found peace in supporting political causes in Pakistan.

It might be heretical to say this, but perhaps Faiz would have been happier in the more politically variegated soil of India, where his poetry is as much admired as it is in Pakistan. In India, only a crippled form of socialist politics breathes, but at least it exists. I concede that to suggest another home for Faiz, particularly India, will be tantamount to committing blasphemy in the eyes of some. It is cruel to Faiz, too. He lives on wherever Urdu remains alive. And yet, it is important to remember one more time that Faiz grew into adulthood and recognition in an undivided Subcontinent amid its dreams.

The communist, the rebel, the secularist, the romantic poet, the happy lover of alcohol – all had in the end become a Pakistani. So it was that when he visited Dhaka in 1974 with Bhutto, it was only to find that many of his friends had been killed or disappeared by the same forces he represented in Bangladesh. The chasm became infinite and complete: he visited accompanied by those with whom his Bangladeshi friends could no longer associate.

People who dream of a better world are often condemned to become what history demands of them.

Afsan Chowdury is a multi-media journalist, filmmaker, environmental advocate, human rights specialist, social communicator and researcher. Chowdhury has worked with BRAC (world's largest NGO based in Bangladesh), UNICEF, OXFAM and South Asia Panos Institute among others in Bangladesh, Nepal, Nigeria, Uganda, Sri Lanka, India and Turkmenistan. The article in this publication was previously appeared in the on-line journal: Himal Southasia.

Faiz with Chilean Nobel Laureate poet Pablo Narua at Sochi, Black Sea, Georgia, 1962

Chapter 6

Faiz-Neruda: Great Contemporary Poets, Friends and Humanists

IKRAMUL HAQ AND HUZAIMA BUKHARI

Pablo Neruda (1904-1973) and Faiz Ahmad Faiz (1910-1984)—
contemporary poets, friends and outstanding humanists—have
left lasting impression on the world of literature. Their works
won global recognition—Neruda was honoured with Nobel
Prize for literature in 1971 and Faiz won Lenin Peace Prize in
1962. Both Neruda and Faiz, like many others, notably Nazim
Hikmet and Mahmoud Darwish, were essentially humanists,
anti-colonialists and anti-imperialists. Their great struggle and
works were interwoven—these were inseparable. Their work
complimented their struggle and vice versa.

The life and work of Neruda has amazing similarities with that
of Faiz.

Neruda (real name Neftalí Ricardo Reyes Basoalto), was born
on 12 July, 1904, in the town of Parral in Chile. His father was
a railway employee and his mother, who died shortly after his
birth, a teacher. Some years later his father, who had then
moved to the town of Temuco, remarried Doña Trinidad
Candia Malverde. The poet spent his childhood and youth in
Temuco, where he also got to know Gabriela Mistral, head of
the girls' secondary school, who took a liking to him. At the
early age of thirteen he began to contribute some articles to
the daily *La Mañana*, among them, Entusiasmo y Perseverancia
–his first publication– and his first poem. In 1920, he became
a contributor to the literary journal *Selva Austral* under the
pen name of Pablo Neruda, which he adopted in memory of
the Czechoslovak poet Jan Neruda (1834-1891). Some of the
poems Neruda wrote at that time are to be found in his first
published book: Crepusculario (1923). The following year saw
the publication of *Veinte poemas de amor y una cancion
desesperada*, one of his best-known and most translated works.
Alongside his literary activities, Neruda studied French and
pedagogy at the University of Chile in Santiago.

Between 1927 and 1935, the government put him in charge of
a number of honorary consulships, which took him to Burma,
Ceylon, Java, Singapore, Buenos Aires, Barcelona, and Madrid.
His poetic work during that difficult period included, among
other works, the collection of esoteric surrealistic poems,
Residencia en la tierra (1933), which marked his literary
breakthrough.

The Spanish Civil War and the murder of García Lorca, whom
Neruda knew, affected him strongly and made him join the
Republican movement, first in Spain, and later in France, where

he started working on his collection of poems *España en el Corazón* (1937). The same year he returned to his native country, to which he had been recalled, and his poetry during the following period was characterized by an orientation towards political and social matters. *España en el Corazón* had a great impact by virtue of its being printed in the middle of the front during the civil war.

In 1939, Neruda was appointed consul for the Spanish emigration, residing in Paris, and, shortly afterwards, Consul General in Mexico, where he rewrote his *Canto General de Chile*, transforming it into an epic poem about the whole South American continent, its nature, its people and its historical destiny. This work, entitled *Canto General*, was published in Mexico 1950, and also underground in Chile. It consists of approximately 250 poems brought together into fifteen literary cycles and constitutes the central part of Neruda's literary work. Shortly after its publication, *Canto General* was translated into some ten languages. Nearly all these poems were created in a difficult situation, when Neruda was living abroad.

In 1943, Neruda returned to Chile, and in 1945 he was elected senator of the Republic, also joining the Communist Party of Chile. Due to his protests against President González Videla's repressive policy against striking miners in 1947, he had to live underground in his own country for two years until he managed to leave in 1949. After living in different European countries he returned home in 1952. A great deal of what he published during that period bears the stamp of his political activities; one example is *Las Uvas y el Viento* (1954), which can be regarded as the diary of Neruda's exile. In *Odas elementales* (1954- 1959) his message is expanded into a more extensive description of the world, where the objects of the hymns –things, events and relations—are duly presented in alphabetic form.

In July 1957, Neruda travelled to Colombo, Sri Lanka (then Ceylon) and took part in the Peace Supporters World Congress. He went to India and Burma together with Jorge Amado and Zelia Gattai. Later visited China from the Kuo-Ming province. During this trip he worked on his books *Navegaciones y Regresos and Estravagario*. He returned to Europe with Matilde and embarked on brief trips to the Soviet Union, Czechoslovakia and East Germany. In September, he settled in Paris to continue working on *Estravagario and Cien Sonetos de Amor*.

In 1958, he was actively involved in Salvador Allende's second presidential campaign and took part in the 11th Congress of the Chilean Communist Party. Neruda was elected member of its Central Committee during the September session.

In January 26, 1959, he had encounter with Fidel Castro at Cuba's Caracas embassy. He also made short trips through different areas of Venezuela, going back to Chile in April. In November Navegaciones y regresos was released by Losada publishers, Buenos Aires. In mid November 1959, he travelled to the cities of Rancagua, San Fernando, Parral and Linares with a Communist Party delegation. The next few years' activities included travels to various countries, especially to then USSR in 1970 to take part in the deliberations of the Lenin Prize. The Book *Canción de Gesta* was published by the Imprenta Nacional de Cuba in a 25.000 copies edition. On March 30, 1960, he was given the grade of honorary academic member of the Universidad de Chile Faculty of Philosophy and Education. At the induction ceremony, he read a speech titled "Mariano Latorre, Pedro Prado and my own shadow".

In June 1965, Neruda travelled to the US with Matilde Urrutia. He offered recitals in New Yorok, Berkeley and Washington, also took part in PEN Club meetings, besides doing a record for the Congress Library. The same year on 31st July, Cuban writers and intellectuals published "Open letter to Pablo Neruda", in which they accused him of "having allowed being used by the United States of America. He responded: "… in the US and elsewhere I've been heard and respected for what I am and will ever be: a poet who does not hide his thinking and who has devoted his life and work to our people's liberation".

On October 28, 1966, he married Matilde Urrutia in a simple and private ceremony in the Isla Negra House, with only a few very close friends attending. This year the Art Friends Society published in Santiago his *Arte de pájaros* with illustrations by Nemesio Antúnez, Héctor Herrera, Mario Carreño and MarioToral.

In 1967, like every year, he travelled in May to Europe to attend the meetings of the Lenin Prize jury in Moscow. He also was declared guest of the Fourth Soviet Writers Congress. He received the International Literary Prize of Viaréggio-Versilia in Italy. This was the first version of the award, devoted to world personalities working for the culture and understanding among people.

During his visit to Columbia in 1968, he participated in the First Latin-American Festival of College Drama in the city of Manizales. He refused to accept the San Carlos Order's Great Cross from Colombian President Carlos Lleras Restrepo. He offered poetry recitals at the National University of Colombia and the Colombian Language Academy .On October 15 in the Bogotá campus of the Inca University, he received the grade of Doctor Honoris Causa from the Karl Mark University in Leipzig, GDR.

In February 1969, he took part in the Communist Party legislative election campaign. He was made "Honorary member" of the Chilean Language Academy. On June 30, he gave a long TV interview for the show "Reunión con la Pernsa" on Universidad de Chile's Channel 9. On July 12, he celebrated his 65th birthday in the company of secretaries of state, journalists, artists and intellectuals. On August 21 he received the grade of Doctor Scientiae et Honoris Causa from the Pontificia Universidad Católica de Chile. On September 1, the Senate honoured him with the Illustrious Sons of Chile Silver Medal. On September 30, he was nominated as presidential pre-candidate by the Chilean Communist Party.

On January 3, 1970, he abandoned his candidacy after the nomination of Dr. Salvador Allende as the Unidad Popular's only candidate. Allende was elected President of Chile on September 4, 1970.

On January 21, 1971, the Chilean Senate approved his nomination as Chile's ambassador in Paris. In July that year, he experienced the first the symptoms of the disease diagnosed to him two years ago: the appearance of nodules and prostrate growth. On October 1, he was awarded the Literature Nobel Prize. On December 7, he arrived in Stockholm with Matilde Urrutia to attend the ceremony of the Nobel Prize presentation, held on 10th. In his memoirs, the poet remembers: "The old king shook the hands of everyone, gave us the diploma, the medal, the check (…) It is said (or so it was said to Matilde just to impress her) that the king spent more time with me than with other laureates, that he shook my hand with evident sympathy. It was perhaps a reminiscence of the old kindness of monarchs towards bards".

In March 1972, he attended as a guest the XIII Italian Communist Party Congress in Milan. On December 5, on his return to homeland, the Chilean people gave the poet a rousing welcome and great tribute at the Estadio Nacional. This proved to be his last public appearance. In early part of 1973, due to health difficulties, Neruda quitted his position as Chile's Ambassador in France. 12 days after the Coup d'état in Chile, he died at 10.30 PM in Santiago's Clínica Santa María. On September 25, in an atmosphere of tension and collective mourning, a big crowd accompanied Pablo Neruda's body to the Cementerio General. Once in the cemetery, provocative shouts in his honour and Salvador Allende's were heard. He was provisionally buried in the Dittborn family's mausoleum.

On December 11, 1999, Matilde Urrutia and Neruda's remains were exhumed and carried to a ceremonial wake in the ex National Congress Honour Room. The next day, the poet's wills was accomplished 19 years after his death: his body was buried in Isla Negra, facing the sea he loved and sang about so much. The ceremony's only speech was pronounced by President Patricio Aylwin.

Neruda's work is exceptionally extensive. For example, his *Obras Completas*, constantly republished, comprised 459 pages in 1951; in 1962 the number of pages was 1,925, and in 1968 it amounted to 3,237, in two volumes. Among his works of the last few years can be mentioned *Cien sonetos de amor* (1959), which includes poems dedicated to his wife Matilde Urrutia, *Memorial de Isla Negra,* a poetic work of an autobiographic character in five volumes, published on the occasion of his sixtieth birthday, *Arte de pajáros* (1966), La Barcarola (1967), the play *Fulgor y muerte de Joaquín Murieta* (1967), *Las manos del día* (1968), *Fin del mundo* (1969), *Las piedras del cielo* (1970), and *La espada encendida.*

Pablo Neruda, a basic anthology is published in England by The Dolphins Book. It is an excellent anthology for English readers put together by Robert Pring-Mill, friend of the poet and very familiar with his work. This selection also includes a long preliminary study, also by Pring-Mill. Alain Sicard's *La pensee poetique de Pablo Neruda,* one of the most complete and deep studies on the poet's work, is published in France. The Spanish translation, *El pensamiento poético de Pablo Neruda,* is published in 1981 by Gredos.

Faiz Ahmed Faiz was born in Sialkot in the Punjab, then a part of India under British rule. He hailed from a well-to-do landowner's family. Faiz's father was a prominent lawyer, who was interested in literature, and whose friends included several prominent literary figures, including Muhammad Iqbal (1873-1938), national poet of Pakistan. Faiz received his education at mission schools in Sialkot in the English language, but he also learned Urdu, Persian, and Arabic. He studied English and Arabic literatures at Government College, Lahore, receiving in 1932 his M.A. in English, and in Arabic from Oriental College, Lahore. Besides formal studies, Faiz actively participated in the literary circles, which held meetings at homes of established writers. After graduating, he worked as a teacher from the mid-1930s in Amritsar and Lahore.

In the 1930s, Faiz joined the famous leftist progressive movement under the leadership of Sajjad Zaheer (1905-1973). During World War II, Faiz served in the Indian army in Delhi, and in 1944, he was promoted to the rank of Lieutenant Colonel. With the division of the subcontinent in 1947, Faiz resigned from the army and moved to Pakistan with his family. Alys Faiz (died in 2003), whom he had married in 1941, later published a book of memoirs, *Over My Shoulder* (1993). Faiz became editor of the English daily, the *Pakistan Times.* He also worked as managing editor of the Urdu daily *Imroz,* and was actively involved in organizing trade unions.

In 1951, Faiz and a number of army officers were implicated in the so-called Rawalpindi Conspiracy case and arrested under Safety Act. The government authorities alleged that Faiz and others were planning a coup d'état. He spent four years

in prison under a sentence of death and was released in 1955. Faiz became the secretary of the National Council of the Arts, and in 1962 he was awarded the Lenin Peace Prize by the Soviet Union. After the military takeover of General Ziaul Haq on July 5, 1977, Faiz was once again under trouble and was forced to exile. After a period of exile in war-torn Lebanon from 1979 to 1982, Faiz returned to Pakistan and died in Lahore on November 20, 1984.

Celebration event at The Pakistan Times, Lahore, 1955

Faiz's first collections of poetry, *Naqsh-e faryadi* (1943), *Dast-e saba* (1952), and *Zindan Namah* (1956), include his experience of imprisonment. Faiz describes his life behind the walls, in confinement, finding consolation in the thought that 'though tyrants may command that lamps be smashed / in rooms where lovers are destined to meet / they cannot snuff out the moon...'

Faiz has written extensively. His contribution in poetry and prose is enormous. *In Culture and Identity*: Selected English Writings of Faiz, Sheema Majeed and Mohammad Reza Kazimi have presented valuable work of Faiz.

Both Neruda and Faiz were actively involved in freedom movements. Their poetry, musical, lyrical and inspiring, stem from the main theme of making their homelands and the world at large a better place for the downtrodden – 'the wretched of the earth', a phrase masterly coined by Franz Fanon.

The remarkable thing about Neruda and Faiz was that in spite of their overwhelming revolutionary ideas, they never allowed ideological epiphany to burden their poems with shoddy rhetoric. They were masters of art and craft – a quality lacked by many revolutionary poets of their time. Neruda-Faiz legacy is universal and everlasting – both for nearly six decades inimitably articulated the suffering of their people, the agony of dispossession and exile.

Today, Ismail Kadare – winner of 2009 Spanish literary prize who considered as one of the greatest writers and intellectuals of the 20th century – narrates in the same masterly language and style the tragedy of his land (Albania), an incessant battleground. It is, in fact, not a story of one land alone. It is tragedy of millions of others as well—living in troubled lands around the globe where wars, civil strife, hunger, terrorism and militancy are posing problems of day to day survival. Today, Pablo Neruda and Faiz Ahmad Faiz are not alive, but the courage they demonstrated in their work is source of inspiration for all the leading poets and writers of the world.

Pablo Neruda and Faiz Ahmad Faiz were intimate friends, a fact little known in Chile and Pakistan. Chile and Pakistan are geographically far apart, but share amazing socio-political similarities in their post independence period. Both the countries produced charismatic leaders like Salvador Allende and Zulfikar Ali Bhutto. Tragically, they met the same fate— deposed and eliminated by military dictators at the behest of their imperialist masters. Pablo Neruda supported Allende and served under his government as did Faiz Ahmad Faiz under Bhutto. Pablo did not survive long after the 1973 US-backed military coup by Augusto Pinochet attacking the presidential palace and killing Allende. Zulfikar Ali Bhutto was arrested by General Ziaul Haq on July 5, 1977 and after a dubious kangaroo trial was hanged on April 4, 1979.

Since Allende and Bhutto pursued pro-people policies in countries long dominated by the military, they were overthrown by the collaborators of the neo-imperialists, killed at the behest of the military juntas of Pinochet and Zia and followed by long spells of repressive Military regimes which did not retreat until the Cold War drew to an end. Neruda and Faiz participated in the long-drawn struggle for freedom— both in colonial and post-independence eras – and their poetry is epitome of message of hope and commitment for creating a true democratic polity in which the forces of exploitation have no role to play. Their dream was common – to see human beings living in peace and tranquility. Neruda and Faiz were messengers of peace, equality and justice. Their commitment to their cause was infallible. Their poetry reflects the aspirations of masses. From literary point of view, they were masters of their craft. They were not mere revolutionary slogan-mongering who lacked in their work classical authenticity and modern sensibility. On the contrary, both Faiz

and Neruda are considered even by their critics, great masters of poetic expression and authentic builders of new tradition of resistance in literature.

Faiz with Nazim Hikmat, Parbhar Kaur, Hafeez Jallundhari, Dr. Mulk Raj Anand, Tashkent, 1958

In the post-independence period and during the Cold War era, both Neruda and Faiz were still struggling as oligarchy of the rich and mighty, created by colonial masters, captured power denying people their due rights. Both used poetry as a means of resistance against colonial and post-colonial legacy of control, exploitation and denial of rights to the masses. They remained active players in the entire struggle and not mere idealist poets, sitting on the other side of the fence, criticizing others. This makes them distinguishable from many contemporary poets and writers, who believed in "art for the sake of art" and sided with the rulers of the day, either by their silence or inactions.

Faiz during his exile, had a chance of editing the magazine, *Lotus*, of Afro-Asian Writers' Association. In *Lotus* English translations of Pablo Neruda's poems appeared frequently. Faiz, in his many editorials while paying tributes to Neruda, aptly called him poet of humanity, 'great voice of our time', 'true representative of masses' and 'poet of all times to come'. The message of Neruda, according to Faiz, is not only meant for his countrymen but all those who were once subjugated and then struggled for freedom but soon realized their liberation was myth and not reality as colonial masters left behind their cronies who proved to be more cruel than their masters. The poetry of Faiz and Neruda is realization of this myth of independence—title of the book by

46

Zulfikar Ali Bhutto—and how to win real freedom—to undo colonial legacy, defeat the forces of exploitation and establish a just system for all.

How long will this struggle continue? The answer came from Edward W. Said, the great intellectual of our time. In an interview, while elaborating the legacy of Neruda and Faiz, Professor Said pointed out that "in a world so long might is right, the powerful in the global politics want the perpetuation of their control through handpicked cronies and lackeys in different countries, we will need poets like Faiz and Neruda to expose them and give us courage to fight against them".

Professor Said always admired Faiz for his courage and resilience. Faiz, while in prison, expressed remarkably the love for his homeland and struggle against oppression in the following poem:

> I give my life to your alleys, oh nation, where custom now
> dictates that one walk with head bowed, when a lover leaves on
> a pilgrimage to love,
> he must guard his eye, his body, his life. Here, then, is the new
> order of freedom, oh heart
> Stones and bricks are in captivity and dogs run free. Many are
> the pretenses for the oppressor's hand
> for the few who, in madness, take your name
> the ones crazed by lust are both the accusers and the judges
> who can we get to make our case? From whom can we seek
> justice? Yet the days go by for those who can,
> in your separation, turn dusk to dawn. Now that the prison's
> window has turned off
> we know that stars must have decorated your hair.
> Now that these chains are sparkling
> we know that the day must has illuminated your face.
> And so we live, imagining dawns and dusks
> And so we live, gripped by the shadow of these prison walls
> Such has always been, this struggle between oppressor and
> oppressed
> Neither are their customs new, nor our paths new
> Such has always been, that we grew flowers amid fire
> Neither is their defeat new, nor is our triumph new.
> Which is why, we don't offer complains to the sky
> Which is why, we don't mourn being away from you
> If today we are apart, tomorrow we will be together this
> separation for a night is nothing,
> If today the rival's sun is high, so what?
> This good for four days is nothing.
> Those who maintain their oath of fidelity to you they possess the
> cure for the circulation of night and day.

Faiz Ahmed Faiz, Wind's Palm (1953)

The poems of Neruda are still a source of inspiration for many in Pakistan, as in the elsewhere in the world. In Pakistan, translations of his famous works have been made in different regional languages, Urdu, Punjabi, Sindhi and Baluchi. He is hero of all nationalist-revolutionaries who still believe to be working to regain freedom from the occupant forces. Wherever there is injustice, denial of rights of peoples and violence, Neruda is

47

understood and cherished as epitome of courage and source of limitless encouragement. Anwer Zahidi (born July 9, 1946), a Pakistani, has translated Neruda's autobiography, which is certainly an invaluable addition to Urdu letters. The following poem of Neruda is translated in almost all the local languages of Pakistan:

"Because I love my country
I claim you, essential brother,
old Walt Whitman with your gray hands.

So that, with your special help line by line, we will tear out the
roots and destroy the bloodthirsty
President Nixon.

There can be no happy man on earth, no one can work well on
this planet while that nose continues to breathe in Washington.

Asking the old bard to confer with me
I assume the duties of a poet
armed with a terrorist's sonnet

Because I must carry out with no regrets
this sentence, never before witnessed,
of shooting a criminal under siege,

Who in spite of his trips to the moon
has killed so many here on earth
that the paper flies up and the pen is unsheathed

To set down the name of this villain
who practises genocide from the White"

The lines of these poems written way back in 1973 are still relevant. The wars in Afghanistan and Iraq, genocides in various parts of the world, use of religion for killing others, exploitation of world resources by a few—no man can be happy on the earth unless forces in Washington stop their unjust policies. We need another Neruda—a poet with a 'terrorist's sonnet' to counter men with guns killing each other in the name of religion or self-assumed "national interest"(sic).

Huzaima Bukhari and Dr. Ikramul Haq are partners in an international tax law firm. Both of them have published numerous articles and books on a range of current issues including literature. The writers specialise in studying global heroin economy. They are visiting Professor at Lahore University of Management Sciences (LUMS).

ainting of Faiz Ahmed Faiz by Hasan Mehdi, Karachi, 2011

Faiz in Lahore, 1948

Chapter 7

From home to the world

ALI MIR & RAZA MIR

Faiz Ahmed Faiz's internationalist vision was based on working-class movements and the struggles of colonised peoples everywhere.

In March 1955, Faiz Ahmed Faiz, still imprisoned in Rawalpindi's Montgomery Jail where he had been interred since 1951 for 'seditious activities,' wrote Aa Jaao Africa (Come, Africa), a poem based on a phrase he had heard as a rallying cry among African anti-colonial rebels:

> *Aa jaao main ne sun li tere dhol ki tarang*
> *Aa jaao mast ho gayi mere lahu ki chaal ...*
>
> *Come, that I have heard the sounds of your drum*
> *Come that my blood flows to its rhythm*
> *Come, Africa.*
> *Come, for I have raised my forehead from the dust*
> *Scraped away the hide of grief from my eyes*
> *Broken away from the grip of pain*
> *Torn away the web of helplessness*
> *Come, Africa!*
> *The earth's heart beats with mine, Africa*
> *The river dances while the moon keeps time*
> *I am Africa, for I have taken on your form*
> *I am you, and my gait is your lion-walk.*
> *Come, Africa*
> *Come with a lion-walk*
> *Come, Africa!*

We always felt intrigued by the poem, not least because it troubled us. While Faiz's solidarity with Africa was obvious in the lines, the image of the continent was primal, wild, invoking jungles and wild animals. Our latter-day sensibilities could not reconcile Faiz's obvious commitment to international humanism with the image he obviously harboured of Africans as primal beings. It was much later that we learned that far from invoking racialised stereotypes, Faiz's imagery had been inspired by the poetic aesthetics developed by writers and intellectuals of the Negritude movement, which sought to reclaim the metaphors of blackness in the service of an international solidarity amongst people of colour. Faiz's friendship with African poets such as Aimé Césaire of Martinique must have led him to adopt these metaphors, which he then brought to the Subcontinent. Ultimately, other Urdu poets like Ali Sardar Jafri would use similar imagery in

their poems celebrating black revolutionaries across the world.

The story of *Aa Jaao Africa* in many ways frames Faiz's role as someone who helped the progressive aesthetic of Urdu poetry add an internationalist ethos. His travels across the world in the 1950s and 1960s brought Faiz to far more interesting places than the standard sojourn to the island of Vilayat by his peers. He developed relationships with a variety of peers, who in their poems wrote of the oppressed in their lands: the Chilean Pablo Neruda, Langston Hughes of the Harlem Renaissance, and Nazim Hikmet of Turkey (whose work he translated into Urdu). Also, while leftists across the Subcontinent were well aware of Soviet poets like Mayakovski; their exposure was limited to Russians who wrote in a European style. Thanks to Faiz, we have Urdu translations from the 'lesser Soviets' such as Kazakhstan's Olzhas Suleimenov, or Daghestan's Rasul Gamzatov.

Faiz with other writers an at Afro-Asian Writers' conference, Tashkent, 1978.

At odds with the state

Faiz was an internationalist partly by inclination, and partly out of circumstance. His relationship with the nation-state was doomed on 15 August 1947, with the partition of the country. The promised independence arrived, but its crimson hue was not that of the awaited socialist 'red dawn' but came from the blood of the dead of Partition violence. Faiz's poem *Subh-e Aazadi* (The dawn of freedom) was an anthem for the defeat of progressive politics at the moment of decolonisation. *Ye dagh dagh ujaala, ye shab-gazeeda sahar* (This pock-marked light, this night-inflected morning), carried the voice of all progressives regarding the catastrophe of partition. The poem ended with the call to continue the unfinished journey:

> *Abhi giraani-e-shab mein kami nahin aayi*
> *Najaat-e deeda-o dil ki ghadi nahin aayi*
> *Chale chalo, ke wo manzil abhi nahin aayi*
>
> *Don't be fooled, the abatement of the darkness is*
> *not here yet*
> *The deliverance of the eye and the heart is not here yet*
> *Keep moving, for the awaited destination is not here yet.*

Faiz's relationship with the nation-state was rendered even more contingent when he was arrested in 1951 by the Ayub Khan regime in the Rawalpindi Conspiracy Case. The charges of working to overthrow the government led to a longish prison stint, and incidentally laid the foundation for the banning of the Communist Party of Pakistan and its various fronts in 1954. Faiz's poems during those days, collected in his book *Zindan-naama* (Letters from Prison) perhaps reflect his best work:

> *Nisaar main teri galiyon pe ai vatan, ke jahaan*
> *Chali hai rasm ke koi na sar utha ke chale*
>
> *I sacrifice myself to your lanes, my country*
> *Where it has been decreed that none should walk with head*
> *held high.*

It was here that he developed his trademark poetic metaphors, where the qafas (cage) encloses the prisoner, who then depends on the breeze (*saba*) to get news of the homeland. As the two poem snippets below show, Faiz's poetry seemed to enter a reflective state, combining the passion of classic love poetry with revolutionary idiom, which is what makes him unique among the progressives.

Citizen of the world

> *Chaman mein ghaarat-e gulcheen se jaane kya guzri*
> *Qafas se aaj saba beqaraar guzri hai*
>
> *I wonder what wrath the flower-picker wreaked on the garden*
> *For the zephyr has passed through my cage rather agitated*
>
> *Qafas hai bas mein tumhaare, tumhaare bas mein nahin*
> *Chaman mein aatish-e gul ke nikhaar ka mausam*
> *Bala se hum ne na dekha to aur dekhenge*
> *Furogh-e gulshan-o saut-e hazaar ka mausam*

The cage may be in your power, but you do not control
The season of the flowering of the bright rose
And so what if we do not see it? For the ones following us
will witness
The brightness of the garden, the singing of
the nightingale

While Faiz's poems are a vibrant example of the internationalist ethos of progressive Urdu poetry, the internationalism itself is not really exceptional. The internationalist commitment of the progressive movement was apparent since its very beginning. The anti-fascist struggles of European literary figures had enthused the Progressives, and one of the first activities of the newly formed Progressive Writers' Association (PWA), in 1935, was to send Sajjad Zaheer and Mulk Raj Anand as their representatives to London to participate in the conference of 'International Writers for the Defense of Culture' Poets like Mohammad Iqbal had been expanding the horizons of Urdu literature's engagement with the world for a while. The PWA poets besides Faiz, however, took the internationalism to new levels. The Association had come into being at a time when the freedom movement was at its height, and the initial writings of its members were focused on the struggle against British occupation. Overtures to internationalism took two forms: an interrogation and critique of colonialism and its related issues (the Second World War, for instance), and an expression of admiration for the Soviet revolution accompanied by a hope that India's freedom would result in a similar socialist society.

Faiz with Alys and Afro-Asian writers, Tashkent, 1978

The emergence of the Non-Aligned Movement at Bandung, Indonesia in 1955 (the year of the writing of *Aa Jaao Africa*), concretised the idea of Third World solidarity, and provided another arena of expression for progressive poetry. Sahir wrote several poems in appreciation of Lenin, Makhdoom wrote moving elegies to Patrice Lumumba and Martin Luther King, Ali Sardar Jafri composed odes to Paul Robeson, and Kaifi Azmi wrote poems critiquing the US involvement in Vietnam. The cultural exchange fostered by the Non-Aligned and Afro-Asian movements led to the translation of many of Faiz's poems into Swahili, Chinese and Vietnamese, while the works of progressive poets from around the world were translated into Urdu.

This period of Third World solidarity saw the Progressives composing poems on issues such as the struggles of Iranian students in 1959, the McCarthy era of repression of dissent in the United States, the European student uprisings in the 1960s, the Algerian freedom movement, the Palestinian struggle and the anti-apartheid movement in South Africa. Faiz weighed in on a variety of global debates of the time, but with a lyricism that was unmatched. When Julius and Ethel Rosenberg were executed in 1953 by the US government on the charge of being Soviet spies, Faiz was inspired to write a poem. But, rather than write it as a protest against the injustice, he framed it as a lyrical tribute to their love, as they stubbornly refused to betray each other despite inducements, threats, incarceration, and ultimately, execution. His tribute is heartbreakingly titled *Hum jo tareek raahon mein maare gaye* (We who were executed on dark highways). Here is an excerpt:

> *Tere honton ke phoolon ki chaahat mein hum*
> *Daar ki khushk tahni pe vaare gaye*
> *Tere haathon ki shammom ki hasrat mein hum*
> *Neem-tareek raahon mein maare gaye…*
> *Jab ghuli teri raahon mein shaam-e sitam*
> *Hum chale aaye laaye jahaañ tak qadam*
> *Lab pe harf-e ghazal, dil meiñ qandeel-e-gham*
> *Apna gham tha gavaahi tere husn ki*
> *Dekh khaayam rahe is gavaahi pe hum*
> *Hum jo tareek raahon mein maare gaye*

> *In the desire for the flowers that were your lips*
> *We were sacrificed on the dry branch of the scaffold*
> *In the yearning for the light of your hands*
> *We were killed in the darkening streets...*
> *As the evening of tyranny dissolved in your memory*
> *We walked on as far as our feet could carry us*
> *A song on our lips, a lamp of sadness in our heart*
> *Our grief bore witness to our love for your beauty*
> *Look, we remained true to that love*
> *We, who were executed in the dark lanes.*

Inauguration of Lotus magazine: Faiz with Yasser Arafat, Beirut, 1979

Faiz's travels resumed when he went into self-exile in Lebanon during the dictatorship of Zia-ul-Haq. It was in Beirut that he wrote several poems on the Middle East conflict: a piece on Beirut itself *(Ishq Apne Mujrimoñ Ko Pabajaulaañ Le Chala /* Love Leads its Prisoners Away in Chains), an anthem for Palestinian freedom-fighters *(Ek Taraana Filastini Mujaahidoñ Ke Naam /* An Anthem for Palestinian Revolutionaries), a dirge for the Palestinian dead *(Filastini Shohada Jo Pardes Meiñ Kaam Aaye /* Palestinian Martyrs Who Died Abroad), and perhaps the most famous, a lullaby to a Palestinian orphan *(Mat Ro Bachche /* Weep Not, Child). Faiz dedicated his book *Mere Dil, Mere Musaafir* (My Heart, My Wanderer) to the Palestinian leader, Yasser Arafat. But the great sensitivity of Faiz was to relate the Palestinian condition back to South Asia, using the victory of Israel as a metaphor for the victory of capitalist elites in India and Pakistan, often in collusion with religious elites. Following the defeat of the Arab forces in the June 1967 war, his *Sar-e Vaadi-e Seena* (Atop the Sinai Valley) was, among other things, a scathing indictment of the hypocrisy of elitist Islamists. The poem exhorts people to cast off the chains of theocratic exploitation:

> *Phir barq farozaan hai sar-e vaadi-e Sina*
> *Ai deeda-e beena*
> *Phir dil ko musaffa karo is lauh pe, shaayad*
> *Maabain-e man-o tu naya paimaan koi utre*
> *Ab rasm-e sitam hikmat-e khaasaan-e zameen hai*
> *Taaeed-e sitam maslehat-e mufti-e deen hai*
> *Ab sadiyon ke iqraar-e itaa'at ko badalne*
> *Laazim hai ke inkaar ka farmaan koi utre*
>
> *Yet again, lightning shimmers atop the Sinai valley*
> *O seeing eye*
> *Ask the hearts to line up again*

56

> *That between you and me, a new promise may descend*
> *For now, the elite of the earth have decreed*
> *Tyranny to be normal*
> *And the mufti has pronounced Oppression worth obeying*
> *To break this centuries-old cycle of acquiescence*
> *A new proclamation must descend, the proclamation of dissent*

Some of Faiz's contemporaries were even more direct. Using a similar metaphor, but with far great irony, Habib Jalib taunted Zia-ul-Huq in a poem that set the tone for the critique of the regime that chose to deploy Islam as a tool of ensuring domestic acquiescence, but was slow to take on Israeli imperialism for fear of angering the US:

> *Jahaan qatre mein hai Islam, us maidan mein jaao*
> *Hamari jaan ke dar pe ho kyon, Lebnaan mein jaao*
> *Ijaazat maangte hain hum bhi jab Beirut jaane ki*
> *To ahl e hukm ye kahte hain tum zindaan mein jaao*
>
> *If you must save Islam, go where it is in danger*
> *Why darken our doors, go to Lebanon*
> *And when we ask for permission to go to Beirut*
> *Our rulers instead send us to the dungeons.*

Ultimately, Faiz's internationalist vision, and indeed, that of the other PWA poets like Faiz, Majaz, Makhdoom, Kaifi and others, came directly out of the politics and the general sensibility of the time. The realities of colonialism, and later neocolonialism/neo-imperialism, both required and provided a global frame of reference and a basis for shared political engagement with other colonised and/or oppressed peoples. Internationalism in this period, however, was not homogeneous; the internationalism of Faiz and the Progressives, for example, was a far cry from the pan-Islamism of Iqbal and his followers. While Iqbal was motivated more by the need to find common heritage across Muslims of the world, Faiz's understanding was informed more by an understanding of the shared material conditions of oppression and struggle and was inspired by the international working-class movements and the struggles of colonised peoples across the world. For them, internationalism meant a common struggle against imperialism and for a new world order.

Ali Mir and Raza Mir are originally from Hyderabad, India and now teach at universities in the US. Both of them are renowned writers and poets. Their book: Anthems of Resistance is described as the finest critical account of the Progressive Writers' Association that was established in India in 1936. The article in this publication was previously appeared in the on-line journal: Himal Southasia

Faiz Ahmed Faiz, 1956

Chapter 8

How not to read Faiz Ahmed Faiz

GOPI CHAND NARANG

How not to read Faiz does imply how Faiz[1] must not be read, or how Faiz be read. But this is not what is intended here. To say how Faiz be read or how it should not be read sounds prescriptive, and it is not the role of criticism to be prescriptive. There are readings and readings. Faiz is a popular poet and who can tell his admirers how to read and how not to read Faiz. It is besides the point that there is no dearth of critics who take such stance without realizing that their writing is neither of any use for literature nor for literary criticism. Notwithstanding, all sorts of readers read the poetry of Faiz, and the graph of his popularity stays pretty stable. It is also understandable that the camp followers of a particular breed use the poetry of Faiz to shield their own shortcomings.

Popularity has its own downside, because the crowd of admirers comprise the majority of those who do not know why they like their hero. Do they admire him because of their genuine appreciation of his text or simply because others admire him? The popularity of Faiz, intact even today, was established in the second half of the twentieth century, and this is not a short period for the firming of a poet's significance. During this period, much has been written about Faiz, but it is a sad fact that many of his admirers admire him for wrong reasons; they have written little about his poetic worth. In this regard, Faiz deserves our sympathy.

The poetry of Faiz deserves appreciation from those as well who understand the dynamics of reading and how poetry functions. Reading is an open-ended project and the problem arises only when a lobby insists on a particular reading so much so that, that reading restricts the semantic play of the text. To say the least, it is a disservice to the poet. Faiz no doubt is a committed poet and nobody can deny his ideological leanings.

But mere ideological readings do not fit his aesthetic structure and the main question is that how this structure signifies within the framework of his ideological project. As reading implies freedom, by employing a negative 'how not' we are not impeding the free flow of interpretation, rather stressing that conflict within the ideological project needs to be attended to, and any reading that avoids conflict in the ideological project is restrictive and does not do justice to the appreciation of Faiz.

Popularity is usually the result of several factors, such as personal charisma, romantic image and biographical data (especially if it involves political confinement or exile or any such restriction). However, when the cruel hand of time

creates a gap, all such subjective signages are washed away, and what remains is the spotless spring of the text; and it is this that is not fully considered by admirers of Faiz. If they do consider, they do so in a cursory manner. True poetry is a world in itself, but if literary criticism is not open to dissent and difference in interpretation, then the door of the magic of the poetry cannot open. In my earlier writings, I have alluded to the sensuous nature of the aesthetic effect in Faiz's poetry along with its peculiar semantic range. There is no need to repeat all that now. In this piece, I would like to point out briefly that in reading a text, one must not only pay attention to the presence (of words) but also heed to the silences and absences in the text, in the way as Pierre Macherey or Roland Barthes usually suggest. This in my opinion is a necessary prerequisite to appreciate the aesthetic dynamics of Faiz's poetry.

It should be noted that ideology as discussed by Althusser[2] is not an abstraction which people carry around in their minds or a treatise of abstract ideas. Instead it refers to human beings' necessary condition of action in a social formation. He had argued that ideology is represented by discourses governing the practices how we live our lives, i.e., it is in the condition of human existence. It is characteristic of the ideology that in a social formation at one end of the scale lies the ideology, on the other is science & technology, and somewhere in between is the world of art and literature marked by the aesthetic effect. All the three domains are inter-dependent yet relatively autonomous. Science leads to the 'knowledge effect', ideology to the 'ideological effect', and art and literature to the 'aesthetic effect', and this last effect holds the key to the appreciation of Faiz. All the three effects, while each playing an autonomous role in its domain in the superstructure, do overlap and play a determinant role; and despite the inconsistencies and contradictions inherent in them, they do tend to resolve the inherent conflict. Having said this, now let's turn to the text of Faiz.

Faiz reciting at the All Pakistan Urdu-Sindhi Mushaira, Karachi, 1973

Let's see how it is usually read and whether or not such reading is incomplete or misleading. Merleau-Ponty, an important interpreter of phenomenology who has been almost forgotten by the moderns, had noted:

"But what if language speaks as much by what is between words as by the words themselves? As much what it 'does not say' as by what it 'says'!"

In other words, it is beyond doubt that it is the characteristic of language that what it says through words, it also says through gaps and silences. Probably, from the point of view of meaning, this is a clear parallel to the oriental concept of 'bain-ussutoor' (literary between lines), but perhaps no one in the oriental rhetoric ever tried to theorise this.

Mark it that we are not talking of mere silence between lines or words, rather what is intended is the silence between the absent and present meaning. If we read once again what Merleau-Ponty said, we will appreciate the inference that words speak through what they reveal, as well as through what they hide or do not reveal. As if the dark areas of language are as instrumental in evoking meaning and aesthetic effect as the bright areas. Let's take a look at Faiz's poem "Dast-e Teh-e Sang Amada" (A Hand Trapped Under a Rock) from his collection with the same title. (The translation is deliberately literal so that it stays as close to the original as possible):

Bezaar faza

*darpa-i aazaar saba hai
Yun hai ke har ik hamdam-i dairina khafa hai*

*The morning breeze hurts, and the atmosphere is displeased;
It seems as if every old friend is angry with me.*

*Haan baada kasho aaya hai ab rang pe mausam
Ab sair ke qaabi ravish-i aab-o hava hai*

*Yes, fellow drinkers, the time is just right for drinking;
The weather appears just right for a stroll through the garden.*

*Umdi hai har ik simt se ilzaam ki barsaat
Chhaai hui har daang malaamat ki ghata hai*

*The rainstorm of accusations is gathering fast;
The clouds of reproach spread in every direction.*

*Voh cheez bhari hai ke sulagti hai suraahi
Har kaasa-i mai zehr-i halaahal se bhara hai*

*The flask simmer due to its contents;
Every cup of wine brims with deadly poison.*

*Haan jaam uthaao ke ba-yaad-i lab-i sheerin
Yeh zehr to yaaron ne kai baar piya hai*

*Let's raise our glasses in memory of sweet lips;
We have drunk this poison many times before.*

*Is jazba-i dil ki na saza hai na jaza hai
Maqsood-i rah-i shauq vafa hai na jafa hai*

*The emotions of heart are neither to be punished, nor rewarded;
The destination of the journey of desire is neither love nor misery.*

Ehsaas-i gham-i dil jo gham-i dil ka silaa hai

Us husn ka ehsaas hai jo teri ata hai

The gift of the feelings of the heart is grief itself:
A generous gift of your beauty.

Har subh-i gulistaan hai tira ru-i bahaarin
Har phool tiri yaad ka naqsh-i kaf-i paa hai

Every morning of the rose garden is your fresh face;
Every flower: a footprint of your memory.

Har bheegi hui raat tiri zulf ki shabnam
Dhalta hua suraj tire hunton ki taza hai

Every wet night is the dew of your tresses;
Every setting sun: the scene of your lips.

Har raah pahunchti hai tiri chaah ke dar tak
Har harf-i tamanna tire qadmon ki sada hai

Every pathway leads to the door of your love;
Every word of desire: the sound of your footsteps.

Ta'zeer-i siyasat hai na ghairon ki khata hai
Voh zulm jo ham ne dil-i vehshi pe kiya hai

It is neither the punishment of events, nor the tyranny
of adversaries:
This tyranny, we have inflicted ourselves on our poor untamed
heart.

Zindaan-i rah-i yaar main paa-band hue ham
Zanjeer ba-kaf hai na koi band-ba paa hai

We are trapped in the prison of the longing for our beloved;
We wear neither handcuffs, nor are shackled.

Majburi-o va'daa-I giraftaari-i ulfat
Dast-i tah-i sang aamda paimaan-i vafa hai

Helplessness and the pledge to be captured by love:
They are nothing, but a hand trapped under a rock.

On the surface, there is no complexity in the poem, which towards the close cites the ghazal verse of Ghalib: the pledge to love is nothing but a hand trapped under a rock. If one is helpless in love, then the pledge to love means nothing, as one makes a pledge by one's own freewill, and here there is no freewill. Metaphorically, the hand is trapped under a rock, and this is what the pledge is. The pain and agony of the hand under a rock suggests a terrible feeling of helplessness. In short, there is no choice, only helplessness as the hand is trapped under a rock. There are many aspects of helplessness, and Ghalib is a poet of that calibre, whereas said by Meer[4], every word has many dimensions to it. Instead of trying to further dilate the literal meaning, I merely want to hint that the poem, which revolves around the helplessness of love, is not a love poem, nor it is an overtly political poem. Let's note that before tagging Ghalib, Faiz had established the following semantic field in the poem:

> *Every pathway leads to the door of your love;*
> *Every word of desire: the sound of your footsteps.*
> *It is neither the punishment of events, nor the tyranny of*
> *adversaries:*
> *This tyranny, we have inflicted ourselves on our poor untamed*
> *heart.*
> *We are trapped in the prison of the longing for our beloved;*
> *We wear neither handcuffs, nor are shackled.*

The leading of the pathway to the door of love, punishment of events, prison of the longing for beloved, wearing handcuffs: these references undoubtedly evoke a picture of love for a cause. It goes without saying that what is being implied is the love for some ideal, some commitment, maybe freedom of country from army rule or any such oppression. These meanings may suggest themselves at a close reading. Now, let us see the beginning of the poem again:

> The morning breeze hurts, and the atmosphere is displeased;
> It seems as if every old friend is angry (with me).
> Yes, fellow drinkers, the time is just right for drinking;
> The weather appears just right for a stroll through the garden.
> The rainstorm of accusations is gathering fast;
> The clouds of reproach spread in every direction.

Once the parameter of love changes from personal to social, and it is realized that Faiz is a poet with social consciousness, it becomes easy to multiply the obvious with the metaphorical. After such realization, effortlessly every figure of speech starts revolving around a socio-political axis in accordance with expectations. For example, 'displeased atmosphere' becomes the tyrannical environment, the 'breeze that hurts' becomes the unjust order and its oppression, 'fellow drinkers' are fellows with social consciousness, and the 'old friends' are either those not in synch with the revolutionary creed or those who are content to become part of the anti-people regime. Since 'madness and humiliation' are something to be proud of when one is in love (as per the Indo-Persian poetic convention), 'the rainstorm of accusations' and 'the clouds of reproach everywhere' are quite in keeping with the patriotic expectations. Further, the cup and the flask are evoking the passion for freedom. In the act of reading, much has been said about the role of expectations of the reader; besides the text these expectations as well may be generated by the name, creed or ideology of the poet, or by the title or subtitle of the poem. The tagged verse of Ghalib, as suggested before, also has its role.

Faiz addressing railway workers, Lahore, 1948

63

In this discourse, it is not intended to go into the details of the psychology of reading; nonetheless, we have already seen that in the first place we could not have read Ghalib's verse in any other way than as a romantic verse, but when tagged to Faiz's poem, its semantic axis changed, and in this context it now reads for revolutionary zeal and suffering for a social cause. In other words when we started reading the poem with expectations of reading a text loaded with ideology, the non-political nature of Ghalib's verse changed in keeping with the interpretation of the key words in the poem. At one time, Ali Sardar Jafri[5] and his progressive friends used to discuss with fervour the concept of 'revolutionary romanticism'. I wish at that stage if they had paid a little attention to the poetic implications of either romanticism or revolution, the Urdu world would have been spared from the one-dimensional flat poetry that flooded in the forties and fifties.

Let's once again turn back to the obvious or not so obvious meanings of Faiz's poem. Is the poetry of Faiz important because it is the poetry of the given political meaning? If the answer to this question is in the affirmative, then it will be very difficult to defend Faiz as a great poet. Does everyone read Faiz because he is a poet of the given or of the obvious or of preconceived ideas? In our humble opinion, the answer to this question is in the negative. Matters of like and dislike of poetry are complex, similar to the matters of beauty and love. We have discussed earlier that in good poetry, words say as much as what they do not want to say. In the dynamics of poetic aesthetics, both the said and the unsaid interact and intermingle to create a touch of mystery. Does any such thing happen in the poetry of Faiz? If it does, then is the poetry of Faiz only confined to the meanings discussed earlier and which our friends with preconceived notions like best?

Undoubtedly, the obvious meanings are what have been discussed, but the matter does not end there, because if it were so, then Faiz would have been an ordinary poet, and the roots of his popularity would not go very deep. The meanings discussed earlier are clearly motivated by given political agenda, or ideology. As referred to earlier, ideology is not a treatise of doctrine or abstract theory of beliefs. It is also not the official document of social truths, nor the manifesto or 'partynost' done by an Andrey Zhdanov. Perhaps few will disagree that the progressive ideology of the times of Faiz was not much different from the nationalist ideology of the period of struggle for freedom; it was not in conflict with cultural aesthetics generated at the level of the elite which favoured nationalism. Because of this, the progressive ideology in the subcontinent was not restrictive; its real conflict was with oppression, colonial exploitation and denial of freedom. In this context, the obvious meanings discussed above are the given meaning. However, we should not forget that the aesthetics of

Faiz was entrenched in the oriental tradition, so much so that it was rooted in the classical Farsi and Indo-Persian influences.

Strictly speaking, in leftist terminology, this aesthetics is 'bourgeois', and thus supposedly is in conflict with the ideological project. But the fact is that Faiz had inherited and was the guardian of a tradition of aesthetics, whose blood was flowing in his veins. It was part of his conscious, as well as a part of his sub-conscious mind. The ideology is a matter of choice, the rejection or acceptance of which is in one's conscious control. But the aesthetics are not optional as it is part of the creative personality or the sub-conscious mind. Althusser, whom we quoted earlier, has pointed out that ideology and art and literature play relatively independent roles in social formation; and let's not forgot that while overlapping with each other, they also define each other. Ideology by nature tends to discourage difference, and its relation to any sort of play of freedom, be that of aesthetics, is that of repression. The silences and absences find their way into the text because of this repressive relationship. In this context, if we re-examine the poem of Faiz, we shall discover a whole range of repressed meanings. Although it is argued by some that devices of poetic expression, such as figures of speech, similes, metaphors, etc. which are used to create play of meaning and aesthetic effect, are part of baggage of bourgeois pleasure, Faiz is not burdened by this argument, rather it is in this expression that the appeal of Faiz's poetry lies. Needless to say that the aesthetics of Faiz is grounded in the metaphorical edifice of the oriental tradition. This aesthetics is part of his sub-consciousness, and penetrates profusely into his poetry, often moulding his ideological concerns into its own cast. For example, after establishing the political underpinning of the poem with the rainstorm of accusations, clouds of reproach, etc., Faiz comes down to the gay abandon of the sub-conscious, and the wine in the flask of aesthetics spills over, thus weaving magic and casting a spell. To say the least, if such style were taken away from his poetry, Faiz could not be recognized. After the opening three stanzas, read the following:

Let's raise our glasses in memory of sweet lips;
We have drunk this poison many times before.
The emotions of heart are neither to be punished, nor rewarded;
The destination of the journey of desire is neither
love nor misery.
The gift of the feelings of the heart is grief itself:
A generous gift of your beauty.
Each morning of the rose garden is like the charm of
your fresh face;
Every flower: a footprint of your memory.
Every wet night is the dew of your tresses;
Every setting sun: the scene of your lips.
Every pathway leads to the door of your love;
Every word of desire: the sound of your footsteps.

65

It hardly needs stressing that the above lines form the core of the poem. The core thus is drenched in the aesthetic flavour of Faiz, and this cannot be denied that without which Faiz simply is not Faiz. It is not just the matter of ideology yielding to the aesthetic call, there is much more to it. It is worth examining why the ideological project allows repression by the so called 'bourgeois' aesthetics, thus creating silences in the text.

What the French literary critic Pierre Macherey says discussing the fiction of Jules Verne is not irrelevant here:

> 'If Verne's 19th century readers did not identify the repressed in the text, if they did not recognise the silence with which the work finally confronts its own ideological project, it was because they read from within the same ideological framework, shared the same repressions and took for granted the same silences.'[6]

Faiz with Sibte Hasan at the Press Club, Karachi, 1984

So if we are used to the silences in the repressed ideological project, it is firstly because of the fact that the act of our reading is within the same framework; secondly, we tolerate the repression because we ourselves derive aesthetic pleasure in the process. The central portion of the poem begins with 'Let's raise our glasses in the memory of sweet lips.' Glasses of what? Here, the reference is not to the glass of wine.

It can be said that the meaning of wine has been repressed. Similarly, 'sweet lips' should invoke the lips of the beloved, but the human beloved is not being referred to here. The image of the form and beauty of the beloved, which sneaked in through the doorway of aesthetics, wants to take over the poem, but the ideological project represses it. The repressed meaning wants to come to surface; but when it cannot, its form changes.

Repressed by ideology it turns into absence or silence. For example, consider: 'A generous gift of your beauty'. Whose beauty? Or: 'Each morning of the rose garden is your fresh face. Every flower: a footprint of your memory'. Whose fresh face? The flower of whose memory? Consider further: 'Every wet night is the dew of your tresses. Every setting sun: the scene of your lips'. The dew-touch of whose tresses? The scene of whose lips? The answers to these and other such questions lie hidden in the silences and absences of the text. One can say that Faiz permits repression in his poetic expression because the rhetorical conventions of the oriental aesthetics are an integral part of his consciousness. It is known that Faiz as a poet had made his mark with the publication of his first collection *Naqsh-e Faryadi*[7] . The later collections *Dast-e Saba*[8] and *Zindan Nama*[9] completed the poetic identity of Faiz. There was all along an inner contradiction within Faiz himself, even if he wanted to close the hidden door of subconscious or the innate pull of the Indo-Persian aesthetics of ruby lips and rose garden, he could not do so. As a result, those portions are most compelling where the repression runs wild, or where absences and silences speak in their repressed language, or where the text between-the-lines glows with pleasure. The effect in such cases is fascinating.

It should be noted that what has been said is not limited to the nazm (poem) under consideration. Most of the other poetry of Faiz is replete with these characteristics.

Further examples in defence of the discourse are not necessary.

I would like to make one last point: The Indo-Persian aesthetics is the aesthetics of peeping from behind a curtain.

Consider the following segments of a nazm from Naqsh-e Faryadi :

> *Unka aanchal hai ki rukhsaar ki pairahan hai*
> *Kuch to hai jis se hui Juuti hui chilman rangeen?*
>
> *Is it the scarf, the face, or the robe*
> *That makes the reed-curtain so colourful?*
>
> *Sandali haath pe dhundhli si hina ki tahreer ....*
>
> *The faint marks of henna on the sandal coloured hands....*

These fleeting images can best be described by the phrase, / *saaf chupte bhi nahin saamne aate bhi nahi* / (she doesn't hide herself either, nor does she come in front')[10]. This is the hide-and-seek of an aesthetics, which becomes all the more compelling in an environ of repression. Roland Barthes, the author of The Pleasure of Text, writes:

> *"Is not the body's most erotic zone there,*
> *Where the garment leaves gaps?"*

As far as Faiz's repressed aesthetics bursting through the ideological seams is concerned, it does not need any further elaboration. The seams in Faiz generally come undone, exposing the pull of aesthetics. No doubt, Faiz enjoys the construct too. This is the act of the eloquence of silence. If such were not the case, Faiz would not have dwelt so much on the wildness of the untamed heart:

> *It is neither the punishment of events, nor the*
> *tyranny of adversaries:*
> *This tyranny, we have inflicted ourselves on our*
> *poor untamed heart.:*
>
> *Khub parda hai ke chilman se lage baithe hain*
> *Saaf chhupte bhi nahin saamne aate bhi nahin*
>
> *What strange modesty: she sits by the reed-curtain;*
> *Doesn't hide herself completely, nor does she come in front.*
> *finds its resolve through undone seams.*

It can be said that the act of repression and peeping through of aesthetics, having its own peculiar effect, creates the allure and beauty that the poetry of Faiz is known for, and which undoubtedly enlarge the circle of his admirers. The popularity of Faiz deserves further attention, but the current discussion is, as explained earlier, restricted only to the conflict between his ideological project and the subconscious aesthetics that finds its resolve through undone seams. The ghazal in which Faiz speaks about his poetic 'style' becoming accepted as the 'mode of expression in the rose-garden', also has a reference to the tyranny of the cage of the bird-trapper and the flower-picker. It is a matter of subverting expectations. This verse, which is against political oppression, can also be read against the oppression of ideology. No matter how strong an ideology may be, no matter if aesthetics is condemned as bourgeois,

68

the subconscious has its own ways of resolving conflicts. To write poetry or to enjoy poetry, one must accept the pull of aesthetics, yield to a mystery within. Despite the harshness of the so-called bird-trappers and the flower-pickers, the fragrance of the rose and the song of the nightingale could not be stopped. Faiz celebrates life, and it is in the course of this spontaneous celebration that the seams come undone and the silence speaks.

(This article was translated by Baidar Bakht from the original Urdu.)

Dast-e saiyaad bhi aajiz hai, kaf-i gulchin bhi
Bu-i gul thehri, na bulbul ki zabaan thehri hai

The hands of the bird-trapper are as helpless as those of flower-picker;
The fragrance of rose can't be arrested, nor can the song of the nightingale.

Ham ne jo tarz-i fughaan ki hai qafas main ijaad
Faiz gulshan main vohi tarz-i bayaan thehri hai

Faiz, the style of wailing that I invented in the cage
Has now become the mode of expression in the rose-garden

References

[1] Faiz Ahmed Faiz (1911-1984).
[2] For details, see : For Marx by Louis Althusser, New Left Books, London, 1977; and "Ideology and Ideological State Apparatuses" in Lenin and Philosophy and Other Essays, by Louis Althusser, New Left Books, London, 1977.
[3] These four lines are tagged from a ghazal verse of Ghalib (1797-1869)
[4] Meer Taqi Meer (1723-1810), generally regarded as the 'God of Urdu Poesy'.
[5] Ali Sardar Jafri (1913-2000) was one of the last leaders of the Urdu Progressive Writers' Movement.
[6] A Theory of Literary Production by Pierre Macherey, translated by G. Wal, Routledge & Kegan, London, 1978
[7] The first poetry collection of Faiz, first published in 1941.
[8] The second poetry collection of Faiz, first published in 1953.
[9] The third poetry collection of Faiz, first published in 1956.
[10] Reference to an Urdu ghazal verse by Daagh Dehlavi (1831-1905). [11] The two verses of the ghazal referred to here are given below followed by literal translation :

Gopi Chand Narang is currently a Professor Emeritus at University of New Delhi. He is a leading scholar of Urdu language and literature. He has many academic awards, honours and achievements. His famous quote is 'Language is being; it is also the interface of culture. Language is not the medium it is the condition of literature'. He wrote over 40 books mainly on Urdu literature.

Faiz giving an interview at Urdu Markaz, London, 1984

Chapter 9

Dipped in the Heart's Blood

RAKHSHANDA JALIL

Faiz's English-language prose, on the whole, does not carry the resonance of his Urdu poetry. Politics and history are commensurate. At the worst of times, when upheaval and change are the order of the day, so are politics and poetry. There can be no better example of this axiom in the 20th century than the poetry of Faiz Ahmad Faiz, who wrote prolifically and compellingly on the events that shaped today's Subcontinent. Apart from his prodigious output as a poet, Faiz also wrote newspaper editorials and articles, and gave interviews on a range of subjects that, taken together, reveal a highly political mind beneath the poet's persona and demonstrate the astonishing range of his concerns and interests. Our interest here is in Faiz's prose writings and the similarities and differences with his poetry. While admittedly the comparison itself – between prose and poetry – is unfair and the two are, by their very nature, as unlike as apples and oranges, when the writings come from the same pen they inevitably arouse curiosity and critique.

Faiz with the editorial staff of The Pakistan Times, Lahore, 1947.

The War in Europe affected India and Indians in strange ways. After the Nazi invasion of the Soviet Union in 1941, Faiz's pacifism changed. He joined the welfare department of the British army in 1942 and was put in charge of publicity. He served in the army till 1947 and was given an MBE for his services, and raised to the rank of lieutenant-colonel. He wore a uniform and served His Majesty's Government, not for guts or glory but simply because he believed fascism had to be fought at all costs and by whatever means available. But with the war over and his teaching days behind him, Faiz found himself in search of a regular job.

Sometime in early 1947, the Progressive Papers Limited was established in Lahore by Mian Iftikharuddin, and Faiz was offered the job of editing *Pakistan Times* and heading the editorial board of its sister publications, the Urdu daily *Imroze* and the literary and political weekly *Lail-o-Nahar*. Faiz was then only 37 years old. As the editor of the *Pakistan Times*, the English-language left-leaning newspaper from Lahore, he wrote on an array of issues from 1947 until his arrest in the Rawalpindi Conspiracy Case in 1951.

To instruct and inform

It is in these English writings that one gets a taste of what Faiz had set out to do when he, along with a group of like-minded young men, established the *Halqa-e-Arbab-e-Zauq* or the Circle of Men of Good Taste. Set up in 1939, the members of the *Halqa* set themselves up as the arbiters of good taste in matters of poetry, prose and politics, and continued to exercise a prominent influence on the Pakistani literary scene long after the waning of the PWA. The Halqa demanded nothing of its members save a vaguely defined aestheticism that did not shy away from individualism and subjectivity (both, incidentally, anathema to the 'hard-core' progressives). To the modern reader the name of this loose coalition of 'literary types' – many of whom had overlapping membership with the PWA – may seem pretentious and snobbish but it was, during its time, a much-needed corrective for the progressives who held all matters of 'good taste' in lofty disdain and prized ideology above all else. It might, for this reason, be instructive to read Faiz's editorials in the context in which they were written. Their purpose was not merely to raise a voice of dissent or create a platform of resistance for the sake of a laid-down ideology; their purpose was, I think, to instruct and inform, and when his conscience so demanded, offer a critique.

In an editorial entitled 'What Price Liberty?' written in April

1948, we see Faiz at his most trenchant:

> There are no halfway houses between liberty and thraldom. The public have to choose and decide whether they are going to permit this and similar inroads on their hard-won freedom [referring to the infamous Public Safety Act that gave unbridled powers to the State] or whether they are content to live in daily fear for their freedom and honour. The weapon of the Safety Act that they have placed into the hands of their Government is a dangerous weapon and is not a fit thing for children or sadists to play with. It should either be taken back or the people entrusted with it should be taught its proper use. It must be realized that a weapon like this cannot be used properly either by men who are cursed with the vindictiveness of an elephant and the ferocity of a wolf or by men who lack the guts of a rat and the courage of a sparrow.

From the writings of this period, perhaps the most moving is the editorial of 23 March 1949 titled 'Progress of a Dream'. Declaring Partition a way 'to end the vertical division that separated the two major peoples of the sub-continent ... by a horizontal division so that the divided halves could each develop an internal harmony that the undivided whole lacked,' Faiz goes on to say, 'The dream is as yet unfulfilled. The division has come but neither half is as yet completely at peace, either with itself or with its neighbour.' Faiz saves his strongest words of criticism for those 'selfish packs of men' who 'mock at the nobility of freedom'.

However, it seems hard to reconcile – at least for me, as an Indian – the glowing tribute to Muhammad Ali Jinnah, captioned *'To God We Return'*, written upon the Quaid-e-Azam's death on 13 September 1948, with the poet who wrote *Ye daagh daagh ujaala, ye shabgazeeda sehar, Vo intezaar tha jis ka, ye vo sehar to nahin?* Was this the same man who lamented in the poem *Subah-e-Azadi* (Freedom's Dawn) the 'stained light and the night-bitten dawn' that greeted those who had yearned for freedom? For a man like Faiz to write such an unqualified obituary of a political leader whom he calls 'friend and counsellor, the guide and confidante, the comrade and leader all combined into one' seems excessive, to say the least. Moreover, in comparing the loss of India and Pakistan who were 'in quick succession deprived of the two wisest and most humane men in the sub-continent' (referring to Gandhi and Jinnah in the same breath), he goes on to say, incredibly enough: 'Ours is very much the greater and the more grievous

loss.' Was Faiz being prophetic? Was he implying that Pakistan's loss was greater, not because Jinnah's stature was greater than Gandhi's, but that India would, or could, move beyond the Mahatma's death, while for Pakistan it would prove to be a grievous body blow?

To be fair, writing shortly after Gandhi's assassination in an editorial dated 3 February 1948 titled *'Grave Challenge'*, Faiz described Gandhi's murder as 'one of the darkest crimes in history ... comparable only to the crucifixion of Jesus.' But in the very next breath he goes on to make a remark that, in modern parlance, can only be called politically incorrect:

> The Jews have not been forgiven [for the crucifixion], and their lot through the centuries has been little better than that of fugitives and vagabonds. It is our earnest hope and prayer that India may be spared the nemesis to which an entire people is sometimes landed by the doings of its misguided fanatics.

A different medium

Faiz's English prose, much like his Urdu poetry, is powerful and passionate and concerned deeply and ardently with the past and the present; like his poetry it looks at the future with hope and not just a little foreboding. However, unlike the poetry – and one says this with some trepidation regarding someone of Faiz's stature – the prose is occasionally long-winded and just a trifle ponderous. Where the Urdu poetry enchants and beckons, spilling out a kaleidoscope of images and metaphors, calling out to the readers to find common cause against injustice, exploitation and a host of social and political issues, the English prose is occasionally weighed down by its own rhetoric. Where the poetry lilts and soars with effortless ease, conjuring up the most evocative and lyrical images to record or condemn the most grisly events in the history of the Subcontinent, the prose harks back to an older style of writing that was self-consciously pedantic, even sometimes arcane.

It is not just a difference of style; there is the matter of substance, too. In real life, it must be remembered, while Faiz had his sympathies with the poor and downtrodden, he was clearly never one of them. Perhaps, constrained to walk a tightrope between ideology and good taste, between art and propaganda, between his role as an editor and a free thinker, between being a citizen of a Pakistan increasingly moving in the direction of sectarianism and fundamentalism and a world

whose borders were dissolving, Faiz must have felt the tug of nationalism and the voice of his conscience. There must have been occasions when the liberal, progressive ideology that runs like a shaft of translucent light through his poetry gets dimmed in the prism of his prose.

As Faiz increasingly got drawn into the trade union and civil rights movements, he was often called upon to act as a spokesperson for his people and make himself known as an opponent of oppression. 'The wretched of the earth', a phrase popularised by Franz Fanon, continued to interest him but then he did occasionally feel compelled to also write what was expected of him. For instance, there is the account of life in the Soviet Union entitled *Mah-o-Saal-e-Aashnai* (Months and Years of Friendship), which, ostensibly written as a memoir by a sympathetic fellow-traveller, falls barely short of propaganda.

Poetry, on the other hand, allowed him to use classical imagery for political themes, and to evolve a trope of metaphors and symbols that made profoundly radical, even subversive, comments in the guise of a time-honoured repertoire that was familiar both to him and his readers. In this, he borrowed from the best tradition of the centuries-old *shehr ashob* (literally 'lament of the city', this refers to a school of poetry that concerned itself with social and political decline), as well as poets of protest like Chakbast and Hasrat Mohani. It allowed him, for instance, to write deeply political poems, especially during his imprisonment from 1951-55 when the threat of death hung over him. Prose, that too in English, has no such leeway; a spade has to be called a spade or else left alone. The limitation – if it may be called that – is, to my mind, of the medium in such cases and not of the pen.

Faiz at home from his relese from prison, Karachi, 1956.

75

Faiz called his second and third volumes of poetry – *Dast-e Saba* (The Breeze's Hand, 1953), and *Zindan Nama* (Poems from Prison, 1956) – a 'tribute' to captivity: 'Confinement, like love, is a fundamental experience. It opens many new windows on the soul,' he said. Deprived of pen and paper in the early days of solitary confinement, he wrote qatas (four-lined rhymed verse) that he could memorise; later he evolved a complex system of images, drawn from the classical Persian tradition that seemed on the face of it 'harmless' enough. Shortly before his death, while addressing the Asian Study Group, he revealed the subtle ways he was forced to evolve to evade censorship. For instance, when speaking of ehd-e-junoon (period of obsession) or *chaman ki udasi* (sorrow of the garden), he was actually referring to oppression and injustice.

Prose, unfortunately, has no such provisions; it certainly has no time-honoured 'formula' for transforming the lament of a lover for his beloved into the agonised call of the conscience. Also, the very nature of an editorial, bound as it is by the compulsions of time and circumstance, sometimes makes it a knee-jerk response. That might also explain the rawness of thought in some of the editorials. The profound sorrow and solidarity expressed in some of Faiz's poems that came, evidently from reflection, are missing in these editorials. *Hum jo tareek rahon mein mare gaye* (We who were executed in the dark lanes), written for Ethel and Julius Rosenberg, and *Dhaka sewapsi* (Return from Dhaka) resonate with a deep sympathy and profound sensitivity that can only come from long hours of contemplation, even meditation. Even in some of his outright political poems, Faiz could be philosophical, even mystical; he could appeal to the senses and also stir one's thoughts; he could use imagery that was at once oblique, even radically new, or use classical imagery to mean totally new things. The tangled skeins of modernism (jadidyat) and progressivism (taraqqui-pasandi) ran through his poetry and show the influence as much of Hafiz and the Persian masters as Stephen Spender and W H Auden.

The pull of nation

The charges against Faiz during the Rawalpindi Conspiracy Case brought his career as a Pakistani news editor to a halt. When he emerged from jail in 1955, he found the world a changed place *(chhute aseer to badla hua zamana tha)*. The years of the Cold War saw him involved with the International Peace Committee. Between periods of exile he served first the

Pakistan Arts Council (where he wrote radio plays and film scripts) and then the Lok Virsa (National Institute of Folk and Traditional Heritage) as a 'cultural bureaucrat'. It was only during his self-imposed exile in war-torn Beirut, as editor of *Lotus*, the journal of the Afro-Asian Writers' Association, that he once again wielded the prose writer's pen. From 1979-1982, he not only published translations of the poetry of his close friend and fellow-poet, Pablo Neruda, and a host of new voices from the Third World, but also wrote on a range of subjects dear to him. The *Lotus* years show him as a man consistently and compulsively engaged with all those who, like him, longed for freedom from oppression and injustice. These years also show him contributing to the growing movement for anti and post-colonial writings which lay at the heart of the Afro-Asian Writers' Association formed by Faiz and others in the early 1950s and whose first conference he had attended in Tashkent in 1958 as the delegate from Pakistan (with Hafiz Jallundhari as fellow-delegate).

At the same time, since the creation of Pakistan, we see an increasingly nationalistic tone in both his prose and poetry, though never in the jingoistic or chauvinistic sense. Despite all his scathing editorials on the goings-on in the government, the hauntingly evocative ghazals on the bloodbath in East Pakistan by the West Pakistani armed forces, his iconic song to the slain soldier after the 1965 war with India, and his many years in exile, Faiz was essentially a nationalist. He remained one no matter where he lived – in Lahore, London, or Beirut.

The *laila-o-watan* (the beloved who is the country) whom he courted with such ardour in his poetry coloured his prose as well. The effect, so enticing and bewitching in the poetry, is less so in the prose. The small matter of effect aside, together both the prose and poetry consistently show the anti-imperial, anti-colonial and humane outlook that was quintessential to Faiz's worldview.

Rakshanda Jalil is an author, academic, journalist and social activist. She is well known for her literary contributions including Invisible City: The Hidden Monuments of Delhi. She works at Jamia Millia Islamia University at as Director of Media and Culture. The article in this publication was previously appeared in the on-line journal: Himal Southasia.

Faiz Ahmed Faiz, Lahore, 1956

Section Two
Selected Writings of Faiz Ahmed Faiz

Faiz with Alys, Lahore, 1968

Painting of Faiz Ahmed Faiz by Hasan Mehdi, Karachi, 2011

Chapter 10

Autobiographical notes
FAIZ AHMED FAIZ

There were two brothers, Kala and Qadir. No one knows who they were, but a very small village bearing their name existed in Tehsil Narowal of district Sialkot. Village Kala Qadir. My father saw the light of day in a destitute family of this village, a family where, to conserve the oil, the light of the clay lamp was put out early in the evening. There was a primary school nearby and some boys from our village too used to attend it. Our grandfather, Sahibzada Khan, was a small-time peasant, and too poor to afford for our father a share in the fountain of knowledge that spouted there. My Father, used to tell us that he envied those children. When he saw them going to school he felt his heart would break but he couldn't do anything.

In keeping with the ways of the poor he was trained to earn his living when he was five years old instead of being taught to read and write. The village people engaged him to graze their cattle, and ensured his daily bread as compensation. Early in the morning, Father would leave with the herd and tend them outside the village. While the animals grazed he sat in the shade of some tree and looked with longing at the boys in the distant school. One can imagine what went on in his heart. One day he left the cows in the field and went up to the school. The schoolmaster asked why he had come. Father replied boldly, "I want to study." The teacher looked at the cowherd's son who was waiting for his answer with expectant eyes and said, "All right, come every day." Father was struck dumb with surprise and ecstasy. He used to tell us that he was mad with happiness. "The words, 'All right, come every day' gave me a thousand times greater pleasure than the sighting of the Eid moon. Drunk with rapture I ran to the herd and took the animals home. Everyone in the house felt that I was changed. I could hardly contain my excitement. The next morning I collected the animals, left them in the field to appease their hunger while I strove to quench my raving thirst with the first drop of learning that the school gave me. For me the alphabet was like a beautiful dress for a naked child, a grand feast for a starving person or the gift of eyesight for a blind man."

"When the teacher gave me my first lesson it was difficult for me to hold myself still. He was somewhat perturbed and said, 'Boy, do you want to study or graze buffaloes?' I collected my wits and said, "Sir, I want to do both." "Then learn to pay attention," he said. :This is a tough job." The words seared my brain, 'This is a tough job.' I have never forgotten them.

I began to study in school-time and revised my lesson while tending the cattle. This combination of study and cattle-grazing went on for years.

Then, with a sense of thrill I sat for the final primary exam. When the result came the teacher told me I had stood first and would get a scholarship."

Faiz and Alys on the poet's last birthday party, Lahore, 1984.

Father's Scholarship and Education

In those times the monthly scholarship was two rupees. Yes, two rupees. Father was given another two rupees every month by the village people in the form of wheat. Now this distinction further whetted his appetite for learning, but there was no middle school anywhere in the vicinity. The nearest was a few miles away in a village called Maddo. But the problem was that if Father went to that school he couldn't look after the village cattle and would lose the two rupees he received for the work. So he told his father that he would pay the scholarship amount towards household expenses, and thus prevailed upon him to agree to his admission in middle school. The village people too had no objection to this, and so Father began his new journey in life.

Father walked about four miles every day to the new school. He romped and frolicked on the way, and his old friends, the buffaloes, would look up and moo when he passed by. In middle school again he passed the final exam with credit. But again his fate seemed to be darkened by the fact that there was no high school in the entire area. I don't know how he found out that inside Mochi Gate in Lahore there was a mosque known as Chinianwali Masjid where small cubicles were available free for poor students and other destitutes and food was also provided. Father had developed a will of iron. He determined to go to Mochi Gate and "conquer" the Chinianwali mosque and secure admission in the high school there. No one in the village was pleased at this decision.

However, he made up a small package for the journey. It included some barley bread and gur and a few books, and set off for Chinianwali Masjid. He had been correctly informed. He was given permission to reside in a hujra, and came to know that the people of the locality subscribed jointly to sending food for those staying in the mosque. While other travellers came and went, Father, the youngest of them, was to stay there permanently. Impressed by his bright intellect, the Imam Masjid got him admission in the high school. Now, apart from praying in the mosque he also began to perform its daily chores. He recited the Quran in a melodious voice. Very soon the residents of the locality became his fervent admirers, his schoolmasters doted on him, while the Imam Masjid couldn't stop praising his sagacity and good manners. Thus, in a short while he was able to achieve what I have not been able to do till now.

Hard work and the Afghan Counsellor

Father spent the day in school. In the afternoon and evening he did routine work in the mosque. After his evening meal, provided by the mohalla people, and saying the isha prayer, he would set off for the railway station and, till late in the night, work there as a coolie. Whatever he earned from this job he sent home. One day Sardar Amir Muhammad Khan, Counsellor for Afghanistan, came to the mosque for the Friday prayer and incidentally met my father. By now Father could speak both Persian and English. The Counsellor was very pleased and began to take lessons in English from him. After some time he began to give him work of translating documents from Persian into English.

The Afghan Counsellor was a devotee of the Sirhind Sharif shrine which had also been visited once by Amir Abdul Rahman, the Afghan king. I am told that one Abdul Halim from Chiniot had built an Afghan palace there which is probably still in place. One year the Counsellor took Father along on his pilgrimage to Sirhind Sharif and later he went with him many times.

On one such visit he was saying the isha prayer in the company of Sardar Amir Muhammad Khan when he fell unconscious, and, in his dream, heard the Sirhind divine tell him that one day he would be a minister in Afghanistan. When he awoke, he smiled at the state of his present fortunes, recalling the humble dwelling in Chinianwali Masjid, his bed of straw and the earthenware drinking cup. He got up to have some water and then continued with his prayer.

In Afghanistan's royal court

Then the Counsellor had to leave suddenly for Afghanistan, but he took Father with him. There he was introduced to Amir Abdur Rahman and he was given a job as a translator. Gradually he became the custodian of the king's correspondence. His duties were to translate letters from English into Persian and render the Amir's Persian letters into English.

Maybe that is how he acquired proficiency in the two languages and how he became intimately acquainted with the diplomatic politics of the age. Amir Abdur Rahman was very happy with Father's work and showered him with many gifts and rewards. He literally rolled in precious stones.

He was now a man of influence, and, with the passage of time, his fortunes multiplied, till one day he was married off to a niece of the Amir. He was also appointed tutor to the heir apparent, Mir Habibullah. But there are all kinds of persons in a royal court and jealousy breeds enemies. They began to poison the Amir's mind against Father, but he was such a favourite with the monarch that all their efforts were wasted.

Faiz with family, Lahore, 1955.

84

Dr Hamilton

There was an Englishwoman in Kabul by the name of Dr Lillies Hamilton. She was a highly educated lady and she became friendly with Father. The two would often discuss local events and advise each other. One day she said to Father that nobody could depend on kings for ever. The monarch who is in control today can be an exile tomorrow, reduced to a nonentity and without a penny to his name. The new king may spare your life but he will certainly not be your patron. It is also possible that the conspiracies of your enemies may bear fruit, and the monarch who is so beneficent towards you today may be carried away by the poisonous words of your enemies. Therefore it is necessary that you should think of the future.

Father found wisdom in Dr Hamilton's remarks. It was decided, therefore, that all the wealth that he had accumulated should be deposited in the lady's account in a London bank so that he could benefit from it in the coming days. Thus, the lady became his finance minister.

Return from Kabul and imprisonment

When Father had gone to Afghanistan he had taken with him a man from the village, probably a chowkidar. His name was Imam Bakhsh and he always remained loyal and helpful. One day Father discussed the situation with him in view of the mounting conspiracies in the court and the fact that the Amir's relations and other courtiers were now after his blood. Imam Bakhsh agreed to do whatever Father decided.

One dark night they saddled their horses, changed their dress to disguise themselves and took the road to India. They rode at night only and, one morning, they crossed the border. The British government became suspicious because Father had come back without informing any of its officers so they sent him to prison as a spy of Afghanistan. On his part the Amir was also amazed at what Father had done since he wanted him back in Kabul. Father was a man of infinite resource and courage. Somehow he established contact with Dr Hamilton who was now in London and wrote her a detailed letter. That good lady managed to get him released from jail.

Journey to London

The lady insisted that he should come over to London, and Father thought this was the best way out for him. In those days there was no formality about passport and visa, nor did one require a No Objection Certificate from anyone to travel abroad. On reaching England Father took admission in Cambridge. Later he was elected Fellow of the Royal Geographical Society There was no shortage of money The lady handed over his savings to him. Now he studied and played polo, among others with the Prince of Wales who later was crowned as King Edward VII, and moved in high society and was recognised as an important person.

Meantime the Amir of Afghanistan came to know that he was in London and engaged in studies He wrote to Father and offered him the post of Afghan Ambassador to Britain. He said Father need not come over to Kabul if he did not want to and work as his representative to the British government. Father accepted this and became ambassador. After finishing with Cambridge he got interested in the law and enrolled himself as barrister. This was the time when people like Allama Iqbal, Sir Muhammad Shafi, Sir Fazl-e-Husain and Sir Abdul Qadir were also in London, all aiming at becoming barristers. Father was friendly with all of them but his was a life of pomp and luxury while they were students and always short of funds. On the other hand, Father had the wealth he had accumulated in Kabul and also received a salary from the Afghan government. He passed his law exam with ease and comfort.

Return from London

Now the question that faced him was whether he should go back to Afghanistan or to India. He decided on the latter, and leaving London, headed straight for Jhelum. On arriving in Jhelum he began his practice as a lawyer. In those days Jhelum was a small town although in history it occupies a prominent status, for this is the place where Alexander had been confronted by Raja Porus. This ancient town was rather backward in its life style and its economy. Being on the route for invaders from the north-west it could not flourish to the extent that it deserved, while the British used it as a military feeding area. Anyway, Father went to the courts in a phaeton drawn by four horses. The poor town and its citizens were hardly equipped to provide Father with an income commensurate with his taste and life-style, so he decided to move – this time to Sialkot. Here he began active practice and lived in opulence, and also married the daughter of a rich man who lived in a village close to ours.

This was his fifth marriage and I was born from this wife. There is no record of the others.

Faiz and Alys, Nathiagali, 1956

Mammun the Gambler and other personalities

At that time Sialkot was known for a striking social personality called Mammun the Gambler. His real name was Muhammad Bakhsh but everyone knew him and called him by his alias. He was a sort of local Robin Hood, and patronised gambling and smuggling and was king of the underworld. At the same time he was a member of the Municipal Committee and was associated with every organisation set up for improvement of the city. He also donated generously to all good causes. A strange man really. Then there was Maulvi Ibrahim, a rich man in his own right, who had grown a beard, taken up the imamat of a mosque and had begun to teach children. He became my teacher too, and I started going to the mosque to read the Urdu primer.

Maulvi Ibrahim's classes were rather novel. Here he was teaching me ABC and, at the same time, coaching a student of the third class. Another boy is being taught the hadees, while still another is on fiqh. He gave equal attention to all. He had a commanding manner and we were terrified of him. He was a big good-looking man but at heart gentle and affectionate. He had no children of his own. You know, I learned the Quran from him with translation for full seven years. Then there was Maulana Mir Hasan, the famous teacher of Allama Iqbal. His madressah was in another part of the city.

And, of course Baba Kharak Singh was also from Sialkot. He was a great man and the founder of the Sikhs' Akali Movement. In those days the gurudwaras were all controlled by the British Indian government and the high priests of the gurudwaras were also appointed by it. Baba Kharak Singh's movement was mainly to transfer control of Sikh temples to the Sikh community. It was an anti-imperialist movement and its suppression involved firing on the workers a number of times. Later the community joined up with the Khilafat Movement and gave the rulers a tough time in conjunction with the Indian

National Congress. Baba Kharak Singh is a hero of Sikh nationalism.

Personality and character

My father had a highly impressive personality. I remember once how the mirasi delegated the duty of bringing the goats for the Eid-ul-Azha sacrifice did not turn up on time. Father shouted at him why he had been so late. The poor mirasi was so overawed by his loud and peremptory manner that he fell backwards against a wall and fainted with fear. Along with his brilliant intellect and his height and girth, Father always used the power of his voice to dominate company.

He was a truly handsome man and overpowering in his effect on people. Don't try to imagine him from my height and features, for I seem to have acquired my looks from my mother's family. He loved his village and the land of his birth. Sir Abdul Qadir, Sir Muhammad Shafi and others implored him many times to shift to Lahore but he declined, and till the last never left the people of his area. He purchased much property, both in Sialkot and in Lahore's Mochi Gate. We led a life of plenty and never knew what poverty or want could be like.

Father was the presiding spirit of every organisation in the city and was the leader where welfare work was concerned. He was the first to come up with donations for schools and mosques. Among his children he loved me the most. Once he said to me, "Its good that you are writing poetry. You will bring honour to my name. But do go into the ICS." I was in third year of college at that time.

That English lady wrote a novel about him which was published. It was called *The Wazir's Daughter* and is very interesting.

Death

I was still in college when my father died. As we finished with his last rites, people whom he owed money began to turn up; all the sahukars and money-lenders of the city. Then we came to know that he had left debts to the tune of eighty thousand rupees, a lot of money in those times. He had never told us that all his generosity and philanthropy flowed from borrowed wealth. This disclosure left us stunned. Brother Tufail was a noble soul and said to me, "We'll pay all these debts," although I couldn't see how this was going to be done. People advised us to forget the matter, but my brother said a firm no to the idea. Then property began to be sold and the burden of debt began to be relieved. Finally it was all over, and we entered a life of poverty.

Birth

I was born in Kala Qadir, though I do not know my date of birth. In the school documents it is 7 January 1911 at one place and 7 January 1912 at another. I am told that in those days the dates of birth entered in school registers were invariably false. It was always calculated that a boy would pass his matriculation in such-and-such year and for entry into the service of the British the age should be less than the real one. Some time ago I had requested a friend to find but the correct date from the municipal record of births. His effort revealed the date as 13 February 1911.

Faiz and Alys with daughter Salima and grandchildren, Lahore, 1978

First day in school

My childhood was spent in Sialkot, and I went to study in the Scotch Mission School. In my studies my tutor was Shams-ul-Ulema Maulvi Mir Hasan who coached me in Arabic grammar. But I was closer to Maulvi Ibrahim Mir Sialkoti, a very learned person, who taught me the Arabic alphabet and the primers. Later he also gave me lessons in the Quran and Hadith. So that is how I passed my childhood.

I was not sent to school to start with. Father had said that I should first read the Quran, that is memorise it. Then I should

89

go to the mosque and study Arabic and Persian. School would come later. So, assisted by a Hafiz Sahib I began to learn the Quran by heart, I had only done three siparahs when I developed inflammation of the eyes. Then I started on the alphabet with my mother. This was followed by finishing the first primer of Urdu with the help of Maulvi Ibrahim Sahib in a nearby mosque.

I was in the fourth class when I was finally sent to school. This is quite a story, for whenever I recall the event I start feeling uncomfortable. For my first day there my elder sisters got me ready. I was dressed up in velvet, with a red waistcoat and matching shorts, silk socks and new fancy shoes. I had never seen a school from inside and had no idea what went on there. It was an Islamia primary school. What did I see there? There were four boys in my class, one in dirty torn clothes, another without shoes and still another without a cap, and all four sitting on the floor. They stared at me as if I was a strange animal.

In those times desks were only provided in the higher classes, while children in the junior classes sat on straw matting. I felt uncomfortable. I didn't want to sit on the floor and that too on a soiled piece of matting. The boys looked me up and down with a mixture of sarcasm and contempt. The next day I went dressed like them and never wore that velvet suit to school again. One should look like the people one consorts with, and not so out of place as to make them feel that you are showing off your wealth and status. That is bad manners.

Oldest, dim memories

For me the years 1918 to 1920 are just a hazy memory, and the earliest, for what do dates mean at that age? World War I had ended. On their part the British rulers and their toadies were celebrating victory, with streets decorated with coloured bunting, cannon being fired, bands playing and soldiers parading; while, on the other side, the freedom movement was picking up. Every other day there was a new procession and the air was rent with various slogans like *Jo bole so nihal, sat siri akal; Allah-o-Akbar; Bande mataram; Down with the toadies; and Freedom is our birthright.* Famous leaders drove around the city in flower bedecked carriages. This is Moti Lal Nehru, here are the Brothers Muhammad Ali and Shaukat Ali, now comes Maulana Azad, there is Baba Kharak Singh and Dr Kitchlew. Welcome arches have been erected all over the city and the streets and bazaars are crowded with enthusiastic onlookers. One day the city is illuminated to mark a victory of the Turks, and the next day a popular leader's arrest covers it with a pall of gloom.

Mixed with these sights and sounds are the banner headlines of dailies and the shouts of newspaper hawkers: 'Czar overthrown in Russia,' 'Lenin sets up workers' government," 'The red revolution has arrived.' People all over are discussing events — in the sitting room of our house, in the school staff room, in the mosque of the locality, everywhere it is the talk of the town. How did the Russian revolution come about? Will the revolutionary forces also come to India to get us freedom? What is a government of workers and peasants like?

When Father left for the courts in the morning, people who had shops or ran some trade in the neighbourhood would gather on the platform outside our house where benches and stools had been paced for his clients. On sighting a customer they would hurry to deal with him and then come Allah Diya the wrestler, Chiragh Din the oilman, Allah Rakha the butcher, Khushia the barber and their pals spent 19 hours chatting and discussing Indian and world politics. "Have you heard," one would say, "Mahatma Gandhi and the Ali Brothers have announced that within a year all British governors and commissioners and DCs will be expelled and their place taken by our own people." Another would give the news, "They say the Turkish army is coming through Afghanistan after defeating the British." "Yes," would add another, "and the Russian forces have joined the Turks and overthrown their own king. They have a new leader called Lenin who has set up an army of workers, made the king run away and distributed ail wealth among the people. They have a workers' government now." An enthusiastic listener would shout, "Buck up, you son of a lion! I say, let's ask our Agha Safdar to do something similar. (Agha Safdar was a political leader of the city.) What a great thing it would be if this could happen here. Imagine the wealth of Lala Harjan Rai, the money-lender, being distributed among us all!"

This was the first time in those old days when we heard of Russia and Lenin and the red revolution. I don't recall now what impact these words had on our childish minds and what we thought about them. As I grew a bit older, I got absorbed in my studies in school and other interests, soon forgetting these foreign names and events.

Faiz and Alys, Lahore, 1956

Childhood

Our poets constantly complain that the world has failed to recognise their merit. This is a perennial topic with them. My case is otherwise. I am given so much honour, so much affection, by friends and acquaintances, and by those unknown to me, that I often feel guilty. I believe that in order to be worthy of all this adulation I should have done much more than what I have been able to achieve in life. And this is not a recent feeling. It was always like this from my very childhood.

When I was very small and went to school, almost the same kind of relationship had built up with the other boys. For some reason they began to treat me as a leader although I never possessed the attributes usually associated with leaders. One had to be either the aggressive type to hold sway over the boys or exceptionally clever in studies. I was all right in class, and could also hold my own in games. But I never did anything extraordinary by way of academic distinction to make others look up to me or draw their attention. .

When I ruminate over my childhood there's one thing that I recall in particular. Our house was full of women. We were three brothers. The younger Inayat and the elder Tufail never listened to these women and remained engrossed in romping about. I was the only one caught in their snare. This had a good effect as well as a sorry one. The benefit was that these ladies obliged me to spend my days as a well-behaved boy. Never would a vulgar word pass my lips, and that is true even today. But I often regret that I was thus kept aloof from the childish pranks and the carelessness that characterise that young age.

For instance, a boy is flying a kite in the street, another is spinning a top, some boys are playing marbles, but I was oblivious to all these fun-giving activities. Just a silent spectator who dare not join in these sports because they were not considered fit for boys of noble families.

My teachers were also good to me. I don't know about these times, but in our days severe beating was resorted to in schools. Our teachers were proper tyrants. I was not only spared capital punishment but was made class monitor every time. I was also delegated the function of administering punishment to my class fellows. "Pull that boys' ears," or "Give a resounding slap to that one." I found this most irksome, and, as far as possible, tried to be lenient in pulling ears and slapping my companions so that they should not fell the pain. But whenever the teacher found this out I would be admonished and told to use proper force.

Two memories are etched sharply on my mind. One that I was deprived of indulging in childish interests and the other, that I received from my class fellows and teachers the same affection

92

and sincerity that was my lot in later life from mends and contemporaries, and which continues to this day.

I used to go to the mosque for the morning prayer with my father. My routine was to get up with the azaan before dawn, go to the mosque with Father, say my prayer and then for an hour or two listen to the lesson from the Quran from Maulvi Ibrahim Mir Sialkoti who was a truly learned person. Then Father and I would go for a walk for about two hours, followed by school. At night Father would send for me to write his letters, for at that time he felt some difficulty in doing it himself So I acted as his secretary. I also read out the newspaper to him. Because of being involved in these activities I gained a lot, because reading Urdu and English newspapers and writing letters was a really profitable exercise for me.

All this revives another memory. Adjacent to our house was a shop where you could get books on hire. One paid two pice (paisas) per book. The owner was called Brother by everyone. Brother's shop was a great treasury of Urdu literature. The books that we read while studying in the sixth and seventh class are no longer to be found; books like Tilism-e-Hoshruba, Fasana-e-Azad and the novels of Abdul Haleem Sharar. I went through all these at that age. Then I went on to the verses of poets. I read Dagh, but couldn't make head or tail of Ghalib. Even the other poets were only half comprehensible to me, but they all left a kind of impact on my mind as if I was losing my breath.

This variety of reading made me take to poetry instinctively and I developed a lasting interest in literature. My father's clerk also acted as a sort of manager of the household. If I managed to displease him in something he would threaten to tell Father that I secretly read novels and other useless books instead of school books. I used to be afraid of him and would beg him not to tell Father, but one day he did report me. Father called me and asked me if I read novels. I admitted that I did. On which he said, "If you must read novels then read those of English. Urdu novels are not good. Go to the fort library in the city and get English novels from there."

Thus I began to read English novels. I went through the whole of Dickens and Hardy and God knows what else. In this case too, I could comprehend only half of what I read, but this vastly improved my English. By the time I was in tenth class, I began to catch my teachers making mistakes of English and ventured to correct them. I didn't get a beating on this but they did feel annoyed and used to say, "If you know better English why don't you take this class? Why learn from us?"

The bed-bugs of Abbottabad

The bed-bugs of Abbottabad were famous all over. I remember

them from the time when I once visited Abbottabad in my childhood. What a long time ago that was but it seems like yesterday. Hameed Bhai's only sister, a very beautiful girl who died when she was still young, was married in Hazara. My brother Tufail and I once went to her place for the summer vacations, and her husband Pir Sahib took us on a trip to Abbottabad. The bed-bugs there were so virulent, and in such profusion, that I was badly bitten all over the body. As a result I got high fever and was laid up for many days.

I had never before seen mountains and streams and fresh-water springs and I was simply enchanted. Everything was pleasurable. In the courtyard of the hujra, my cousin's husband, who was a local khan, is practising with his pistol, The verandah and rooms are decorated with swords and daggers and other old weapons, Pir Sahib's aged mother is dishing out amulets to village women, and when the men were out of sight the belles of the village could be seen bathing, in scanty dress, in the hill stream.

Faiz with grandchildren, Lahore, 1978

An adventure

What memories of our ancestral village! The intoxicating aroma of a sugarcane field, the sight and smells of citrus blossoms, the golden tassels of the amaltaas flower, the sun-drenched wheat crop and mustard flowers reminiscent of Van Gogh's paintings, the henna-coloured light of the day after a shower, the cool air in the heat under the shisham trees, the

94

feel of soft grass on the body – all these created the same excitement that one felt at that age on hearing the whistle and chuck chuck of the railway engine or by floating paper boats in flowing water.

Days that made you hold your breath with rapture. Also days that were sometimes darkened by fear and sometimes seemed as sharp as a sword because of illness. I went to our village for the first time as a rich boy along with elder brother Haji Tufail Ahmed. Brother Tufail was commonly addressed as Haji because when he was very small Father had taken him along for the holy pilgrimage. We were the sons of a Khan Bahadur but our relations in the village were poor. In any case everyone in the village could not be a Khan Bahadur. We were cosseted and made much of and everyone paid his tribute in the form of affection and genuine adulation, especially the women. This was a novel experience for me. We had been raised in luxury and opulence while our relations presented a picture of poverty and deprivation, living in dark hovels with nothing to distinguish them as homes. Most of them were barefooted, dressed in a single piece of clothing, with the men wearing a tattered piece of cloth as turban and women whose dopattas were in shreds. These were men and women whose bodies smelt of the original human odour, who had never known a soap or a detergent, who scrubbed their dirty utensils clean with the grit of fire-ash and sometimes washed their hands too with the same ashes. They came in hordes, somewhat abashed and fearful, blessing us with both hands while looking into our eyes. Boys and girls of our age, pale and lean, dressed in rags and without shoes of any kind, glared at us from a distance and giggled among themselves.

God knows what they said about us and what made them laugh. We were at a loss in all this, but the fear and hesitation of the poor people soon turned into a deluge of love. Moved by these waves of affection a woman kissed me with a loud smack that could have been heard from afar; I came to know what a kiss could be. Someone said, "Faiz, this is your aunt, your father's sister." I almost fainted with this new experience. For the first time in my life I realised why kings were kings, and how kings transform the poor like these into naive and oppressed human beings full of love and devotion to royalty. I learned at that young age how easy it is to be a prince or princess. All that is required is the seed of a monarch. But what a lot of sacrifice and artless sincerity is needed to become like these poor souls!

All of a sudden I began to look down upon my father's title of

Khan Bahadur and it became irksome to me. At the same time my heart went out to the common man. Our aunts in the village gathered me to themselves, and I too felt a kinship for them. Women of all ages have always appealed to me. Truly, womankind is a great blessing. In the village I saw a flour-mill, a chakki, for the first time. What a strange device it seemed, grinding grain of all kinds, and that too through the strength of a woman's hand! One night the two of us decided to rotate it ourselves. I took up a fistful of grain while Bhai Tufail lifted the heavy topstone of the mill. Before I could pull away my hand the topstone fell from my brother's hand and one of my fingers was crushed under it. Blood streamed from the chakki instead of flour. Brother Tufail was terribly frightened, and so was I. We agreed that no one should know about this, and not the Khan Bahadur in any case. Silently we lay down in our beds. I think Brother went to sleep worrying about what would happen in the morning and making schemes to face the situation. I couldn't think of anything for the pain which was intense and was spreading all over the body. I didn't sleep a wink. In the morning I saw that my aunt's snow white bed-sheet was soaked in blood. It seems that my finger had bled the whole night but I lay quietly without making a sound. When my aunt and other women came to wake me up I was lying with my eyes open and didn't say anything. They were bewildered by the sight. Anyway we were caught, and when asked about what had happened told the truth.

Another childhood memory

I recall how under the dense trees in the Eidgah, my father was reading out the khutba. (Always it was he who delivered this Arabic sermon.) Tufail and I were in the front row, wearing velvet coats. After the Eid prayer our phaeton leaves the place of congregation. The bells in the harness of the horse tinkle merrily. The coachman is throwing fistfuls of ' small change on both sides of the road, and excited screaming children are running along with the carriage. Then I recall the moment when we enter the courtyard of the zenana which is jam-packed with women – our sisters, their children, serving maids, and the poor female guests from the village. As soon as Father enters the courtyard there is pin-drop silence.

Everyone kisses his hand by turn. Then our grandmother gropes her way out of her room and our father bows his haughty head before her. She places her hand on his head and gives him her blessing, after which he leaves the courtyard for the male quarters. The silence breaks and then everyone starts talking and laughing and shouting to their hearts' content.

Beginnings of poetry

I ventured into versifying when I was in Class VII. It was like this. My elder brother, who is now dead, had a mend by the name of Nazir Ahmed Mahmud, who later became a judge of the High Court. They were both in tenth class. This Nazir Ahmed said to me one day, "I say, you are so good at Urdu, have you ever made any verses?" I replied that I had never 'made' any verses. So he wanted me to make some. On my asking how that was to be done, he said, "There is a boy in our class called Chhaiju Ram. He is a nuisance for us. You write me a poem against him. It should have verses that compare his head with a cooking pot, his stomach with a pitcher, his legs with stalks and you must say similar things about his hands and his eyes and his nose." I "manufactured" a poem of seven or eight lines. Nazir Ahmed read it out in class and it became famous in the whole school. Then I thought that I had not been fair to Chhaiju Ram as all those derogatory verses must have hurt him. I should go and apologise to him. I asked my brother to show me the Chhaiju in question. So I went up to him and said, "Friend, you must forgive me. I don't even know you and I have written all that rot about you." But Chhaiju asked me not to apologise and said, "There is nothing to be sorry about. Because of you I have become known in the whole school. In fact I am very happy." That is how it was, though it was after a long time that I actually started writing poetry.

Again, in school one day our headmaster had the idea that there should be poetry competition among the boys. Well, not exactly poetry but versification. He gave us a verse which we were to use as the rhyme, a misra-e-tarha. In the first competition of the kind the judge was Shamsululema Maulvi Mir Hasan Sahib. By chance I was judged the best and received a cash award. More than that I cherished the medal that I was given. I remember that the award was one rupee.

These two events caused me to misunderstand that I could do something in this line. Next to our house there was a palatial mansion, an oldfashioned haveli, where poetic symposiums, mushairas, were regularly held. In those days in Sialkot there was a gentleman by the name of Munshi Raj Narayan Armaan Dehlvi. Maybe you have heard of him. Later he went away to live in Lahore. Well he had set up a poetic society and this society arranged mushairas on a regular basis in the haveli which were presided over by the late Munshi Siraj Din, a mend of Allama Iqbal's. (His name is mentioned in some of the Allama' s writings.) He was mir munshi in the residency

in Kashmir and he used to move over to Sialkot with the residency. A flood of mushairas would start with his arrival. For five or six months poetry would flourish.

I too used to go to these sessions. Ghazals had to be composed on a misra-e-tarha. For a long time I could not pick up courage to participate for fear of Munshi Siraj's biting sense of humour. It usually happened that as a poet's turn came and he read out a couplet, Munshi Sahib would fire away a dozen couplets of the masters on the same subject. One day I did venture and read out a ghazal. Unexpectedly Munshi Sahib exclaimed, "Young man that was not bad." But it was more or less a shot in the dark at that age. Urdu and Persian were commonly spoken at home. I was of a tender age when I built up a world of the intellect in my mind and began to write poetry. But from the very beginning the words and sounds of Punjabi songs echoed in my memory. During the First World War people used to go about in the streets singing popular songs. It is only now that I have given Punjabi poetic form to the tunes that lay buried in my consciousness. I am a Sialkoti, but Father had lands in Sargodha. There the tenants joined in singing Punjabi folk songs at night. And there I listened to Waris Shah's Heer, and the kafis of Bullhe Shah, and the epic poems Sohni Mahinwal and Mirza Sahiban. I very much wanted to write in Punjabi but then how could I match the old masters? Actually I had not read the Punjabi poets in depth, but from whatever I had listened to I knew I could never write like Waris Shah. In those days I was sometimes overtaken by a strange feeling. It was as if the colour of the sky had changed, and some things have distanced themselves from me, the sunshine had acquired a henna-like hue, and whatever was in the range of my sight had taken a different form. It was somewhat like a motion picture. This feeling would occur now and then, but I experience it no longer. Meeting with Iqbal I had the honour and pleasure of meeting Iqbal many times. For one we were from the same city, and he was also my father's friend and contemporary. In England too they had been together. I first saw him in my childhood, when I was six or seven years old. I recollect clearly the annual sessions of the Anjumane-Islamia in Sialkot. The Anjuman had a school of its own and the Allama sometimes came to attend its annual day, as also the functions of some other schools. My first sight of him was at the annual session of the Anjuman. I was required to be there because I was a student of its Islamia School and had to recite from the Quran at the session. I recollect that someone lifted me up and stood me on the table.

98

Painting of Faiz Ahmed Faiz by Hasan Mehdi, Karachi, 2011

99

Faiz with daughter Moneeza, Lahore, 1950.

Chapter 11

Lenin Peace Prize Acceptance Rendition

FAIZ AHMED FAIZ

Creating words and shaping them in an orderly form is the vocation of poets and men of letters. But there are occasions in life when one is left speechless. This is one such occasion for me; I don't have the words with which to adequately thank the Lenin Peace Prize Committee, as well as other Soviet institutions and friends, for the honour they have conferred upon me. The Peace Prize is invaluable because it carries Lenin's honoured and sacred name with it. Lenin is the most revered standardbearer of liberty and peace in our time, peace which is a prerequisite for human life and its beauty and excellence. I do not find anything in my life and work which should have made me worthy of this single honour.

However, I can think of one reason: the fervent yearning for peace and independence which has motivated me and my colleagues. There is such glory in the desire itself that even the humblest votaries of peace and independence are considered worthy of respect and recognition.

Faiz receiving the Lenin Peace Price, Moscow, 1962

All except those who are affected by dementia or are given to crime are agreed that peace and independence are beautiful ideals. All can visualise that peace is reflected in the wheat fields, in poplar trees, in the brides veil, in the laughing hands of children, in the poet's pen, artists brush. All of us can visualise that independence guarantees all these and servitude kills all qualities which distinguish man from beast-- qualities of intellect and intelligence, truth and justice, dignity and valour, piety and forbearance. Therefore, there should logically be no difference of opinion among reasonable people regarding the achievement and consolidation of peace and independence. Unfortunately, however, that common understanding is lacking because, from the beginning of time, contending forces have been at work. These forces are the forces of creation and destruction, of light and darkness, of justice and injustice. The interplay of these contrary forces continues to this day. At the same time, the problems with which we are faced today are different in character than the one that used to tax us in the past. War today does not mean bloody tribal strife. Nor, do we mean by peace today merely, that bloodshed should come to an end. Today, war means the annihilation of the human race itself. Today, peace is the precondition for the survival of humanity as such. On these two words – annihilation or survival – depends the continuation or culmination of human history. On these two words depends the destruction or survival of the human habitat. Again, man did not have, until our own time, sufficient control over natural resources and the forces of production to take care of the needs of all groups and clans.

Faiz receiving his medal at the Lenin Peace Price ceremony, 1962

Thus, there was some justification in the past for the grab-and-run loot which has been so much a part of human history. That is not the situation today. Human inventiveness has taken science and technology to such high levels of efficiency that all mouths can be fed, all physical feeds can be met, provided that the limitless bounties of nature, the infinite means of production at the disposal of mankind, are geared not to satisfy the avarice or monopolists or special interest groups but to ensure the welfare of all, and provided also that the scientific and industrial abilities of the human race are put to constructive rather than destructive purposes.

All this is possible only under a social structure raised upon the foundations of justice, equality, independence and the collective good, and not on avarice, exploitation and monopoly interests. This is something to work for and not merely to talk about. This requires practical effort and in this effort, the struggle for peace and the struggle for independence converge and become indivisible. This is so because the forces which work for peace are also the forces which work for independence, and the forces working against independence are also the forces working for the destruction of peace. On the one hand there are the imperialist forces, whose interests and whose monopolies can survive only through force and thrive only through jealous competitions. Pitted against them are those who value human life more than banks and factories, those who love to work together rather than to order others about. In short, in politics and morality, in literature and art, in day-today life, this struggle between constructive and destructive forces is being waged on several fronts, in myriad shapes. For those who cherish independence and love peace, it is necessary to be vigilant on every front.

For instance, even apart from this inevitable conflict between imperialist and non-imperialist forces, there are violent differences among countries which attained independence recently. Such differences exist between Pakistan and neighboring India, between one Arab state and another, and between one African state and another. It is obvious that only those powers can benefit from these differences which are opposed to world peace and universal brotherhood. It is essential, therefore, that peace loving peoples should think about these differences and help find just solutions.

A few days ago, when the whole world was excited by the latest Soviet achievements in space, the thought came to my mind that now that we could have a glimpse of our own planet from other stars, how foolish are these small meannesses, this desire to cut up the world into small parcels of land, this desire to dominate small groups of people. Isn't there even a small group of aware, honest and just human beings among us who can convince the others that now that the passageways to the entire universe are being opened up in front of our very eyes, and the riches of all creation are there for humanity to use, we should dismantle all the military bases and throw these bombs and rockets and guns into the sea, so that we may go forth together to conquer this wide universe where there is room enough for all mankind, where no one need fight anyone else, where there is limitless space and worlds without number? I am convinced that despite numerous difficulties on the way, we can succeed in convincing humankind of these simple truths. I am convinced that the humankind which has never surrendered to its enemies, will emerge victorious yet, and that, at long last, hatred, repression and war will give way to peace and universal brotherhood. I am convinced that we shall all live together in harmony as Hafiz, the Persian poet, had wanted us to live long ago:

> *Khalal pazir bawad har bina ki mi bini*
> *Bajuz bina-i-mohabbat ki khali as khalal ast.*
>
> *Every foundation that we have seen has been flawed,*
> *but for the foundation of love, for love alone is flawless*

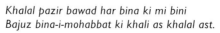

103

Faiz with poet Mustafa Zaidi, Lahore 1960

Chapter 12

On problems of cultural planning in Asia, Pakistan

FAIZ AHMED FAIZ

Alien imperialist domination of Asian countries was not merely a passive process of pure political supremacy. It was also an active process of social and cultural subversion

The vast land mass known as Asia encompasses numerous countries and peoples and the cultural patterns specific to different lands do not easily yield to broad generalizations. Thus, we have in Asia a number of Socialist States where cultural planning obviously takes on a completely different orientation from other countries operating under a different socio-political organization. Then there are countries which have escaped direct foreign colonial domination or occupation and where the continuity of cultural traditions was not radically subverted by foreign influences. Lastly, there is a group to which my country - Pakistan - belongs who have been only recently liberated after a prolonged era of subjugation. This paper is mainly relevant to the cultural problems of the last group, although some of these problems may be shared in some measure by the other groups as well because dominative western influences have been operative there as well at some stage of their political history.

Culture in the broad sense is commonly defined today as the whole way of life of a given human community. In a more restricted sense it comprises finished or stylized expression of this way of life in various forms of creative and artistic expression. For purposes of convenience these two inter-related aspects may be discussed separately.

In the broader sense, culture in human societies has two main aspects: an external formal aspect and an inner ideological one. The external forms of culture, social or artistic, are basically an organized expression of its inner ideological content. Both are integral components of a given social structure. They are changed or modified as this structure changes and because of this organic link they also promote and influence such changes in their present organism. Cultural problems, therefore, cannot be studied or understood or solved in isolation from social problems, i.e. problems of Asian countries also have to be understood and their solutions found in the light of this larger perspective – in the context of their underlying social problems.

Faiz with friends at the Indus Gallery, Karachi, 1983

Very broadly speaking, these problems are primarily the problems of arrested growth: they originated primarily from long years of foreign domination and the remnants of a backward, outmoded social structure. This should not require much elaboration. Todays industrialized or economically powerful western countries caught up with various Asian lands between the 16th and 19th centuries. Some among these were fairly developed feudal societies with ancient traditions of advanced feudal culture. Others had yet to progress beyond primitive pastoral tribalism. The social and cultural development of them all was frozen at the point of their political subjugation and remained so until the advent of political independence. The culture of these ancient feudal societies, in spite of much technical and intellectual excellence, was restricted to a small privileged class which rarely intermingled with the parallel unsophisticated folk culture of the general masses. Primitive tribal culture, in spite of its child-like beauty, had little intellectual content. Both feudal and tribal societies living contiguously in the same homelands were constantly engaged in tribal, racial, religious or other feuds with their tribal and feudal rivals. Foreign colonialist domination accentuated this dual fragmentation, i.e. the division among different tribal and national on the one hand and the division among different classes within the same tribal or national group on the other.

One basic cultural problem which faces many of these countries, therefore, is the problem of cultural integration.

Vertical integration which means providing a common ideological and national basis for a multiplicity of national cultural patterns and horizontal integration which involves educating and elevating the entire body of the people to the same cultural and intellectual level. Thus, the qualitative political change from colonialism to independence was required to be followed by a similar qualitative change in the social structure left behind by the colonialist era.

Alien imperialist domination of Asian countries was not merely a passive process of pure political supremacy. It was also an active process of social and cultural subversion. It tried on the one hand to kill or destroy whatever was good, progressive, and forward looking in the old feudal or pre-feudal structures by way of arts, skills, customs, manners, humanist values or mental enlightenment. It tried to sustain and perpetuate, on the other, whatever was unwholesome, reactionary, or backward looking: ignorance, superstition, servility, and class-exploitation. What was handed back to the newly liberated countries, therefore, was not the original social structure taken over at the point of their subjugation but the perverted and emasculated remnants of this structure. Superimposed on these remnants were cheap, spurious and second-hand imitations of western cultural patterns by way of language, customs, manners, art forms, and ideological values.

Faiz going by train to receive the Lenin Peace Prize, Lahore, 1962

This poses a number of other basic cultural problems for these countries.

First, the problem of salvaging from the debris of their shattered national cultures those elements which are basic to national identity, which can be adjusted and adapted to the needs of a more advanced social structure, and which can help to strengthen and promote progressive social values and attitudes.

Second, to reject and discard those elements which are relevant to a backward and out-moded social structure, which are either irrelevant or repugnant to a more advanced system of social relationships and which hinder the progress of more rational, enlightened human values and attitudes.

Third, to accept and assimilate from imported foreign and western cultures those elements which help to elevate national culture to higher technical, aesthetic and intellectual standards.

Fourth, to repudiate those elements among these imports which are deliberately aimed at promoting degeneracy, decadence, and social reaction. Roughly speaking, these problems may be termed. Problems of new cultural adaptation, assimilation, emancipation, and purification.

In addition to the above, political independence has also given rise to certain new attitudes, subjective as well as social, which also require rectification and reorientation, e.g. the craze for chauvinistic revivalism and the craze for indiscriminate modernism. Thus, certain social groups insist that it is not only the good and valuable element of traditional, cultural and social practice which should be revived and revitalized but also the bad and worthless elements. Conversely, not only the bad and worthless elements of modern western culture must be discarded and repudiated but the useful and progressive elements as well. The baby must be thrown out with the bath water! The motivation of these schools is primarily not cultural but political, i.e. to hamper the progress of rational social awareness and to confirm the exploiting classes in their interests and privileges. Secondly, political and commercial entrepreneurs from the more advanced western countries have sought to fill the cultural vacuum confronting newly liberated countries with a deluge of cultural, or more correctly, anti-cultural trash in the form of debased literature, magazines, music, dances, fashion, etc. which extol and glorify crimes, violence, cynicism, perversion, and profligacy. A good deal of this trash has been indiscriminately accepted by certain other sections of these communities under the mistaken notion of modernism.

From this point of view some of the major cultural problems of Asian countries, e.g. arrested growth, uneven distribution, internal contradictions, imitativeness, etc. are primarily social problems related to the organization, values, judgments, and social practices of a backward social structure. Their solution, therefore, lies outside the domain of a purely cultural endeavor and falls within the domain of political and socio-economic reforms.

Notwithstanding what has been said above, it should also be borne in mind that while national culture cannot transcend the limitations of a given social structure it can certainly lag behind it. In other words, while cultural activity cannot go beyond the progressive potentialities of a particular society it can certainly fall short of what is both possible and desirable within the limitations of this society. It can accept or reject attitudes; it can adopt or ignore measures in the cultural field which are conducive to social progress and intellectual enlightenment within its own social framework. This is particularly true of those forms of human culture which are alienable to deliberate planning and conscious promotional effort, e.g. creative skills and the body of the arts. It is in this context that I would like to speak about the situation in my own country and the and solutions that have been, or are being faced and attempted.

In May 1968, the then Government of Pakistan set up a Committee under the chairmanship of the writer of this paper to investigate and report on these problems and what follows are some of the conclusions arrived at by this Committee. While discussing certain national attitudes inimical to the promotion and development of art and culture it was observed:

Outside the office of The Pakistan Times, from left to right, Ahmed Nadeem Qasmi, Faiz, Iqbal Singh and Alyz Faiz, Lahore, 1957

"There is a school of thinking which holds that all cultural activity in general and the performing arts in particular are immoral and antireligious. The anti-culture, anti-art attitudes fostered by this school mainly derive from the following:

(i) Prolonged colonial subjection subverted the native cultural patterns of our old society and the imperialist rulers sought to replace them by their own cultural imports. Everything native' by way of culture and the arts was held up to contempt and ridicule and their western counterparts held up as the only models fit for imitation. The resultant disruption of national life and impoverishment of all the national arts robbed large sections of our people, particularly the influential section called the Civil Lines', of all love, respect and understanding of their national arts.

(ii) During the declining years of the Mughal Empire in the sub-continent, as elsewhere in similar historical conditions, the arts were seduced to become handmaids of dissolute courts and instruments of their decadent pleasures. This was particularly true of music and dancing which was encouraged to become the monopoly of a socially and morally unacceptable class. After the downfall of the Mughals, the moral indignation evoked by these decadent practices and the social prejudices attaching to the class of 'singing girls' were detached from the social conditions which gave them birth and transferred, in the popular mind, to the arts themselves.

(iii) Since Independence these anti-art attitudes inherited from the past have been seized upon by certain factions in the country for topical political ends. They first sought to equate all music and dancing with the lewd vulgarizations of these arts by inept professionals. From these premises, it was easy to proceed to the conclusion, as has often been done, that all art is immoral, hence anti-religious, hence ideologically unacceptable. Any ideological objection that can be brought against any art, however, must relate to some particular form and content of a particular art and not the art as such. This obvious platitude is deliberately ignored because the basic motivation of this school is neither moral nor religious but socio-political. This motivation seeks to promote attitudes hostile to all agencies of sensitive feeling and enlightened thought, including scientific research and artistic creation.

(iv) The generally negative public and official attitudes towards national art and culture have opened the gates for a resolute cultural invasion by western commercial

and political agencies. Thus, in the last few years many corrupt and perverted versions of western culture focused on sex, violence, and profligacy, have provided the stable cultural fare for the sophisticated Pakistani boy and girl and the main outlet for his or her natural craving for self-expression.

(v) A second fairly influential point in the controversy is that culture and the arts, even though they may not be morally undesirable or ideologically reprehensible, are still something of a luxury which only the rich countries can afford. Developing countries, like Pakistan, must put first things first and devote all their resources to material developments, i.e. agriculture and industry, and let the harp and the fiddle wait until better days come round – just as the poor would put his daily bread before the pleasures of art."

Faiz inaugurating sculptor Shahid Sajjid's first solo exhibition, Karachi, 1965

We are unable to agree with this point of view.

In a developing society, where the paucity of funds hinders all development, education constitutes personal capital and hence counts as a basic factor in development. Similarly, culture which represents the awareness of a society of its values, aims, and aspirations provides an important incentive for a national development. Any development efforts which ignore the emotional and spiritual aid provided by a nation's awareness of its own goals and aspirations are bound to engender antagonistic contradictions between the people and the agencies responsible for such development. Cultural activity in a developing nation is in many ways a form of socio-political activity and it is only through this activity that a people's full participation in nation-building efforts can be ensured.

Secondly, the arts are as much a factor in the material process of production as is education. Just as an investment in national education has a direct bearing on national productivity through creating superior skills, an investment in the arts has a direct role in improving the standards and qualities of many forms of industrial production by superior fashioning and designing.

Thirdly, in the world of today, advertising and public relations are no longer regarded as a luxury but an important change in industrial revenues. Nations do their advertising and public relations through cultural exchange, i.e. exchanges of art products and performances.

Before the inception of Pakistan there was, understandably, no such entity as a Pakistani nation. Politically, the people of present-day Pakistan (leaving aside some minority groups) were part of the Indian Muslim Community. Ethnically and geographically they were called after the areas they inhabited, i.e. Bengalis, Punjabis, Sindhis, Baluchis, Pathans, etc.

Understandably, therefore, the culture of the new Pakistani nation when it emerged was not a finished, ready-made unified entity. The differences in social development among different regions of the country, differences of climate and geographical habitat, ethnic and historical factors and administrative divisions enforced by foreign rulers, all combined to make the culture of the people of the present-day Pakistan a composite of diversified patterns.

Nevertheless, these people in all parts of Pakistan shared a common historical experience as well as those common ethical and cultural mores which originated from the religion they professed. It was this common religion and the sum total of these values and their expression in social life which made the Muslims of the sub-continent emerge as a separate and distinct cultural entity over a long period of history.

There is considerable difference of opinion on how precisely this culture should be defined. There appears to be some agreement, however, that the culture of the people of Pakistan includes everything which has been integrated into the bloodstream of the social and historical life of our people. This conglomeration is principally composed of (a) the religion of Islam which provides the ethical and ideological basis for the people's way of life; (b) the indigenous cultures of different linguistic regions inherited from their own specific cultural

112

past; and (c) elements of western culture absorbed since the days of British occupation.

Added to the above are the distinctive cultures of minority groups who form a part of the Pakistan nation.

This raises some debatable issues, e.g. the issues of regional cultures. The basic and characteristic vocabulary of our people's culture, i.e. language, dress, customs, architecture, music, folk arts, etc. has naturally been better preserved in our villages and the countryside of the various regions than in big towns where dominative foreign influences have introduced a cosmopolitanism composed of many elements and characteristics which are not exclusively national. The growth of these folk cultures was arrested at various levels of development with the disintegration of feudal societies, the withdrawal of feudal patronage, and the concentration of power, wealth and educational and cultural facilities in the big towns. A reversal of this process of stagnation, therefore, and a revival of these regional cultures – the most authentic storehouse of what is distinctively Pakistani – seems obviously called for.

This raises two issues: first, whether such a revival would promote centrifugal tendencies of narrow regionalism and militate against the goals of national integration; and secondly, whether such a revival and the development of regional cultures would yield to some sort of a synthesis on the national plane.

Faiz taking to workers and Kashmiri leader K. H. Khurshaid at the office of The Pakistan Times, Lahore, 1950

The consensus of the opinions can be summarized as follows:

(a) In as such as all regional cultures are an organic part of the totality of our national culture, love for the part does not preclude, and, in fact, predicates love for the whole. The confusion of thought which continues to plague this subject stems from one basic fallacy which seeks to counterpose national and regional cultures as antagonistic rivals and thus postulates that one can or would develop only at the expense of the other. This fallacy can be dispelled by a clear understanding of the obvious fact that just as the country is a geographical union of its constituent regions and the nation is a political union of the people inhabiting these regions, similarly, national culture is an aggregate of these regional cultures plus the unifying bonds of faith and history.

(b) A genuine synthesis of diverse forms of regional cultures into national patterns cannot be brought about by any forcible impositions through administrative means. It can only evolve through a gradual accumulation of affinities and a gradual assimilation of "sympathetic elements into a new compound." This is possible only if "diversity" is not misinterpreted as disunity and the natural process of the growth of diverse elements is not perverted or stifled by an impatience for immediate results.

The problem of national identity also relates to the classical tradition of the arts. And this presents a different set of problems.

(A) Since this tradition, particularly in arts like music and dancing, is much older than the Muslim era, it contains many ingredients unrelated to Muslim social traditions.

(B) Since the Indo-Muslin civilization was not confined to the areas which now form Pakistan, it contains many ingredients which transcend our boundaries and cannot be deemed exclusively Pakistani.

Should this tradition, then, be owned and accepted wholesale or should it be recast into a mold nearer to the heart of a Pakistani? There is considerable difference of opinion over this issue. One school holds that to establish a completely different national and ideological identity it is necessary to discard all these ingredients, and if this is not possible with regard to a particular artistic tradition, it is best to do away with this tradition altogether. The opposite view is that by maligning a tradition evolved by Muslim society in the days of their greatest glory, a tradition which represents their main contribution to the cultural history of this subcontinent, we really malign our own history; that we are not justified in taking exception to what our ancestors, in whom we take pride, not only took no exception to but actively sponsored and patronized.

As for territorial limits, it should be obvious that some of the most basic components of our cultural heritage originated and evolved in areas beyond the present geographical boundaries of Pakistan. These include the Urdu language and literature and the whole body of Arabic, Iranian, Central Asian, and various other influences which have been integrated into our cultural tradition.

Lastly, there is the problem of re-valuating our cultural and artistic tradition in the light of contemporary experience, the adjustment of "continuities from the past" with the demands of the present." Western societies, after nearly two hundred years of scientific, industrial, and technological advancement, mainly at the expense of the peoples they dominated, have introduced to the world techniques, methodologies, tools, materials, and modes of production unknown before. These advances, in their turn, have induced new habits of thought and cultural expression, thus modifying or eliminating various traditional elements in social or cultural life. In developing and newly liberated countries, like Pakistan, this process has just begun. And along with it have emerged the horns of a dilemma – of tradition versus modernism.

Faiz with Ustad Daman, Lahore, 1984

This dilemma has generated three tendencies. One, the blind imitativeness of our own past in the name of tradition. Two, the blind imitativeness of everything Western in the name of modernism. Three, the tasteless hodge-podge of the two in order to have the best of both worlds. We are of the opinion that all these attitudes are incorrect, that:

(a) The continuity of tradition does not mean its perpetuation in toto. For instance, the place of our traditional arms, the sword and the spear, is no longer in the battlefield but in the museum. Nevertheless, they should be preserved, loved, and respected as part of our heritage.

(b) The acquisition of scientific, technological, industrial, and intellectual knowledge from the West does not necessitate a negation of our own historic personality.

Therefore, those elements of our traditional culture which were only relevant to another set of conditions in the past and have outlived their utility cannot and should not be artificially perpetuated merely on the grounds of sentiment. The sentiment of love and respect alone should be enough. The application of new techniques in the arts, experimentation with new forms of expression, utilization of new materials, popularization of new artistic concepts should not be discouraged merely because they have originated in the West, provided the artist retains his/her identity as a member of his/her on community.

(c) A living and dynamic culture is one which provides conditions for maximum contribution by national talent for the aesthetic and intellectual enrichment of the community at the highest level of contemporary attainment. Our endeavor should be to create the most favourable conditions for this maximum contribution at appropriate levels.

This article was first published in November, 1984 in the magazine "Pakistan Progressive" by the Department of Economics, University of Wisconsin at Madison USA.

Section Three
Faiz Ahmed Faiz in Europe

Faiz in BBC studio, Birmingham, 1975

Promotional poster produced by Lifting the Lid for Faiz event, Manchester, 2011

118

FABBEH HUSEIN AND MOHSIN ZULFIQAR

Faiz, Citizen of the world

Faiz loved Lahore, 'City of Lights', and his homeland, Pakistan. However, due to prevailing oppressive and toxic political conditions in Pakistan Faiz was forced, many a times, to take refuge in Europe and elsewhere. According to Inder Kumar Gujral, former president of India, Moscow (more specifically the Indian embassy in Moscow) was Faiz's second home[1]. However, Faiz spent noteworthy periods of time in Britain. Apart from his extended stay in Beirut, as the editor of an international literary journal *Lotus*, it was Britain particularly where he found solidarity, acknowledgement, warmth, friendship, admiration, respect, respite and refuge.

After the partition of India, Faiz Ahmed Faiz visited many countries representing his homeland as a journalist, trade union leader, poet, and peace activist. In addition to Soviet Union (as it was in 1980s), Faiz visited Algeria, Angola, Bangladesh, Bulgaria, Britain, Canada, Cuba, Ethiopia, France, India, Indonesia, Iraq, Germany, Lebanon, Kenya, Switzerland, Syria, the Philippines, Tunisia and the USA. Apart from Faiz's own reminiscences of his journeys to Cuba and the Soviet Union, very little has been written about his presence in these countries. Ludmila Vasileva[2], Sibte Hasan[3] and a chapter by Ashfaq Hussain[4] in his book: *Faiz kay Mughrabi Hawley*, have described Faiz's presence in the Soviet Union. Recently, Zulfi's book[5] on the years Faiz spent in Lebanon is a welcome addition. There are some other articles relating to Faiz in Europe and Canada.

Europe: Home, away from home

Perhaps, we can divide the time Faiz spend in Europe into two parts. Firstly, his many visits to Soviet Union and secondly, his long period of stays in Western Europe mainly in Britain. In this brief article we attempt to provide glimpses of his life in Europe.

The present-day Europe is politically very different compare to the times of Faiz Ahmed Faiz. The Soviet Union, which collapsed in 1991, was still the bulwark of socialist ideals across the world. The socialist block provided inspire and hopes to all those who were fighting for justice and equality; a world free from imperialism, neo-colonialism and economic exploitation.

In an ideologically contesting world, Soviet Union, provided access to and an understanding of an alternative for social, economic and political future for Pakistan. As a committed

communist, he welcomed the opportunities for visiting Soviet Union several times during his life. Long visits to Moscow were also punctuated by his detailed observation of the achievement of socialism in many parts of vast Soviet Union. These included his travels to many soviet states with USSR, including Kazakhistan, Azerbaijan, Latvia, and Georgia. His visits to other 'socialist' block countries included People's Republic of China and Cuba. Both of these visits were undertaken as a representative of journalists and writers of Pakistan. The experience of Cuba are summarised in his book: '*Safarnama-e-Cuba*' (Travels in Cuba). In his slightly more voluminous book: *Mah-o-Saal-e-Ashnai* (Months and Years of Acquaintance). In this volume, he described his visits to many Soviet states as well as the opportunities he had in interacting with some of the greatest writers of the time.

Faiz with Ifthikar Arif and Ahmed Faraz at Urdu Murkaz, London 1984

While in Moscow[6], Faiz had the opportunity to meet, converse and become friends with many writers, including Nazim Hikmat (Turkish poet in exile in Soviet Union), Ilya Grigoryevich Ehrenburg, Soviet writer and journalist (1891-1967); Jean-Paul Sartre (1905-1980), French philosopher; novelist and playwright, Saliminov Chyngyz Aitmatov (1928-2008); well known writer from kyrgyzstan, Alberto Moravia (1907-1990), Italian novelist, Nobel Laureate Sir William Gerald Golding (1911-1993), British novelist and poet, famous for his novel Lords of the Flies; Léopold Sédar Senghor (1906-2001), first president of Senegal, a known poet and cultural theorist; Umar Ali Sulaimanow (Kazakh writer) and Chingiz Aitmatow (Kirghiz writer).

Faiz was already well known in the Soviet literary circles. From early 1960, his poems were translated in Russian and other languages and published mainly in journals. The first volumes of his poems were published in 1983; according to Vasileva[7] by late 1980s over 210,000 copies of his books were printed. In addition to his reminiscence of Soviet Union, Faiz penned of some of his better known poems in the comfort of the country. His famous poem: *Teen Awazeen* (Three Voices) was written in Samarkand (the capital of Uzbekistan). The poem portrays the perpetual struggle between 'have' and 'have-not'; between exploiters and exploited and between tyrant and victim. This is how Faiz articulates the voice of the victim[8] questioning the status-quo:

> *Night is the harbinger of pain*
> *And the dawning day its maturity.*
> *At noon every vein burst with agony*
> *And at sunset appears the demon of fear.*
> *Oh God! this cyclic horror of night and day.*
> *This never-ending restless journey of my life.*
> *Was this what you destined for me?*
> *Not even an iota of happiness?*
> *They say that cruelty pleases you*
> *And that injustice is not possible without your consent.*
> *If this is true should I deny your benevolence?*
> *Should I listen to them or should I believe in you?*

His unfinished poem *Intisaab* (Dedication) was written in Moscow in 1967. This powerful poem truly reflects Faiz's political views in respect of the wretched of the world:

> *In the name of this day*
> *and*
> *In the name of this day's sorrow:*
> *Sorrow that stands, disdaining the blossoming garden of Life,*
> *Like a forest of dying leaves*
> *A forest of dying leaves that is my country*
> *An assembly of pain that is my country*
> *In the name of the sad lives of clerks,*
> *In the name of the worm-eaten hearts and the worm-eaten tongues*
> *In the name of the postmen*
> *In the name of the coachmen*
> *In the name of the railway workers*
> *In the name of the workers in the factories.*

Both the poems describe clearly the conditions of Pakistani people in an unequal and unjust society. He also identified those who have the power to propel the society forward and the lines from his poem: *Tum apni kar guzroo* (Do what you have to do), penned in Moscow in 1975. The lines exemplify the resolve of people to deal with the pain of the struggle and overcome the enemy[9].

Why worry now about that day
when the heart will be broken into pieces
and all sorrows will be wiped out.
Throw away on the rubbish heap
of oblivion all our doubts and fears.
If there is laughter we will laugh.
If there is weeping we will weep.
Do what you have to do
and let the future take care of itself.

Faiz, while in the Soviet Union, avoided writing eulogistic poems to praise the achievements of a socialist system. However, elsewhere, Faiz openly acknowledged the achievement of socialism in terms of steps taken to improve the conditions of soviet people in the areas of culture, health, education, construction, etc.

While in Soviet Union, Faiz was optimistic and full of hopes for the people of Pakistan. This optimism remained an integral part of the poetry of Faiz but became mingled with sorrow and pain as he took decision to leave Pakistan under duress. There are three long periods when Faiz decided to leave Pakistan. After the end of his prison sentence, Faiz moved to Britain for year in 1955. Between 1962 to1964, he again stayed in Britain, though this period was also punctuated with short visits to Lebanon, Syria, Iraq, Algeria and Egypt. The takeover of Pakistan by yet another militarily dictator, General Zia-ul-Haq, in July 1977, compelled Faiz to leave home. This time the destination was Beirut, where Faiz stayed till the invasion of the country by Israel. He left war-torn Beirut to Britain where he stayed till 1982.

Faiz in Britain

His extended stay in Britain is understandable. Faiz found that there was a large settled South Asian community. He was well supported by an established community of political activists who themselves had escaped military rule in Pakistan. Faiz was the icon of cultural resistance against the corrupt inequitable system and military dictatorship in Pakistan. As such he was a symbol of hope for millions of Pakistanis both at home and in Europe. His unassuming manners and 'ordinariness' endeared him to all sections of the Pakistani diaspora. He was a popular freedom fighter, indeed.

BBC Television Mushaira, London, 1980

The South Asian communities in Britain loved his poetry. They organised and flocked to many a mushairas (poetry sessions) where Faiz was received as a living legend. So, here was Faiz buoyed by fellow South Asians. It was not home but it was a surrogate home.

His visits to Britain seem to coincide with frequent troubles in Pakistan or whenever he felt a looming imprisonment or limitations to him being able to express freely or when he was invited by the South Asian diaspora to attend literary events or speak to Indian Workers Association amongst other organisations.

On one of these occasions of leaving Pakistan, Alys Faiz[10] observed that Faiz simply flew out of Lahore. This happened when in August 1977 General Zia led a military coup against the Bhutto government to end a relatively calm period of life for Faiz. According to her, the government and all civil institutions were suspended, all political and trade union activity was banned, arrest began and, for Faiz, it was déjà vu all over again. He was again put under constant police surveillance. His every move watched. He could be arrested at any time, and finally decided to leave the country on his flight out of the country.

According to Alys Faiz "he, cigarette in hand, strolled out of his house. The policeman on duty thought he was going for his regular morning stroll and paid him no attention. Faiz went straight to the airport and flew out of the country. In his own words, this was his 'self-exile'. He had not been forced to leave. He just did not want to stay and risk imprisonment again. He later said, 'It is not that one has no fight left. It is only that I am not as young as I once was and it is difficult to physical punishment when you are older. The soul is willing but the body is not."

From Lahore, Faiz flew to Delhi and then to Moscow. He made several visits to Britain before going to Beirut. When war broke out in Beirut he did not feel safe. Ideally, he wanted to go back to Lahore but those were Ziaul Haq years, so he stayed in London instead'.[11]

'After receiving the Lenin award, London became Faiz's permanent residence; because Ayub's Martial Law put a ban on people writing freely, also all the doors for working to earn were closed[12].' 'Wherever he lived, the memories of the homeland continued to haunt him. He was also disillusioned with the conditions in Pakistan. His love for the homeland grew proportionally as the conditions in the country turned from bad to worst[13]. '... He was a like a fish outside water – uninvited guest in strange lands.

However, his optimism and zest for life enabled him to engage with others from literary, arts and political circles. He would often stay up late nights with close friends and sometimes ' just start talking about Sialkot and the old days, speak very admiringly of Iqbal[14], Maulvi Mir Hasan[15], Sufi Tabassum[16], etc.'

Faiz with American poet Naomi Lazard at Urdu Markaz, London, 1982

124

Sayeed Hasan Khan[17] recalls: 'He (Faiz) was always invited during his visits to London by the BBC Urdu service to recite his poems. Later on we would sit with him in the club and spend hours talking. One day we came out of the Bush house and were waiting for the taxi when a Pakistani from Lahore saw us and recognised Faiz. He approached us, and after introducing himself insisted on take us out to dinner at a restaurant he owned. Faiz in his usual way accepted the offer as he hated to say no to anybody'.

Sayed Hasan Khan adds that 'Many of us have cherished memories of listening to his poetry in Mushairas[18] and in privately organized poetry sessions in the major cities of Britain including Birmingham, London and Manchester. He made frequent appearances on BBC's Urdu Service programmes. He had many close friends living in Britain including Dr. Ayub Mirza (author of a major book on Faiz: *Hum Kay theray ajnabi)*; Ifthikar Arif (who was Director of Urdu Murkaz in London and Faiz's letters to him has been recently published under the title: *Faiz banam Ifthikar Arif); Raza Ali Abidi* (from BBC who hosted many radio programmes with Faiz); the film-maker, Yavar Abbas; and among his personal friends were Syed Badar-ud-din from Birmingham and once London-based, well known Urdu poetess, Zehra Nigah. Among his friends were many progressive British and European writers and political activists. The Scottish Communist writer, Victor Kiernan, was a close friend and the first one to translate Faiz Ahmed Faiz into English'

Faiz spent two years in Britain. During this time Salima and Moneeza attended school and Alys worked. Faiz did not have the opportunity to work. He experienced immense psychological and emotional traumas as a result of growing sense of loneliness and isolation. For example, the poem: *Dil-e-mun, Mussafar-e-mun* (O Traveller! My Heart) written in London in 1978, capsulate his loss and displacement[19].

> The decree was passed for us,
> to leave this beloved land,
> to cry and weep in distant lands.
> Sitting in alien cities,
> we search for the postman
> to bring us letters from our land.
> From every stranger we seek
> the fate of our left over dwellings.
> In this land of unknown people
> we have been ordained to spend our days and nights.
> Oh Heart! Pass this time by talking to this or that fellow.
> Do not ask us the pangs and agony of
> this terrible evening of sorrow.
> Even this living was better Heart!
> If only we were made to know for how many days more.
> For us even death was not unwelcome
> Should it visit once only?
> Oh Traveller! My Heart!

Faiz wrote many other poems whilst in Britain. In the same year penned: *Phool murjha gaye sarey* (All the flowers have wilted)[20]

All the flowers are wilted
The sky's tears will not stop;
The candles have gone dark,
The mirrors lie shattered;
No more music do instruments make,
The anklets that sang once are now asleep.

And behind those clouds,
Far, far in the distance,
Twinkles a star,
The star of pain,
But it makes music,
It smiles.

It is instructive to note that the poems demonstrate a strain in his optimism. In the early 1960s his poems expressed a sense of hope. Towards the late 1970s his optimism seems to be tampered by exile, isolation and dislocation. And yet, the late Edward Said saw the indefatigable and resilient spirit in Faiz.

Edward Said[21] wrote, 'To see a poet in exile – as opposed to reading the poetry of exile – is to see exile's antinomies embodied and endured with a unique intensity. Several years ago I spent some time with Faiz Ahmed Faiz, the greatest contemporary Urdu poet. He was exiled from his native Pakistan by Zia's military regime, and found a welcome of a sort in strife-torn Beirut. Naturally his closest friends were Palestinian, but I sensed that, although there was an affinity of spirit between them, nothing quite matched – language, poetic conventions, or life-history. Only once, when Eqbal Ahmad, a Pakistani friend and a fellow-exile, came to Beirut, did Faiz seem to overcome his sense of constant estrangement. The three of us sat in a dingy Beirut restaurant late one night, while Faiz recited poems. After a time, he and Eqbal stopped translating his verses for my benefit, but as the night wore on it did not matter. What I watched required no translation: it was an enactment of homecoming expressed through defiance and loss, as if to say, Zia, we are here.'

Many a close friends have outlived Faiz and remember him fondly. Amongst such is Georges Fisher. Faiz had a very close and life long friendship with Georges Fischer. They met each other in Geneva in 1949. Now in his nineties, Fischer recalled in a letter[22] to a mutual friend of Faiz, Syed Badar Uddin Beider, a patron of Faiz Centenary Organising Committee, UK, that 'Faiz was a very dear friend. I met him in 1949 at ILO (International Labour Organisation) in Geneva, Switzerland, where I was representative of the World Federation of Trade Unions'. They also met each other fairly frequently in Pakistan, India, Britain and France. In the 1980s, Fischer permanently moved to a country house in France, where Faiz stayed for ten days in March 1984, 'Trados', 600 kilometres to the south of Paris. Fischer being an ardent communist and trade unionist had a close affinity with Faiz as they both played important roles in developing strategies to forge close co-operation among the international trade union movement.

Being friends, they naturally kept regularly in touch with each other through letters and recently Beider requested Fischer

126

to send him any copies of Faiz's letters he may still have. Fischer responded that 'I don't dare send you several letters of Faiz. They are in a bad shape, so I send you only the copies of his two letters and copies of two letters from Alys, two newspaper articles, and two speeches by me.'

George Fischer was in New Delhi when he heard the news of Faiz's death. On December 4, 1984, Fischer attended a memorial meeting in Delhi and recalled his long association with Faiz. He shared the platform, among others, with I. K. Gujral, Amrita Prtam, Som Nath Chib, Dr. Bhishan Sahni, Ghulam Rabbani Taban, Dr. Qamar Rais, Kartar Singh Duggal, Professor Mumtaz Hussain and Dr. Gyula Csak.

A few days after Faiz's death, Alys Faiz received a card from Fischer. In response, Alys Faiz, in a letter dated December 16, 1984, wrote[23]:

'I was most touched to receive your card – and actually wept for times past – conditions here are not good so one hardly smiles for the future'. In the same letter, Alys describes one of the commemoration events held after Faiz's death in Lahore, 'on this 21st the theatre was crowded and the last item was arranged by Salima – recitations of Faiz's poems illustrated with slides which she took in Central Asia this summer – it was most poignant – last of all his most famous poem 'Prayer' in his own voice and with a magnificent slide of him – all in a darkened hall. There was hardly a dry eye there.'

In an another letter[24] to Fischer, Alys Faiz wrote about a mutual friend and biographer of Faiz, Auyb Mirza who was settled in Britain, 'I am sorry I have no news of Ayub he seems to be very angry and that makes me sad – he has said he will never come to Lahore now that Faiz is not here – that really is too bad – one has so few good friends and he was one.' In the same letter, Alys informed Fischer that the Faiz Foundation had been registered and they were now able to call for donations – 'anyway we have been given 10,000 rupees by the Old Ravians of Government College and 40,000 from somewhere else. So we have a starting fund.' Even after the death of Faiz, Fischer and Alys remained in touch with each other, until Alys' own death in 2003.

M. H. Askari in his commemorative article in The Daily Dawn on November 14, 1986 on the second anniversary of Faiz's death, wrote, 'Faiz's circle of friends and admirers in Paris included Professor Georges Fischer of Paris University ... Georges Fischer was a very special friend, as he had known Faiz as a trade unionist at the ILO in Geneva.' Fischer was then the Director of Research at the Centre Nationale de la Recherche Scientifique in Paris.

Another very close friend of Faiz was in Europe was Syed Badar Uddin Beider.

Beider, born in the Kota state of Rajasthan, British India in 1934, was enriched by his family, from Lucknow, by being steeped in literature and culture since birth. When the family migrated to Pakistan in 1948, Beider's access to the world of

Faiz's poetry came about just a few years later in the 1950s and he was an instant admirer. Incidentally, Beider's chosen profession, working for a travel agency, soon brought him into contact with Faiz in the late 1950s. Faiz, who was travelling to Paris with Alys Faiz to attend a UNESCO conference, was issued an air ticket with PIA (Pakistan International Airlines) but the flight was cancelled so Beider took it upon himself to change his ticket, to fly with Air France so he could make the conference on time. He presented Faiz with the new travel arrangements, only for them to be rejected as Faiz refused to fly with Air France stating that he was representing Pakistan and so will travel with the national carrier. True to his word, Faiz waited for a later PIA flight while Beider again changed his ticket. Beider described this first encounter as one that made a lasting impression of Faiz being a man of principle.

Just a few years later, Beider left Pakistan and worked in several different countries, including the Soviet Union, picking up on and communicating with the world and people around him, before settling in Britain. He recounts his story of moving to Birmingham and beginning his long association of Faiz in the 1960s. 'The poet Ahmed Faraz[25] came to Birmingham in 1971 to attend a *Mushaira* and before the event he was invited by a local dignitary to attend a dinner at his residence. The host refused to provide alcohol at the dinner, which displeased and upset Faraz.

Salim Shahid, a BBC producer suggested to go and have a drink in his car, which naturally annoyed Faraz as he did not feel like he had to 'sneak away' and hide his true personality. This ultimately let to Faraz refusing to stay at the dinner any longer. 'Salim Shahid promptly contacted me and Faraz arrived at my house late at night around 11.00 p.m. with others in tow – and left ten days later well satisfied[26]'. Faraz had passed on the message to Faiz that he had found a good place to stay in Birmingham and it ensued that the following year Faiz came to visit.

This visit resulted in the beautiful friendship that was stuck between the two and one that lasted for nearly thirty years. Both were so committed to their friendship that even whilst studying at the University of Sussex in the 1970s, Beider travelled every other day to travel from Brighton to London to meet Faiz to talk throughout the dark of the night and into the early hours of the morning. Faiz stayed with Beider countless times for considerable periods; before and after going to Beirut, after being admitted to a sanatorium in Yalta due to ill health and when he journeyed to and from Pakistan. Just hearing how much time these two men spent in each other's company shows the lifelong friendship that transpired by chance. Faiz communicated his thoughts, his world and his feelings to Beider in regular letters, though a collection of around 120-130 of them are now lost. However, Beider is left with a cherished few photographs, letters and postcards from Faiz and an undying love for an intellectual giant of twentieth century.

Following three articles in this section give the reader a further insight into Faiz and his times in Europe.

References

[1] Inder Kumar Gujral, 'Indian embassy in Moscow was Faiz's second home…', http://www.thinkindiaquarterly.org/ thinkindiaquarterly/ ArticleDetails.aspx? ArticleId=320&Id=39.

[2] Ludmila Vasileva, Parwarish-e-Loh-o-Qalam: Faiz, Oxford University Press, Karachi, 2007, p. 245-261.

[3] Sibte Hasan (1987) Sukhn dar Sukhn, Danyal Publications, Karachi, p. 77-86.

[4] Ashfaq Hussain, Faiz kay Mughrabi Hawaley, Jang Publishers, Karachi, 1992.

[5] Tasleem Elahi Zulfi, Faiz Ahmed Faiz Beirut mein (Faiz Ahmed Faiz in Beirut), Pakistan Academy of Letters, Islamabad, 2011, 83pp. .

[6] Faiz Ahmed Faiz, Mah-o-Saal-e-Ashnai (Months and Years of Acquaintance), Muktaba-e-Danyal, Karachi, 1980.

[7] Vasileva, ibid, p.245.

[8] Daud Kamal, Selected Poems of Faiz in English, Pakistan Publishing House, Karachi, 1984, p.5 .

[9] Daud Kamal, ibid, p.17.

[10] Alys Faiz quoted in Ali Madeh Hashmi's article: Childhood and early life, Dawn Faiz Centenary Supplement, Karachi, February .

[11] Zehra Nigha, No one like him, Dawn Faiz Centenary Supplement, Karachi, February 13, 2011.

[12] Sibte Hasan, ibid, p. 57.

[13] Sibte Hasan, ibid, p.58.

[14] Allama Muhammad Iqbal (1877-1938) was one of the leading Urdu poets of his time..

[15] Shams al-'Ulama' ("Sun of Scholars") Syed Mir Hassan (1844–1929) was scholar of Qur'an, Hadith, Sufism and Arabic. He taught Faiz at Scotch Mission College in Sialkot where he was a professor of Arabic..

[16] Sufi Ghulam Tabbasum (1899-1978) was a noted poet and Faiz's teacher who subsequently became his friend..

[17] Sayeed Hasan Khan, An all-embracing man', Dawn Faiz Centenary Supplement, Karachi, February 13, 2011.

[18] Faiz Ahmed Faiz, following the well-established tradition of Mushaira (public recital), participated in many such events in the South Asian sub-continent as well as in a number of countries in Asia, Europe and North America. Mushaira is a poetic symposium. It is a term in Urdu used to describe an event where poets gather to perform their works. A Mushaira is a popular form of literary culture of North India, and it is greatly admired by participants as a forum for free self-expression. .

[19] Translated by A. K. Mota, http://www.a-w-i-p.com/index.php/ poetry/2010/05/25/mere-dil-mere-musaafir-o-traveller-my-he.

[20] Daud Kamal, The Unicorn and the Dancing Girl: Poems of Faiz Ahmed Faiz, Independent Publishing Company, London 1988, p.52 .

[21] Edward Said, 'Reflection on exile', Granta (No. 13, August 1984).

[22] Georges Fischer, Letter to Badar Uddin Beider, May 25, 2011.

[23] Alys Faiz, Letter to Georges Fischer, December 16, 1984.

[24] Alys Faiz, Letter to Georges Fischer, June 6, 1985 .

[25] Ahmed Faraz (1931-2008), a prominent Urdu poet from Pakistan and a close friend of Faiz Ahmed Faiz.

[26] Badar Uddin Beider in a conversion with Mohsin Zulfiqar, June 12, 2011

Fabbeh Husein and Mohsin Zulfiqar, originally from Pakistan, are well-known educationists. Both have worked as lecturers, education advisors and inspectors in Britain and have worked in several European countries on educational programmes. They have participated actively in ant-racist and human right movements locally, nationally and internationally. Both have been involved in Faiz Centenary National Organising Committee (UK). They are authors of several books and articles on education, anti-racism and the history of minority communities in Britain.

129

Faiz in London, 1980

Chapter 14

The Word of Truth
SYED BADAR UDDIN BEIDER

The title of my piece is 'the word of truth'. I am fully aware that it sounds pretentious, but after debating with myself, I find that nothing else is appropriate. Faiz's immense popularity often stands in the way of a proper critical appraisal of his work. His contribution to our language and culture needs no endorsement from me. Faiz may have had some detractors as a poet but as a person he has had the rare distinction of having no enemies. He radiated what can only be described as 'plain goodness.' His warmth and humanity touched all those who had contact with him. Whether they knew him well enough is neither here nor there. People warmed to him. He had a remarkable knack of making you feel that you had known him all your life. This certainly cannot be said about any other man of letters in the context of the sub-continent.

It is perhaps not widely known that Faiz, the great Urdu poet was an extremely clear headed writer of English prose. He wrote precisely and simply. Pakistan Times came into being at about the same time as the country (Pakistan) itself. Faiz was appointed its first editor-in-chief and remained so for the first six years (the English newspaper might not have seen the light of day had Faiz not agreed to take on the editorship.) Under his tutelage the newspaper gained a tremendous amount of prestige and dignity. Faiz's editorials bear witness to the lucid quality of his prose.

Faiz with Badar Uddin Beider, Birmingham, 1970s

Faiz was extremely fortunate that unlike other creative geniuses he didn't have a painful childhood. He was brought up by loving parents in a well-adjusted, happy and caring home. There were no skeletons lurking in the family cupboard. He did not have to seek metaphors to break through the constricting walls of a tortuous relationship with an overbearing father or an over possessive mother. He chose to align himself (and empathise) with the deprived and downtrodden classes although nothing in his childhood or adolescence had prepared him for this course of action. It was not a rebellious gesture; it was a conscious, intellectualised decision on his part.

At a time when the young poets (and not so young) would go on about the effable radiance of comely maiden, Faiz would take a different path. He would begin by paying homage to the time honoured metaphor of 'shall I compare thee to a summer's day?' In his case[1]

> Is that her fringed veil, is it her face, her dress,
> Behind the hanging gauze, that makes it glow –
> And in the vague mist of the rippling tress
> Does the bright earring twinkle still, or no?

Translation by Victor Kiernan

But he would circumvent into grim and starker image[2]

> Bitter threads began to unravel before me
> as I went into alleys and in open markets
> saw bodies plastered with ash, bathed in blood.
> I saw them sold and bought, again and again.
> This too deserves attention. I can't help but look back
> when I return from those alleys – what should one do?
> There are other sorrows in the world,
> comforts other than love.
> Don't ask me, my love, for that love.
> Don't Ask me for that Love Again.

Translation by Agha Shahid Ali

Of all the modern Urdu poets Faiz Ahmed Faiz stands out uniquely if only because, unlike his contemporaries, he did not give up the traditional poetic diction. He had a tranquil and temperate disposition. He was steeped in the classics. Throughout his life he remained the embodiment of patience and forbearance.

Faiz with Badar Uddin Beider and Afzal Bangash, Birmingham, 1970s

Faiz became a leftist as a young man and remained one all his life. He believed passionately in changing the world's social order. He envisaged a world in which man would no longer exploit man. He must have been disillusioned at some stage but he never allowed doubt and despondency to creep into his poetic works. Loyalty was a paramount value in his social and philosophical make-up.

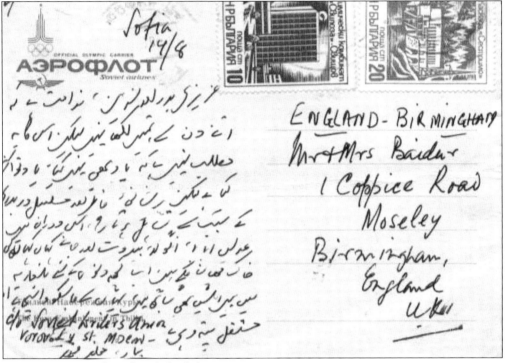

Postcard to Beider from Faiz, Sofia, Bulgaria

Faiz's tone never becomes strident. He speaks gently; he caresses our vulnerabilities, our doubts and more often than not whispers affable sentiments into our ears. His voice is so gentle and so soft that we cannot help but be swayed by it. Only when he stops that we realise what he was uttering was not 'sweet nothings' but a cogent well thought out message. His affable expression portrays the sorrow and anguish that he feels for the human condition[3]:

> In the desert of loneliness, my darling; quivers
> the echo of your voice, the mirage of your lips
> With so much tenderness, my darling your memory has put,
> Just now, its soothing hands on my turbulent heart,
> It appears, although it is still the dawn of separation,
> The day of parting is gone, and has come reunion's night.

Translation by Sian Sucha

or[4]

> O tyrant, busy concocting poison—
> not for you will there be any success today or tomorrow.
> What if you put out the candles
> in our luminous chamber of love—

snuff out the moon
and I'll concede defeat.

Translation by Shiv K. Kumar

The most universal aspect of Faiz's poetry is that given when he talks of the need for bringing sweeping changes in the established order, he employs a language that is couched in traditional religious symbolism. I can think of no other poet in our language who draws so much from the prolific stories of Islamic credo (Josh Malihabadi comes to mind but Josh has high fluting diction which mesmerises us with the panoply of its verbiage). Faiz adopted this manner almost as a stylistic device[5].

In every prison cries of I am the Truth
echoes with the sound of pouring wine,
in every river waves of bloodied hope
flow along with currents of pleasure.

Translation by Leila Sen

Faiz uses symbols of religious dissentions to explore his views. Sometimes he does so quite plainly[6]

Khuda who waqt At last I'll be rid of all concern for
pain or loss—

Also rid of the need to beseech all and sundry.
Never mind if there'll be no wine in hell—
At least the preacher will be nowhere around.

Translation by Shiv K. Kumar

And often, allegorically and metaphorically

Trampling about the streets aimlessly, these pariah dogs,
born to the prerogative of beggary—
their only treasure is the world's scorn
their only wages, the world's reproof.

Translation by Shiv K. Kumar

There is nothing obtuse in Faiz's poetry. Indeed at times, his verse is alarmingly simplistic in the mode of hymn-writer[7]:

We will see,
Certainly we, too, will see
That promised day –
That day ordained
When these colossal mountains
Of tyranny and oppression
Will explode
Into wisps of hay.

Translation by Daud Kamal

It is a hymn all right and you can interpret it as such. Faiz may have had a different connotation. I would like you to bear in mind that Faiz's use of phrases that evoke an ever-present fund of religious references, is a subtle device to articulate his abiding passion for equality and social justice when you hear him say[8]:

Only the name of God
Will remain
Who is both absent
And present –

Both the seen
And the seer.
The cry:
'I am Truth'
Will rend the skies
Which means
You, I, and all of us.
And sovereignty
Will belong to the people
Which means
You, I, and all of us.

Translation by Daud Kamal

He not only reminds you of the history of certain events deeply embedded in the psyche of the Muslims, he also makes a valid justification for the protesting against the inequalities that exist in our society.

Islamic culture, its parables, fables and its symbols assume an aesthetic quality in Faiz's poetry. Faiz's diction often transcends even the ideological goals that he had set himself. His thinking was always a little more refined, a little more chiselled than his creed. His upbringing, his mental conditioning, his cultural growth was soaked in Islamic condition. Few people know that he made a deep study of the Koran (whilst in prison) and this remained evident in his mature verse[9]:

Let's pray that those who follow false gods
Find the courage to defy and the strength to question;
Let those who wait for the sword to fall on their
bowed heads.,
Find the strength to jerk aside the executioner's hand.
Let the love that burns through our being
Be declared to the world so that the heart is at rest.
Let the word of truth that lies like a thorn in the heart
Be expressed so that it will rankle no more.

Prayer. Translation by Khalid Hasan

Faiz with Nasreen and Badar Uddin Beider, Birmingham, 1970s

I am not suggesting that Faiz was an Islamic poet in the sense in which we call T. S. Elliot a Christian poet. I am trying to suggest that Faiz's imagery remains traditional - and like all traditional classic poets (Urdu and Persian) it is ensconced in Islamic symbolism. He was particularly fond of Sauda, Mushafi and Hafiz, and you can detect shades of these poets in his ghazals (love poems).

But Faiz was also his own man and he created his own stamp, his own seal and this seal was culled of scriptural and doctrinal terminology. Faiz wore a deeply human and intensely mellow message of love and good fellowship. You do not find a single example of rancour or bitterness in his verse. He believes in cause, but remains tolerant of those who didn't. It is this tolerance (exquisitely crafted into his diction) that endeared him to millions of people in his land – and many who live beyond[10]:

> Truth's potent word, that keeps pricking the heart like a thorn.
> Make it our own, and the throbbing pain bring to an end.
> Prayer. Translation by Victor Kiernan
> If I were to pinpoint the secret of Faiz's poetic temperament I would quote[11]:
> Let's pray that our poisoned today
> is filled with the sweetness of tomorrow.
> Prayer. Translation by Khalid Hasan
> Love – and utter if you dare the word of truth.

References

[1] Kiernan, Victor (1971) Poems by Faiz, George Allen & Unwin, London, pp. 91

[2] Ali, Agha Shahid (1992) Faiz Ahmed Faiz: The Rebel's Silhoutte, Oxford University Press, Delhi, pp. 5

[3] Sian, Sucha (2011) www.faiz centenary.org

[4] Kumar, Shiv K. (1995) Faiz Ahmed Faiz: Selected Poems, Viking, New Delhi, pp.81

[5] Sen, Leila (2011) Translated especially for this article.

[6] Kumar, Shiv K., Ibid, pp. 31

[7] Kamal, Daud (1984) Selected Poems of Faiz Ahmed Faiz in English, Pakistan Publishing House, Karachi, pp.24

[8] Kamal, Daud, Ibid, pp.24

[9] Hasan Khalid (2008) O City of Lights: Faiz Ahmed Faiz – Selected Poetry and Biographical Notes, Oxford University Press, Karachi, pp.275

[10] Kiernan, Victor, Ibid, pp. 277

[11] Hasan, Khalid, Ibid, pp.275

Badar Uddin Beider was a close friend of Faiz Ahmed Faiz. Faiz stayed with him several times since 1970s. Beider organized and supported progressive events in Birmingham in UK. Previously he ran a successful travel agency in Soviet Union and Britain.

Painting of Faiz Ahmed Faiz by Hasan Mehdi, Karachi, 2011

Faiz being interviewed by Zia Moheyuddin at BBC Urdu Services, London, 1968

Chapter 15

Faiz Ahmed Faiz - Reminiscences

GEORGES FISCHER

I am not competent to speak or write about the poetry, life and activities of Faiz Ahmed Faiz. I can only call to mind the stage of phases of our long and old friendship. A French philosopher and moralist of the 19th century, Joubery, wrote: "When one of my friends is one-eyed, I look at him sideway. Faiz doesn't need this kind of indulgence. From whatever angle you consider him, you always look at his right side." These few lines are intended only to give expression and admiration for Faiz, the human being.

I first met Faiz in 1949. We met three times during that year, at the end of which I visited him in Pakistan. He was already an illustrious poet, journalist, labour and civic leader, life and soul of the Pakistani intelligentsia, knowing everybody and known by all. Thanks for Faiz, I began to understand the problems and difficulties of Pakistan, the complex, and real reasons behind the birth of this singular, new State.

Afterwards we met several times in France and in Pakistan. In-between, news about his imprisonment was worrying us. But Faiz has the wonderful gift to turn up whenever one needs his spiritual; moral and intellectual help the most. (He himself seems to have a large reserve of moral and intellectual strength that he doesn't need outside help.) So all of a sudden, he happened to be at my side in a Paris hospital in 1864 and again at my country-home in the South West of France in 1977 (or 1978.) Thanks to Faiz, I was invited to the 1976 Islamabad Centenary celebration of Mohammed Ali Jinnah, the Quaid-i-Azam. He took me to various clubs and meeting place. It was an exciting experience for a European to see people all around reciting by heart poems writing by Faiz. In 1980, I believe, we met in Delhi where, at the Pakistani Embassy, for the first time, I heard Faiz recite his own poems. Some of his poems were also sung by a charming Indian singer.

Now I wish to bring up two points which left a lasting imprint in my mind.

From 1946 to 1952, I was head of the economic and social department of the World Federation of Trade Unions. As such, I was in close contact with various trade union federations and centres and with International Organisations like the U.N and the I.L.O. I first met Faiz at the International Labour Conference in Geneva, in June 1949. Faiz was there as a labour adviser to the Pakistani worker delegate, representing the Pakistan Trade Union Federation. In this capacity, he has previously attending the 1948 International Labour Conference. We met again during the first days of July of the same year, in Milan, at the Congress of the World Federation of Trade Unions (W.F.T.U.).

In order to truly appreciate Faiz's links with the trade union movement of this country, one has to recall the difficulties encountered by the workers organisation in Pakistan. Immediately after partition, in November 1947, the trade unions in the new county split from the All India Trade Union Congress (A.I.T.U.C.) and the International Federation for Labour (I.F.L.), with the agreement of these two organisation to which they had belonged up until then. After leaving the A.I.T.U.C, the Pakistan Trade Union Federation (P.I.U.F.) was formally set up in January 1948. In his speech at the (W.F.T.U.) Congress, in July 1949, Faiz related clearly and precisely the history of the Pakistani trade union organisations since partition.

Pakistan was then and is still today, industrially poor, without a real industrial tradition. The country, founded in 1947, was geographically divided. Even among workers, the geographical and ethnic divisions are stronger than the feeling of class solidarity. Labour is illiterate and inexperienced. Workers are poor, unions are weak and poorly organised, union dues are not paid, union membership is low. There are many central or regional organisations. Employers are opposed unions and victimise workers who are active in union affairs. In many cases, participation in the unions represents a risk for the worker, a danger for his livelihood.

One American scholar, whom nobody could name as a leftist, wrote: "In Pakistani industries, labour is often thought of as things to be manipulated rather than as people to be led or motivated. Under these circumstances, it is unavoidable that, especially in the beginning, some of the trade union representatives would not be workers but intellectuals.

The same American author acknowledges the important role played by the P.T.U.F., which considered the unions as the expression of class struggle and wanted to develop a class-conscious proletariat. It advocated the overthrow of capitalism, the abolition of landlordism, the confiscation and the nationalisation of foreign factories and banks. It was perhaps at that time too radical a programme. But the P.T.U.F. represented in 1949, more than half of the unionised workers in Pakistan, in spite of the fact that it was victimised by the government. Two years later, its top leaders were arrested, it was banned in 1954 and its headquarters sealed off. But as the American author quoted above recognised: the P.T.U.F. "organised a large number of labour unions within a short period of time."

In his speech to the Congress of the W.F.T.U., on the 8th of July 1949, Faiz explained all this. He exposed the repressive action of the government against the P.T.U.F., the increasing unemployment, the deteriorating living and house conditions of the workers and the fact that meanwhile 67% of the budget was used for military purposed. He described the poverty of the rural masses, the way in which they were exploited. The

P.T.U.F., he said, endeavours, in cooperation with the peasant unions, to provide them with a powerful organisation.

At that time, Faiz's moving voice was that of the workers not only from Pakistan but also of those in many developing countries. I do not intend to analyse here the achievement and the shortcomings of the P.T.U.F., but I do remember my delight, as in intellectual committed to the labour movement, when I listened to a great writer, a great poet, representing a trade union organisation and expressing the grievances an the aims of the fighting wing of Pakistani workers.

It was, I believe, in 1973, in Paris, that Faiz suggested the creation of a French-Pakistani friendship association and of a periodical French-Pakistani colloquium. After many efforts and discussions, the first colloquium was held in Paris, in November 1975 on the following theme: Tradition, National Identity, Development. I still remember some of the remarks made by Faiz during the meeting. He pointed out that the elimination of illiteracy cannot be achieved without the active participation of the masses, without organising them, without their support. The masses knowledge of civil society, of their rights, is sometimes more important than an abstract and often inadequate apprenticeship of writing and reading. He exposed the conservatism of the mullahs, that of the upholders of the Sharia and stressed the need to listen to the people and to understand their needs. He also underlined the importance of the links between, on the one hand, culture and art, and, on the other hand, the people, the masses without whose support the former cannot progress.

The ideas of Faiz on culture and art, especially in the Pakistani setting, were surmised in a booklet published in 1975 in Lahore and entitled *'Problems of National Art and Culture.'* It is made up of extracts from the report of the Standing Committee on Art and Culture. This Committee, of which Faiz was the President, was appointed in 1968 and extracts of that report were published seven years later. Although it is the report of the whole commission, I am sure it reflects some of the views of Faiz. I'll try to give a summary of this very interesting document.

Culture is a whole way of life, evolved by the whole community; it "must be both historical and territorial, although its ideological components may include extra-territorial and supra-temporal elements."

The quality and the complexion of culture "are determined more by what is actually practiced and not so much by what is merely professed." Here one notices that practice is considered more important than ideology. The report goes onto state that culture is fragmented on the pattern of the social fragmentation of the society itself. "To evolve a common or unified culture for such a society must presume the evolution of a unified and equitable social structure."

Art is an agent both of national identity and integration and of international friendship an understanding (it helps "every society to discover underlying universalities in the best contemporary thought and feeling.")

The report sharply criticizes the school of thought which asserts that culture and arts are immoral and anti-religious. First of all, there are objective factors which explain why this view is shared by some people: during the decadence of the Moghul Court, arts were linked to the dissolute Courts and their decedent pleasures; the colonial subjection subverted the native cultural patterns and the Western rulers tried to superimpose their own culture on the ruled; even after independence, the negative public and official attitudes towards national art and culture contributed to the opening of the gates for the cultural invasion of western commercial and political agencies. One sees here how Faiz, even when he fights against an opinion which he opposes strongly, ties to understand the reasons, historical and sociological, which might explain why this opinion is shared by some people.

So the report states that culture and art are not incompatible with morals and religion. The real motivation of those who take the contrary view is neither moral nor religious, but socio-political. "Any ideological objection that can be brought against any art, therefore, must relate to some particular form and content of a particular art and not the art as such." Muslim culture and Islamic civilization show that there is no hostility to artistic and cultural activities in Muslim societies.

In the developing societies, according to the report, culture and art are not a luxury. "Any development efforts which ignore the emotional and spiritual aid provided by a nation's awareness of its own goals and aspirations are bound to engender antagonistic contradictions between the people and the agencies responsible for such a development. Cultural development in a developing nation is in many ways a form of socio-political activity that a people's full participation in nation-building efforts can be assured."

The report deals then with the link between culture and national identity. It rejects the theory according to which Pakistan being an ideological State and its ideology being Islam. Muslim or Islamic culture is an adequate definition of Pakistani culture. There are basic arguments against this view:

> a. It ignores the reality of non-ideological components of culture, such as language, dress, cookery, architecture, arts and crafts, non-religious customs and social observances;
>
> b. The artistic tradition, particularly in music and dancing, is much older than the Muslim era;
>
> c. "since the Indo-Muslim civilization was not confined to the areas which now form Pakistan,

it contains many ingredients which transcend our boundaries and cannot be deemed exclusively Pakistani "

d. Islam cannot count alone for the different cultures of the various Muslim nations: herein lies the problem of nation-hood and culture.

I believe this analysis is extremely important in the light of certain tendencies and schools of thoughts prevailing today in Pakistan and in some parts of the Islamic world.

The report strongly advocates the revival of the regional cultures of Pakistan. This revival, according to the report will promote real national integration: "national culture is a aggregate of these regional cultures plus the unifying bonds of faith and history." The flowering of regional cultures and arts will promote a widespread and consistent exchange of artistic expression, a sharing of collective experience and ultimately national integration, if "diversity is not misinterpreted as disunity." Here again, with unavoidable caution, the report advocates a policy very different from that which was and is carried out in Pakistan. It represents a serious intellectual effort towards the development of a culture founded on traditions of the people, of the masses, an effort also to find in the different cultures of the different peoples, a secular and concrete basis of Pakistani unity.

I believe the report which I have just summarised and which was mainly written by Faiz- even if he had to compromise on several points- is a very outstanding document not only for Pakistan but for all the developing countries. These countries and UNESCO would be well advised to ponder on the ideas contained in the report.

Unfortunately, I am not able to enjoy Faiz's poetry in the original language. I have to read it in French or English, whereby, as for all poetry in translation, it loses part of its flavour. But even so, one can appreciate its beauty, its strength, and first of all its human and humanistic message. Recently, Faiz himself, discussing the development of modern Urdu literature, said: "Some who could be called subjectivists, reverted to traditional poetry, others rejected tradition in toto and called themselves expressionist or symbolists. A few like me took the middle course. We built on tradition or modern sensibility by committing ourselves to the cause of humanity at large."

Faiz is rooted in the soil and blood of his native land. He is one of the few Pakistani intellectuals who never lost contact with the rural world, the village where bulk of the population is living. He and his wife Alys, built up the beautiful folk-art museum in Islamabad. Meanwhile he always showed an unusual wide familiarity with the whole world at large. He is the son of India and Pakistan, a patriot, an Urdu poet, a fighter for beauty, justice and freedom everywhere, a citizen of the world, the voice that sings for all those who suffer and resist. Remember his moving poems about the Rosenbergs, Africa, the foreign students who perished in the struggle for peace and justice, for the Palestinians.

Faiz's life and activities corroborate the assertion of our great Jaures: "A little internationalism leads one away from the fatherland, much internationalism brings one back to it: a little patriotism leads one away from internationalism, much patriotism brings one back to it."

Faiz was never preoccupied with his own difficulties or sufferings. He wrote:

> What others on the road
> Meet, I have met with:
> Prison-cell solitude,
> Marketplace anathemas
> Thundering from pulpits,
> Threats and reviling
> From places of power...
> But this poem ends with fiery assertion:
> My heart that bears every
> Scar, but that of shame.

And you will have noticed that he begins by saying: What others on that road meet, I have met with; he considers his own individual fate as part of the collective destiny of those who struggle for the same ideals:

> I learned of misery, helplessness, despair,
> I learned to be friend of suffering creatures,
> I came to know the torment of the oppressed,
> The truth of sobbing breath and livid features.
>
> When labourers' flesh is sold in chaffing streets
> Or pavements run with poor men's blood, a flame
> That lurks inside me blazes up beyond
> All power quenching; do not ask its name.

Anyway, I never heard him, during our long friendship, complaining about his own problems. He has the gift to see the world as it is and to love it still. I admire in Faiz, the poet, the man, the unusual mixture of the strength of his convictions and the forbearance and patience he shows towards ideas and peoples. This makes him a wonderful friend and a wonderful teacher. He has the blessing to discover in each human being, even in the most unpleasant one, something good, something worthwhile. I think that he feels that the world can and should be changed and that this will produce a change in most of the human beings. It comes from what I would call His realistic optimism. Showing the way, he speaks about the "burning arrows of hope," he asserts that "night's last hour cannot defeat us" that "someday a ripe harvest will be ours," and that

> Others will see, if I do not, that hour
> Of singing nightingales and splendid flower.

We can be grateful to Faiz to carry us- like Schiller and

Beethoven- through sorrow to joy. As he himself wrote: "We have always made flowers blossom in the fire."

One has to be grateful to him for constantly showing the highest degree of courage which according to our Jaures is to seek and tell the truth. The poet Faiz appeals to each of us when he writes:

"Speak for the truth is alive!
"Speak, say whatever is to be said!"

At the end of September 1984, coming from Tunisia, he spent a few days in Paris. We met many times during his stay. We lamented together the "death" of Dr. Ayub Mirza, which was reported to him by phone from London, a report which fortunately turned out to be false. He attended my granddaughter's birthday party, not forgetting to bring a gift and joking so nicely with the children. At a dinner arranged by T.N. Kaul and hosted by Mr. Madanjeet Singh, he recited some of his poems and translated them immediately into English for the benefit of those who didn't understand Urdu.

My wife and myself didn't suspect that this happy encounter will be the last. But we were struck by his extraordinary serenity; maybe he felt that the end was near. He was radiant with the supreme and tranquil joy and contentment of a man who did his duty, who fought the good fight and who has given so much to mankind.

The first thought that occurred to me when I learnt of his death was: the best way to remain faithful to his legacy is to continue the fight against oppression, obscurantism and human suffering, and for changing our world so that everybody shall have his share of beauty, justice and freedom.

Looking back to our many encounters, I remember so many joyful, pleasant and moving events. But I feel like the fisherman of the story, who, his work done, came back every evening to his village, speaking about his meetings with a beautiful Mermaid. One day it happened: he really met the Mermaid. And that day he kept silent. I knew a great poet, a wonderful man, a crusader for the rights of the wretched of the earth; a real and reliable friend and I feel I shouldn't say anything more.

Georges Fischer was a long-standing friend of Faiz Ahmed Faiz. He first met Faiz in 1949 in Switzerland while attending 1949 the International Labour Organisation conference. Fischer was a leading European trade unionist and was the Director of Research at the Centre Nationale de la Recherche Scientifique in Paris.

145

Faiz with interpreter and Urdu scholar Lyudmila Vasilyeva, Tashkent, 1977

Chapter 16

With Faiz in Paris – and in Spring!

M. H. ASKARI

It was in April 1977, while I was posted in France, that a friend rang me up from London and told me that Faiz would be arriving in Paris a couple of days later, and he would like to stay with us. That came as something of a surprise.

While my association with Faiz went back to over 30 years, I could not count myself as being in his close circle of friend. I first met him in Delhi during the war, when he was posted there with the Arm Public Relations setup. I also later used to see quite a lot of him in Karachi.

But somehow I always felt a bit too self-conscious to get into his group of intimates. In any case, I often found in his company people who seemed totally out of place, loud, somewhat upstartish and rather uncouth. To be with Faiz was a sort of status symbol and all kinds of people managed to get close to him. And he was perhaps always too civilised and polite to put them off.

As undergraduates in the forties, we had begun to idolise Faiz and other leaders of the *avant-garde* movement, of Urdu poetry, such as Rashid and Meeraji. Their bold experiments with form and content completely captivated our imagination.

Then, during the war, several of the *niaz-man-dan-e-Lahore* came to live in Delhi. They included Majeed Malik, Ahmed Shah Bokhari Patras, Chiragh Hasan Hasrat and Mohammad Din Taseer. They brought with them their attitude of pleasant rivalry with the *ahl-e-zaban* of Delhi and Uttar Pradesh As a former Delhi-wallah, I sincerely believe that was good for us, because it prompted many of us to come out of our shell of accepted traditions and norms.

A number of Lahore-based intellectuals invariable came to call on my father, Prof. Mirza Muhammad Said, in our ancestral home in old Delhi. He too had a long association with Lahore, having been a student at the Government College there and later, for long years, a teacher of English in his *alma mater*. His rather precocious achievement as a scholar and teacher of English and a pioneer novelist/critic of Urdu endeared him to several generation of Lahore-wallahs. It was after his retirement from the Indian Education Service That he decided to come back to Delhi and live there. Patras was one of the most frequent of the *niaz-mandan* to visit my father.

Faiz got posted to New Delhi in the latter part of the war, and we looked forward to his visit to our home with a great deal of excitement. We found it rather incongruous to see him in

a Major's uniform. He also looked surprising at peace with himself, exuding none of the anger of his poems of *Naqsh-e Farayaadi.*

Faiz had his office in makeshift barracks, one also came across for the first time many other wellknown people belonging to the world of literature and journalism: Upendra Nath Ashk, Kaushalya Ashk, Chiragh Hasan Hasrat, N.M.Rashid, Badruddin Badr, Mian Kifayat Ali Eric Britter (who after the war became the United Nations correspondent of *The Times*, London,) Morris-Jones, who had been a student of Laski's at the London School of Economics and after the warn went back to war went back to teach at the LSE, Prem Bhatia, who has recently retired as Chief Editor of The Tribune of Chandigrah, Leuit-Col 'Bijji' Kaul, who later rose to the rank of Lieut-General in the Indian Army and became somewhat controversial during India's war with China, Desmond Young, former editor of the Pioneer and who later wrote a best-seller biography of Rommel, and Ivor Jehu, who had been the Editor of *The Time of India*, when it was still British-owned.

It was exciting to get to know them. It all seemed like a different world. However, all that was over 30 years ago, and now Faiz was going to be our house guest in Paris.

I must say we felt a bit of apprehension at the prospect of Faiz coming to live with us. We did not know him that well. We were unfamiliar with his routine and habits. We many turn out to be rather inadequate hosts and not come up to his expectation. However, when he actually came, we found him a most undemanding and adorable guest. He showered nothing but affection to my wife, my children and myself and fitted easily into the routine of our home.

In spring, Paris is unmatchable in its charm. Its tree-lined avenue tempts you to go out for long random walks. The cafes along the pavements in the Champs-Elysees, Montmartre and the Latin Quarters, drenched in soft sun, appear irresistibly hospitable. The bridges of the Seine with their quiet elegance fill you with a sense of calm and introspection which make you stand on the sidewalk and gaze at the river flowing below, for hours at end. Time comes to a stop and all seems well with the worlds.

Faiz was never in a rush, and seldom has any specific timetable for his day's outing. He has all the leisure to see Paris, with ourselves as his company. Once when we emerged from the Metro on an avenue close to Arc de Triomphe he stood in utter silence for quite a while looking at what is probably one of the most graceful structures in Paris. Another time, he spent a whole day at the Museum of Rodin.

Ambassador Qizilbash, who informed me that Faiz was his friend from the days of their youth in Lahore, insisted that for all the days that Faiz was going to be in Paris that he along with his hosts, including the children, and his friends and admirers, would be his guest at his house every evening.

Each evening, Faiz relaxed and responded good-humouredly to the persistent demand for the recitation of his poetry, especially his most popular ghazals. The audience doted over him, even though the French among them could not have understood a word of what he recited. The language barrier did not seem to matter, he was universally loved.

Faiz's circle of friends and admirers in Paris included Prof. Georges Fischer of Paris University, Charles and Monique Moraze, a socially well-connected and charming couple who took a lot of interest in trying to promote cultural exchanges between France and Pakistan, Ashfaq Naqvi and Nasin Anwar Beg, who worked with UNESCO, a young Pakistani expatriate Zafar Masud, who had once been active in the journalistic and artistic circle in Karachi and his accomplished wife Paule, and Masud Kohari, the artist and sculptor from Karachi.

Georges Fischer was a very special friend, as he has known Faiz from his days as a trade unionist at the ILO in Geneva. (He also happened to be in Delhi was Faiz died, and went with me to a condolence meeting there. He spoke about Faiz with great love and admiration.)

It was good to be with Faiz in Paris and in such excellent company.

The April of 1977, I may recall, Faiz was rather disturbed in Pakistan. Zulfikar Ali Bhutto had held his elections and was facing a massive upsurge, which he was trying to get under control by firm methods. Accounts of the protest, demonstrations and police excesses reached Paris usually via London, greatly exaggerated and distorted.

Diplomatic correspondent of French newspaper confronted me and my colleagues in the Embassy with their own version of the reports: of Bhutto's adversaries being picked up in the middle of the night, of repressive methods used by peace keeping forced, of petty party leaders strutting about in military style uniforms, of students and trade union leaders being send to jail for detention without trial. It was generally known that Faiz was close to the regime. As a PR man I was worried that his presence in Paris should not lead to some sort of controversy in the Press. But his visit passed off without incident.

During Faiz's stay, my colleague Iqbal, who was Minister in the political wing of the Embassy, often discussed with me certain aspects of Faiz's poetry, the deep anguish that he expressed

against man's brutality upon man, the recurrent theme in his poetry of protest and anger and injustice and repression. Iqbal sometimes wondered whether Faiz was all that committed to his ideals, and, if he was how one could explain his proximity to the Bhutto regime. I tried to suggest that Faiz was a poet and not a political activist and we believed that we had to 'accept' him for what he was, despite what seemed like a contradiction between his idealism and his life-style. However, I could sense that Iqbal was less than satisfied with my 'defence' of Faiz.

One evening, shortly after Faiz had gone back to London, Iqbal phoned me at my house and after the usual polite preliminaries once again brought up the subject of Faiz and his poetry. News of the situation in Pakistan had made him feel eve more perturbed. He asked me a blunt questions: why didn't Faiz come out openly and condemn all that was happened? I said I was sure that Faiz was too sensitive to remain impervious.

The next morning the BBC said that the Minister in the Embassy of Pakistan in Paris had 'defected' and arrived in London, where he had issued a rather strongly worded statement saying that his conscience did not permit him to continue to serve a Government with whose policies and actions he found himself in total disagreement.

So he had decided to quit. I was stunned. It took me quite a while to grasp the full implication of the news. I now realised how intensely Iqbal had felt about the development at home.

It could not have been easy for him to take the decision that he did. He was a diplomat of considerable seniority and ability, and had a promising career before him. However, there was also obviously no link between our endless discussions about Faiz's poetry and Iqbal's decision to quit. There was every indication that Iqbal had been planning his move for quite some time. It was only coincidence that Faiz happened to come to Paris at the time when Iqbal was debating with himself whether he should take the plunge or not.

M. H. Askari is one of the most respected journalists in Pakistan. He is the senior correspondent for the leading Pakistani newspaper: Daily Dawn. He is very versatile journalist and has addressed varied issues. His writings on literary issues have always attracted widespread interest and admiration. He is author of several books including Courtesans' Quarter that he co-edited with Ralph Russell and others.

Section Four

Anthems of Resistance
Selected poems of Faiz Ahmed Faiz

Speak

Speak, your lips are free.
Speak, it is your own tongue.
Speak, it is your own body.
Speak, your life is still yours.

See how in the blacksmith's shop
The flame burns wild, the iron glows red;
The locks open their jaws,
And every chain begins to break.

Speak, this brief hour is long enough
Before the death of body and tongue:
Speak, 'cause the truth is not dead yet,
Speak, speak, whatever you must speak.

Translation by Azfar Hussain

152

بول ۔۔۔

بول، کہ لب آزاد ہیں تیرے
بول، زباں اب تک تیری ہے

تیرا ستواں جسم ہے تیرا
بول کہ جاں اب تک تیری ہے

دیکھ کہ آہن گر کی دکاں میں
تند ہیں شعلے، سرخ ہے آہن

کھلنے لگے قفلوں کے دہانے
پھیلا ہر اک زنجیر کا دامن

بول، یہ تھوڑا وقت بہت ہے
جسم و زباں کی موت سے پہلے

بول کہ سچ زندہ ہے اب تک
بول، جو کچھ کہنا ہے کہہ لے!

153

Do not ask of me

Do not ask of me, my love,
that love I once had for you.

There was a time when
life was bright, and young and blooming,
and your sorrow was much more than
any other pain.
Your beauty gave the Spring everlasting youth;
your eyes, yes your eyes, were everything,
all else was vain.

While you were with me, I thought, the world was mine.
Though now I know that it was an illusion
that's the way I imagined it to be;
for there are other sorrows in the world than love,
and other pleasures, too.

Do not ask of me, my love,
that love I once had for you!

Woven in silk and satin and brocade,
those dark and brutal curses of countless centuries:
bodies bathes in blood, smeared with dust,
sold from market-place to market-place,
bodies risen from the cauldron of diseases
pus dripping from their festering sores -
my eyes must also turn to these.
You're beautiful still, my love
but I'm helpless too;
for there are other sorrows in the world than love,
and other pleasures too.

Do not ask of me, my love,
that love I once had for you!

Translation by Shaheen Sultan Dhanji

154

مجھ سے پہلی سی محبت مری محبوب نہ مانگ

مجھ سے پہلی سی محبت مری محبوب نہ مانگ

میں نے سمجھا تھا کہ تو ہے تو درخشاں ہے حیات

تیرا غم ہے تو غمِ دہر کا جھگڑا کیا ہے

تیری صورت سے ہے عالم میں بہاروں کو ثبات

تیری آنکھوں کے سوا دنیا میں رکھا کیا ہے؟

تو جو مل جائے تو تقدیر نگوں ہو جائے

یوں نہ تھا، میں نے فقط چاہا تھا یوں ہو جائے

اور بھی دکھ ہیں زمانے میں محبت کے سوا

راحتیں اور بھی ہیں وصل کی راحت کے سوا

ان گنت صدیوں کے تاریک بہیمانہ طلسم

ریشم و اطلس و کمخواب میں بُنوائے ہوئے

جا بجا بکتے ہوئے کوچہ و بازار میں جسم

خاک میں لتھڑے ہوئے خون میں نہلائے ہوئے

لوٹ جاتی ہے اُدھر کو بھی نظر کیا کیجے

اب بھی دلکش ہے ترا حسن مگر کیا کیجے

اور بھی دکھ ہیں زمانے میں محبت کے سوا

راحتیں اور بھی ہیں وصل کی راحت کے سوا

مجھ سے پہلی سی محبت مری محبوب نہ مانگ

Our kind

In the mind's hall, holding each his dead lamp,
Turning with trembling nausea from the sun's light,
Huddle in our own darkness, hugging it tight
As if in an endless dreams of sweet face;
Riddle of good and ill and beginning and end,
The old futile inquisition, profitless chase;

Tedium of today's colourless minutes,
Goad of remembrance, chill of tomorrow's fears;
Starved thoughts that come to no conform, blistering tears
That find no way to the eye, a numb misery
Not melting into any song or escaping
From the heart's shadowed crevices; - and a quest,
Visionary, bemused, for remedy;
A thirst for desert and dungeon, for the rent garment.

Translation by Victor Kiernan

ہم لوگ

دل کے ایواں میں لیے گل شدہ شمعوں کی قطار
نورِ خورشید سے سہمے ہوئے اکتائے ہوئے
حسنِ محبوب کے سیال تصور کی طرح
اپنی تاریکی کو بھینچے ہوئے لپٹائے ہوئے

غایت سود و زیاں ، صورت آغاز و مآل
وہی بے سود تجسس، وہی بے کار سوال
مضمحل ساعت امروز کی بے رنگی سے
یاد ماضی سے غم گیں ، دہشت فردا سے نڈھال

تشنۂ افکار جو تسکیں نہیں پاتے ہیں
سوختہ اشک جو آنکھوں میں نہیں آتے ہیں
اک کڑا درد کہ جو گیت میں ڈھلتا ہی نہیں
دل کے تاریک شگافوں سے نکلتا ہی نہیں
اور اک الجھی ہوئی موہوم سی درماں کی تلاش
دشتِ وزنداں کی ہوس، چاکِ گریباں کی تلاش

157

Dogs

These stray dogs in the streets,
Begging – an endowment their only treat
Curses from others, are their total effects,
Abuses by the world are their only assets.
Neither rest at night, nor joy in the day,
Filth is their abode, in gutters do they lay.
If agitated, then turn them on one another,
A piece of dry bread will do this wonder.
Expected to be kicked around by every stranger,

Accustomed to wither away with lingering hunger.
If these poor beasts ever lift up their heads,
Mankind would, then, forget all deeds of rebellion.
If they decide, they can own the universe,
Even chew down the bones of their cruel masters.

Just make them aware of their degradation so deep
Just make them move their tail that has fallen asleep.

Translation by Sian Sucha

کتے

یہ گلیوں کے آوارہ بے کار کتے
کہ بخشا گیا جن کو ذوقِ گدائی
زمانے کی پھٹکار سرمایہ ان کا
جہاں بھر کی دھتکار ان کی کمائی

نہ آرام شب کو، نہ راحت سویرے
غلاظت میں گھر، نالیوں میں بسیرے
جو بگڑیں تو اک دوسرے سے لڑا دو
ذرا ایک روٹی کا ٹکڑا دکھا دو
یہ ہر ایک کی ٹھوکریں کھانے والے
یہ فاقوں سے اکتا کے مر جانے والے

یہ مظلوم مخلوق گر سر اٹھائے
تو انسان سب سرکشی بھول جائے
یہ چاہیں تو دنیا کو اپنا بنا لیں
یہ آقاؤں کی ہڈیاں تک چبا لیں
کوئی ان کو احساس ذلت دلا دے
کوئی ان کی سوئی ہوئی دم ہلا دے

159

May God not bring that time

God never sends a time when you too mourn –
When you too find life easing sleep foreworn,
When joy has spent with you its long bright hour
And left the cup of your existence sour;

When, its bright mirror tarnished with hot tears,
Your mind is filled with swarms of anxious fears,
And thronging misery comes with gnawing tooth,
Till only old dream is left of youth;

When beauty's proud thoughts turn to abjectness,
And you too long through the long night of peace,
While parched eyes strain for comfort no-one brings
And autumn's sad desire thirsts for new springs;

When no more foreheads bowed on your doorstep find you
Have cheated with some sweet tomorrow-vow
And thank for love's humility's display;

God never sends that time that must remind you
Of the poor heart that wait and watch for your today.

Translation by Victor Keirnan

خدا وہ وقت نہ لائے ۰۰۰۰۰

خدا وہ وقت نہ لائے کہ سوگوار ہو تو

سکوں کی نیند تجھے بھی حرام ہو جائے

تری مسرت پیہم تمام ہو جائے

تری حیات تجھے تلخ جام ہو جائے

غموں سے آئینۂ دل گداز ہو تیرا

ہجومِ یاس سے بے تاب ہو کے رہ جائے

وفورِ درد سے سیماب ہو کے رہ جائے

ترا شباب فقط خواب ہو کے رہ جائے

غرورِ حسن سراپا نیاز ہو تیرا

طویل راتوں میں توں بھی قرار کو ترسے

تری نگاہ کسی نغمگسار کو ترسے

خزاں رسیدہ تمنا بہار کو ترسے

کوئی جبیں نہ ترے سنگِ آستاں پہ جھکے

کہ جنسِ عجز و عقیدت سے تجھ کو شاد کرے

فریبِ وعدۂ فردا پہ اعتماد کرے

خدا وہ وقت نہ لائے کہ تجھ کو یاد آئے

وہ دل کہ تیرے لیے بیقرار اب بھی ہے

وہ آنکھ جس کو ترا انتظار اب بھی ہے

161

Poetry's theme

Twilight is burning out and turning chill,
Night come fresh-bathed from where the moon's spring flows;
And now – these eager eyes shall have their will,
These avid fingers feel the touch of those!

Is that her fringed veil, is it her face, her dress,
Behind the hanging gauze, that it makes it glow—
And in the vague mist of that rippling tress
Does the bright earring twinkle still, or no?

Subtly once more her loveliness will speak,
Those pencilled lids, those languorous eyes, again:
Dusted with the faint powder, her pink cheek,
On her pale hand the henna's delicate stains.
Here is the chosen world of rhyme and dream
My muse inhabits, here her darling theme!

Under the black and blood-red mark of ages
How has it fared with Eve's sons all these years?
How shall we fare, where daily combat rages
Of death with life? How fared our forefathers?

Why must those gay streets' swarming progeny
So draw breath that to die is all they crave?
In those rich fields bursting with bounty, why
Must no ripe harvest except hunger wave?

Walls dark with secrets frown on every side,
That countless lamps of youth have sunk behind;
Everywhere scaffolds on which dream have died
That lit unnumbered candles in man's hand.

These too are subjects, more there are; - but oh,
Those limbs that curve so fatally ravishingly!
Oh that sweet wretch, those lips parting so slow –
Tell me where else such witchery could be!
No other theme will ever fit my rhyme;
Nowhere but here is poetry's native clime.

Translation by Victor Kiernan

162

موضوعِ سخن

گل ہوئی جاتی ہے افسردہ سلگتی ہوئی شام
دھل کے نکلے گی ابھی چشمۂ مہتاب سے رات
اور مشتاق نگاہوں کی سنی جائے گی
وران ہاتھوں سے مس ہوں گے یہ ترسے ہوئے ہاتھ

ان کا آنچل ہے، کہ رخسار، کہ پیراہن ہے
کچھ تو ہے جس سے ہوئی جاتی ہے چلمن رنگیں
جانے اس زلف کی موہوم گھنی چھاؤں میں
ٹمٹماتا ہے وہ آویزہ ابھی تک کہ نہیں

آج پھر حسنِ دل آرا کی وہی دھج ہوگی
وہی خوابیدہ سی آنکھیں، وہی کاجل کی لکیر
رنگِ رخسار پہ ہلکا سا وہ غازے کا غبار
صندلی ہاتھ پہ دھندلی سی حنا کی تحریر

اپنے افکار کی، اشعار کی دنیا ہے یہی
جانِ مضموں ہے یہی، شایدِ معنی ہے یہی
آج تک سرخ و سیاہ صدیوں کے سائے کے تلے
آدم و حوّا کی اولاد پہ کیا گزری ہے؟
موت اور زیست کی روزانہ صف آرائی میں
ہم پہ کیا گزرے گی، اجداد پہ کیا گزری ہے؟

ان دمکتے ہوئے شہروں کی فراواں مخلوق
کیوں فقط مرنے کی حسرت میں جیا کرتی ہے؟
یہ حسیں کھیت پھٹا پڑتا ہے جوبن جن کا
کس لیے ان میں فقط بھوک اگا کرتی ہے؟

یہ ہر اک سمت پُراسرار کڑی دیواریں
جل بجھے جن میں ہزاروں کی جوانی کے چراغ
یہ ہر اک گام پہ اُن خوابوں کی مقتل گاہیں
جن کے پرتو سے چراغاں ہیں ہزاروں کے دماغ

یہ بھی ہیں، ایسے کئی اور بھی مضموں ہوں گے
لیکن اس شوخ کے آہستہ سے کھلتے ہوئے ہونٹ
ہائے اس جسم کے کمبخت دلآویز خطوط
آپ ہی کیجئے کہیں ایسے بھی افسوں ہوں گے
اپنا موضوعِ سخن ان کے سوا اور نہیں

163

Loneliness

Someone is at the door again, my weeping heart, no, no one
Perhaps a passerby, who will go somewhere else

The night has passed, waiting, the star-dust is settling
Sleepy candle-flames are flickering in distant palaces
Every pathway has passed into sleep, tired of waiting
Alien dust has smudged all traces of footsteps

Blow out the candles, let the wine and cup flow
Close and lock your sleepless doors

No one, no one will come here now.

Translation by Hamid Rahim Sheikh

تنہائی

پھر کوئی آیا دل زار ! نہیں کوئی نہیں
راہرو ہوگا ، کہیں اور چلا جائے گا
ڈھل چکی رات بکھرنے لگا تاروں کا غبار
لڑکھڑانے لگے ایوانوں میں خوابیدہ چراغ
سو گئی راستہ تک تک کے ہر اک راہگزر
اجنبی خاک نے دھندلا دئیے قدموں کے سراغ
گل کرو شمعیں، بڑھا دو مے و مینا و ایاغ
اپنے بے خواب کواڑوں کو مقفل کر لو
اب یہاں کوئی نہیں، کوئی نہیں آئے گا

Both universes

Having lost both his universe in thy love,
he departs after having spent as if some night of hell.

Dreary is the house of wine and gloomy are the goblets,
your departure has as if displeased the flowering spell.

I have been granted the leisure to sin but merely four days,
In that I have seen the guts of that invincible.

The world prevented me from reminiscing over you,
more mystifying than you are the woes of labour.

Today she did smile though only unwittingly 'Faiz',
ask not about the unrest it created in the heart of a quiet soul.

Translation by Meenakshi Sinha

دونوں جہان تیری محبت میں ہار کے

دونوں جہان تیری محبت میں ہار کے
وہ جا رہا ہے کوئی شبِ غم گزار کے

ویراں ہے میکدہ، خم و ساغر اداس ہیں
تم کیا گئے کہ روٹھ گئے دن بہار کے

اک فرصتِ گناہ ملی، وہ بھی چار دن
دیکھے ہیں ہم نے حوصلے پروردگار کے

دنیا نے تیری یاد سے بیگانہ کر دیا
تجھ سے بھی دلفریب ہیں غم روزگار کے

بھولے سے مسکرا تو دیئے تھے وہ آج فیض
مت پوچھ ولولے دلِ ناکردہ کار کے

167

To the rival

Round you my memories of the fair one twine
Who made my heart a fairies' nursery,
Caught in whose toils I called this busy age
And old wives' tale, and let the world go by.

Familiar with your feet too are those paths
Her youthtime designed to tread, drunk with youth's pride,
While as her beauty's pageant passed, these eyes
Gazed on it worshipping, unsatisfied.

With you too have those darling breeze played
Where fading perfume of her dress still hangs,
On you too from her roof has rained that moonlight
Haunted by long-done nights and bygone pangs.

You who have known that cheek, those lips, that brow
Under whose spell I fleeted life away,
You whom the dreamy magic of those eyes
Has touched, can tell where my years ran astray.

Such gifts as love and love's keen anguish bring,
Gifts beyond counting, side by side we earned:
To whom else could I speak of what that passion
Cost me, or through that passion what I earned?

Translation by Victor Kiernan

رقیب سے!

آ کہ وابستہ ہیں اُس حسن کی یادیں تجھ سے
جس نے اس دل کو پری خانہ بنا رکھا ہے
جس کی الفت میں بھلا رکھی تھی دنیا ہم نے
دہر کو دہر کا افسانہ بنا رکھا تھا

آشنا ہیں ترے قدموں سے وہ راہیں جن پر
اُس کی مدہوش جوانی نے عنایت کی ہے
کارواں گزرے ہیں جن سے اُسی رعنائی کے
جس کی ان آنکھوں نے بے سُود عبادت کی ہے

تجھ سے کھیلی ہیں وہ محبوب ہوائیں جن میں
اُس کے ملبوس کی افسردہ مہک باقی ہے
تجھ پہ بھی برسا ہے اس بام سے مہتاب کا نور
جس میں بیتی ہوئی راتوں کی کسک باقی ہے

تو نے دیکھی ہے وہ پیشانی، ہ رخسار ، وہ ہونٹ
زندگی جن کے تصور میں لٹا دی ہم نے
تجھ پہ اُٹھی وہ کھوئی ہوئی ساحر آنکھیں
تجھ کو معلوم ہے کیوں عمر گنوا دی ہم نے

ہم پہ مشترک کہ ہیں احسان غمِ الفت کے
اتنے احسان کہ گنواؤں تو گنوا نہ سکوں
ہم نے اس عشق میں کیا کھویا ہے کیا پایا ہے
جز ترے اور کو سمجھاؤں تو سمجھا نہ سکوں

Tonight

Do not strike the chord of sorrow tonight!
Days burning with pain turn to ashes.
Who knows what happens tomorrow?
Last night is lost; tomorrow's frontier wiped out:
Who knows if there will be another dawn?
Life is nothing, it's only tonight!
Tonight we can be what the gods are!

Do not strike the sword of sorrow tonight!
Do not repeat stories of sufferings now,
Do not complain, let your fate play its role
Do not think of tomorrows, give a damn—
Shed no tears for seasons gone by,
All sighs and cries wind up their tales,
Oh, do not strike the same chord again!

Translation by Azfar Hussain

آج کی رات

آج کی رات ساز درد نہ چھیڑ

دکھ سے بھرپور دن تمام ہوئے

اور کل کی خبر کسے معلوم؟

دوش و فردا کی مٹ چکی ہیں حدود

ہو نہ ہو اب سحر، کسے معلوم؟

زندگی ہیچ! لیکن آج کی رات

ایذدیت ہے ممکن آج کی رات

آج کی رات ساز درد نہ چھیڑ

اب نہ دُہرا فسانہ ہائے الم

اپنی قسمت پہ سوگوار نہ ہو

فکرِ فردا اتار دے دل سے

عمرِ رفتہ پہ اشکبار نہ ہو

عہد غم کی حکایتیں مت پوچھ

ہو چکی سب شکایتیں مت پوچھ

آج کی رات ساز درد نہ چھیڑ

171

That day is not so far, my love

That day is not so far, my love,
when pain will halt all ways of life
and inner sorrow reach its limit
and yearning eyes will tire of waiting.
My eyes, my tears will all be taken
my youth, my dreams all lost.
You might, my love, think of my love
and make your frail heart sad;
you might some shedding tears upon my grave
and place a few spring flowers on the dust.

You might, my love, just walk over my grave,
Laugh at my senseless devotion
(You will not think much of all this
but my broken heart will soldier on),

You may laugh when all is over
You may cry and weep and scream
You may regret the past, or be glad of it –

Your lover will be asleep, uncaring.

Translation by Mahmood Jamal

آخری خط

وہ وقت میری جان بہت دور نہیں ہے
جب درد سے رُک جائیں گی سب زیست کی راہیں
اور حد سے گزر جائے گا اندوہِ نہانی
تھک جائیں گی ترسی ہوئی ناکام نگاہیں
چھن جائیں گے مجھ سے مرے آنسو مری آہیں
چھن جائے گی مجھ سے مری بے کار جوانی

شاید مری الفت کو بہت یاد کرو گی
اپنے دلِ معصوم کو ناشاد کرو گی
آؤ گی مری گور پہ تم اشک بہانے
نوخیز بہاروں کے حسیں پھول چڑھانے

شاید مری تربت کو بھی ٹھکرا کے چلو گی
شاید مری بے سُود وفاؤں پہ ہنسو گی
اس وضعِ کرم کا بھی تمہیں پاس نہ ہو گا
لیکن دلِ ناکام کو احساس نہ ہو گا

القصہ مآلِ غمِ الفت پہ ہنسو تم
یا اشک بہاتی ہوئی فریاد کو تم
ماضی پہ ندامت ہو تمہیں یا کہ مسرت
خاموش پڑا سوئے گا داماندہِ الفت

173

A few days more

A few days more, my dear, only a few days
Must we gasp in the shadow of tyranny
Bear oppression, writhe and weep.
This is our inherited condition:
Bodies imprisoned, feelings chained,
Thoughts captive and speech punished,
Yet we resolve to go on living.
Is life the coat of a pauper,
Hourly patched with scraps of pain?
But now the tyrant's term expires,
forbear a while, the days of grievance wane.
In this parched wasteland of our age
we must remain, but something will change --
The anonymous burden of foreign hands
We bear today, but not always.
This dust of hardship blurring your beauty,
Defeat on defeat in our transient youth,
The futile anguish of moonlit nights,
Fruitless throbbing of the heart
And the body's wail of despair --
A few days more, my dear, only a few days.

Translation with Ruth L. Schmidt

چند روز اور مری جان!

چند روز اور مری جان! فقط چند ہی روز
ظلم کی چھاؤں میں دم لیے پہ مجبور ہیں ہم
اور کچھ دیر ستم سہ لیں، تڑپ لیں، رو لیں

اپنے اجداد کی میراث ہے معذور ہیں ہم
جسم پہ قید ہے، جذبات پہ زنجیریں ہیں
فکر محبوس ہے، گفتار پہ تعزیریں ہیں
اپنی ہمت ہے کہ ہم پھر بھی جیئے جاتے ہیں
زندگی کیا کسی مفلس کی قبا ہے جس میں

ہر گھڑی درد کے پیوند لگے جاتے ہیں
لیکن اب ظلم کی میعاد کے دن تھوڑے ہیں
اک ذرا صبر کہ فریاد کے دن تھوڑے ہیں
عرصہ دہر کی جلسی ہوئی ویرانی میں

ہم کو رہنا ہے پہ یونہی تو نہیں رہنا ہے
اجنبی ہاتھوں کا بے نام گراں بار ستم
آج سہنا ہے، ہمیشہ تو نہیں سہنا ہے
یہ ترے حسن سے لپٹی ہوئی آلام کی گرد
اپنی دو روزہ جوانی کی شکستوں کا شمار
چاندنی راتوں کا بے کار دہکتا ہوا درد
دل کی بے سود تڑپ، جسم کی مایوس پکار
چند روز اور مری جان! فقط چند ہی روز

175

Last night

Last night your lost memory visited my heart
As spring visits the wilderness quietly,
As the breeze echoes the silence of her footfalls
In the desert,
As peace slowly, softly descends on one's sickness.

Translation by Azfar Hussain

176

رات یوں دل میں تیری کھوئی ہوئی یاد آئی

رات یوں دل میں تری کھوئی ہوئی یاد آئی

جیسے ویرانے میں چپکے سے بہار آ جائے

جیسے صحراؤں میں ہولے سے چلے بادِ نسیم

جیسے بیمار کو بے وجہ قرار آ جائے

An elusive dawn

this trembling light, this night-bitten dawn,
this is not the dawn, we have waited for so long
this is not the dawn whose birth was sired
by so many live, so much blood

generations ago, we started our confident march
our hopes were young, our goals within reach
after all, there must be some limit
to the confusing constellation of stars
in a vast forest of the sea
even the lazy languid waves
must reach at last their appointed shore

and so we wistfully prayed
for a consummate end to our painful search
many a temptation crossed our forbidden path
many inviting bodies, many longing arms
many seductive pleasures beckoned on our way

but we stayed faithful to our distant dream
we kept marching to a different drum
we kept searching for our lost freedom
we kept looking for our elusive dawn

We are told: our new Dawn is already here;
Your tired feet need journey no more
Our rulers whisper seductively
Why this constant struggle? Why, this perpetual search
Come, joun us, enjoy this new-found wealth
Built by the toil of our "liberated" poor

And yet, even today
Our hearts are aflame
Our desires unquenched
Our goals unmet

Was there a streak of light?
Where did it go?
The wayside lamp just blinked unawares

This is yet no relief in the darkness of the night
No liberation yet of our souls and minds

So let us keep marching, my tiring friends

We have yet to find our elusive dawn.

Translation by Mahbub-ul-Haq

صبح آزادی

اگست ۱۹۴۷ء

یہ داغ داغ اجالا، یہ شب گزیدہ سحر
وہ انتظار تھا جس کا، یہ وہ سحر تو نہیں
یہ وہ سحر تو نہیں، جس کی آرزو لے کر
چلے تھے یار کہ مل جائے گی کہیں نہ کہیں
فلک کے دشت میں تاروں کی آخری منزل
کہیں تو ہوگا شب سست موج کا ساحل
کہیں تو جا کے رکے گا سفینۂ غمِ دل

جواں لہو کی پر اسرار شاہراہوں سے
چلے جو یار تو دامن پہ کتنے ہاتھ پڑے
دیارِ حسن کی بےصبر خواب گاہوں سے
پکارتی رہیں باہیں، بدن بلاتے رہے
بہت عزیز تھی لیکن رخِ سحر کی لگن
بہت قریں تھا حسینانِ نور کا دامن
سبک سبک تھی تمنا، دبی دبی تھی تھکن

سنا ہے ہو بھی چکا ہے فراق ظلمت و نور
سنا ہے ہو بھی چکا ہے وصالِ منزل و گام
بدل چکا ہے بہت اہلِ درد کا دستور
نشاطِ وصل حلال و عذابِ ہجر حرام
جگر کی آگ، نظر کی امنگ، دل کی جلن
کسی پہ چارۂ ہجراں کا کچھ اثر ہی نہیں
کہاں سے آئی نگارِ صبا، کدھر کو گئی

ابھی چراغِ سرِ رہ کو کچھ خبر ہی نہیں
ابھی گرانیِ شب میں کمی نہیں آئی
نجاتِ دیدہ و دل کی گھڑی نہیں آئی
چلے چلو کہ وہ منزل ابھی نہیں آئی

179

My salutations to thy sacred streets

My salutations to thy sacred streets, O beloved nation!
Where a tradition has been invented- that none shall walk
with his head held high
If at all one takes a walk, a pilgrimage
One must walk, eyes lowered, the body crouched in fear

The heart in a tumultuous wrench at the sight
Of stones and bricks locked away and mongrels
breathing free

In this tyranny that has many an excuse to perpetuate itself
Those crazy few that have nothing but thy name on their lips
Facing those power crazed that both prosecute and judge,
wonder
To whom does one turn for defence, from whom does one
expect justice?

But those whose fate it is to live through these times
Spend their days in thy mournful memories

When hope begins to dim, my heart has often conjured
Your forehead sprinkled with stars
And when my chains have glittered
I have imagined that dawn must have burst upon thy face

Thus one lives in the memories of thy dawns and dusks
Imprisoned in the shadows of the high prison walls

Thus always has the world grappled with tyranny
Neither their rituals nor our rebellion is new
Thus have we always grown flowers in fire
Neither their defeat, nor our final victory, is new!

Thus we do not blame the heavens
Nor let bitterness seed in our hearts

We are separated today, but one day shall be re- united
This separation that will not last beyond tonight, bears
lightly on us
Today the power of our exalted rivals may touch the zenith
But these four days of omniscience too shall pass

Those that love thee keep, beside them
The cure of the pains of a million heart-breaks

180

نثار میں تری گلیوں کے ۰۰۰

نثار میں تری گلیوں کے اے وطن کہ جہاں

چلی ہے رسم کہ کوئی نہ سر اٹھا کے چلے

جو کوئی چاہنے والا طواف کو نکلے

نظر چرا کے چلے، جسم و جاں بچا کے چلے

اے اہلِ دل کے لیے اب یہ نظم بست و کشاد

کہ سنگ و خشت مقید ہیں اور سگ آزاد

بہت ہے ظلم کہ دستِ بہانہ جو کے لیے

جو چند اہلِ جنوں تیرے نام لیوا ہیں

بنے ہیں اہل، ہوں، مدعی بھی، منصف بھی

کسے وکیل کریں، کس سے منصفی چاہیں

مگر گزارنے والوں کے دن گزرتے ہیں

ترے فراق میں یوں صبح و شام کرتے ہیں

بجھا ہے روزنِ زنداں تو دل یہ سمجھا ہے

کہ تیری مانگ ستاروں سے بھر گئی ہوگی

چمک اٹھے ہیں سلاسل تو ہم نے جانا ہے

کہ اب سحر ترے رخ پر بکھر گئی ہوگی

غرض تصوّرِ شام و سحر میں جیتے ہیں

گرفتِ سایۂ دیوار و در میں جیتے ہیں

یونہی ہمیشہ الجھتی رہی ہے ظلم سے مخلوق

نہ اُن کی رسم نئی ہے، نہ اپنی ریت نئی

یونہی ہمیشہ کھلائے ہیں ہم نے آگ میں پھول

نہ اُن کی ہار نئی ہے نہ اپنی جیت نئی

اسی سبب سے فلک کا گلہ نہیں کرتے

ترے فراق میں ہم دل بُرا نہیں کرتے

گر آج تجھ سے جُدا ہیں تو کل بہم ہوں گے

یہ رات بھر کی جُدائی تو کوئی بات نہیں

گر آج اوج پہ ہے طالعِ رقیب تو کیا

یہ چار دن کی خدائی تو کوئی بات نہیں

جو تجھ سے عہدِ وفا استوار رکھتے ہیں

علاجِ گردشِ لیل و نہار رکھتے ہیں

181

A prison nightfall

The night descends
step by silent step
down the stairway of the stars.
The breeze goes by me
like a kindly whispered phrase.

The homeless trees of the prison yard
are absorbed, making patterns
against the sky.

On the roof's high crest
the loving hand of moonlight rests.
The starry river is drowned in dust
and the sky glows silver with moonlight.
In the dark foliage
shadows play with the wind
as a wave of painful loss
invades the heart.

Defiantly, a thought tells me
how sweet life is at this instant:
Those who brew the poison of cruelty
will not win, tomorrow or today.
They can put out the lamps
where lovers meet;
they cannot blind the moon!

Translated by Mahmood Jamal

زنداں کی ایک شام

شام کے پیچ و خم ستاروں سے
زینہ زینہ اتر رہی ہے رات
یوں صبا پاس سے گزرتی ہے
جیسے کہہ دی کسی نے پیار کی بات
صحن زنداں کے بے وطن اشجار
سر نگوں ، محو ہیں بنانے میں
دامن آسماں پہ نقش و نگار
شانۂ بام پر دمکتا ہے!
مہرباں چاندنی کا دست جمیل
خاک میں گھل گئی ہے آب نجوم
نور میں گھل گیا ہے عرش کا نیل
سبز گوشوں میں نیلگوں سائے
لہلاتے ہیں جس طرح دل میں
موجِ دردِ فراقِ یار آئے

دل سے پیہم خیال کہتا ہے
اتنی شیریں ہے زندگی اس پل
ظلم کا زہر گھولنے والے
کامراں ہو سکیں گے آج نہ کل
جلوہ گاہ وصال کی شمعیں
وہ بجھا بھی چکے اگر تو کیا؟
چاند کو گل کریں تو ہم جانیں

183

A prison daybreak

It was still dark, when standing by my pillow
The moon said to me 'Wake, dawn is here:
The share poured for you of this night's wine of sleep
Has sunk from brim to bottom of the cup.'

I took farewell of my love's image, and gazed
Out over the dim coverlet of the night's
Slow-ebbing flood, where here and there a dance
Of argent ripples flickered, while the stars,
Like lotus-petals fallen from the moon's hand,
Came sinking, floating, fading, opening out;
Daybreak and night lay long in each other's arms.

Golden in the jail yard my comrades' features
Slowly emerging, a glow against the darkness,
Washed clean by oblivion's dews of brooding grief
For loved face lost, or care for native land –
A far-off drum sounding, a shuffle of feat
Off pallid famished guards starting their rounds,
And arm in arm and on and on with them
The angry din of prisoner and complaint.
Light winds still drunk with dream-delights are stirring:
With them, ghostly, a prison's boat full noises:
A distant door opens, another shuts,
A distant chain scrapes sullenly, scrapes and sobs,
Far off a dagger plunges in some lock's vitals,
A shutter rattles, rattles, beating its head.

My mortal foes have risen again from sleep,
Grim monsters welded out of stone and steel,
Fast in whose talons daylong and nightlong wail
Those gossamer spirits, my empty nights and days,
Captives watching and waiting and waiting for their prince
Whose quiver holds the burning arrows of hope.

Translation by Victor Kiernan

زنداں کی ایک صبح

رات باقی تھی ابھی جب سرِ بالیں آ کر
چاند نے مجھ سے کہا_ "جاگ سحر آئی ہے
جاگ اس شب جو مئے خواب ترا حصہ تھی
جام کے لب سے تہِ جام اُتر آئی ہے"
عکسِ جاناں کو ودع کرکے اٹھی میری نظر
شب کے ٹھہرے ہوئے پانی کی سیاہ چادر پر

جا بجا رقص میں آنے لگے چاندی کے بھنور
چاند کے ہاتھ سے تاروں کے کنول گر گر کر
ڈوبتے، تیرتے، مرجھاتے رہے، کھلتے رہے
رات اور صبح بہت دیر گلے ملتے رہے

صحنِ زنداں میں رفیقوں کے سنہرے چہرے
سطحِ ظلمت سے دمکتے ہوئے اُبھرے کم کم
نیند کی اوس نے ان چہروں سے دھو ڈالا تھا
دیس کا درد، فراقِ رخِ محبوب کا غم

دور نوبت ہوئی، پھرنے لگے بیزار قدم
زرد فاقوں کے بتائے ہوئے پہرے والے
اہلِ زنداں کے غضبناک، خروشاں نالے
جن کی باہوں میں پھرا کرتے ہیں بازیں ڈالے

لذتِ خواب سے مخمور ہوائیں جاگیں
جیل کی زہر بھری چور صدائیں جاگیں
دور دروازہ کھلا کوئی، کوئی بند ہوا
دور مچلی کوئی زنجیر، مچل کے روئی
دور اُترا کسی تالے کے جگر میں خنجر
سر ٹکنے لگا رہ رہ کے دریچہ کوئی
گویا پھر خواب سے بیدار ہوئے دشمنِ جاں
سنگ و فولاد سے ڈھالے ہوئے جنّاتِ گراں
جن کے چنگل میں شب و روز ہیں فریاد کناں
میرے بیکار شب و روز کی نازک پریاں
اپنے شہپور کی رہ دیکھ رہی ہیں یہ اسیر
جس کے ترکش میں ہیں اُمید کے جلتے ہوئے تیر

August 1952

It's still distant, but there are hints of springtime:
some flowers, aching to bloom, have torn open their collars.

In this era of autumn, almost winter, leaves can still be heard:
their dry orchestras play, hidden in corners of the garden.

Night is still where it was, but colours at times take flight,
leaving red feathers of dawn on the sky.

Don't regret our breath's use as air, our blood's as oil –
some lamps at last are burning in the night.

Tilt your cup, don't hesitate! Having given up all,
we don't need wine. We've freed ourselves, made Time
irrelevant.

When imprisoned man opens his eyes, cages will dissolve:
air, fire,
water, earth – all have pledged such dawns, such gardens
to him.

Your feet bleed, Faiz, something surely will bloom
as you water the desert simply by walking through it.

Translated by Agha Shahid Ali

186

روشن کہیں بہار کے امکاں ہوئے تو ہیں
گلشن میں چاک چند گریباں ہوئے تو ہیں

اب بھی خزاں کا راج ہے لیکن کہیں کہیں
گوشے رہِ چمن میں غزل خواں ہوئے تو ہیں

ٹھہری ہوئی ہے شب کی سیاہی وہیں مگر
کچھ کچھ سحر کے رنگ پر افشاں ہوئے تو ہیں

ان میں لہو جلا ہو ہمارا کہ جان و دل
محفل میں کچھ چراغ فروزاں ہوئے تو ہیں

ہاں کج کرو کلاہ کہ سب کچھ لٹا کے ہم
اب بے نیازِ گردشِ دوراں ہوئے تو ہیں

اہلِ قفس کی صبحِ چمن میں کھلے گی آنکھ
بادِ صبا سے وعدہ و پیماں ہوئے تو ہیں

ہے دشت اب بھی دشت مگر خوں پا سے فیض
سیراب چند خارِ مغیلاں ہوئے تو ہیں

187

In my heart now well up

In my heart now well up your long-forgotten sorrows
as though some forsaken idol returns to the kaaba.

One by one the stars are coming alive –
your footfalls are drawing close to my destination.

Pep up the tempo of the wine-dance, let the music
swell to its crescendo –
to the tavern come the emissaries of the haram.

It is I alone, who would not seek favours,
Although she is ever willing to oblige.

Tell the night of separation to hold itself awhile,
for the heart now aches less and remembrance too is faint.

Translation by Shiv K. Kumar

دل میں اب یوں ترے بھولے ہوئے غم آتے ہیں
جیسے بچھڑے ہوئے کعبے میں صنم آتے ہیں

ایک اک کر کے ہو جاتے ہیں تارے روشن
میری منزل کی طرف تیرے قدم آتے ہیں

رقصِ مے تیز کرو، سازِ کی لے تیز کرو
سوئے مہ خانہ سفیرانِ حرم آتے ہیں

کچھ ہمیں کو نہیں احسان اٹھانے کا دماغ
وہ تو جب آتے ہیں، مائل بہ کرم آتے ہیں

اور کچھ دیر نہ گزرے شبِ فرقت سے کہو
دل بھی کم دکھتا ہے، وہ یاد بھی کم آتے ہیں

Fragrance is a name for your flowing tresses

Colour is a dress; fragrance is a name for your flowing
tresses.
Your appearance at the window gives the Spring its name.

Say something about this sight, my friends, without which
neither the garden would have colour, nor the tavern have a
name.

Again the eye fills with the scent of flowers, again the heart
is lit with a leaping flame;
Imagination exults, and hesitating no longer, rejoins this
happy company again.

Romance is a trick to set the tongues of the world wagging,
now even those with angel faces must keep their tresses
tamed.

No beloved will now declare her desire openly
for where is the lover who is not defamed?

Praise to the naysayers! for by their grace
the drunkard, bartender, wine, cask and shotglass have
their fame.

Those with the gardens say to us, "You, out there,
why don't you give your wilderness a pretty name?"

Faiz, they demand faith from us now, who
would rather be outsiders than bear a lover's name.

رنگ پیراہن کا خوشبو ، زلف لہرانے کا نام
موسمِ گل ہے تمہارے بام پر آنے کا نام

دوستو، اُس چشم و لب کی کچھ کہو جس کے بغیر
گلستاں کی بات رنگیں ہے ، نہ میخانے کا نام

پھر نظر میں پھول مہکے ،دل میں پھر شمعیں جلیں
پھر تصور نے لیا اُس بزم میں جانے کا نام

(ق)

دلبری ٹھہرا زبانِ خلق کھلوانے کا نام
اب نہیں لیتے پری رو زُلف بکھرانے کا نام
اب کسی لیلیٰ کو بھی اقرار محبوبی نہیں
ان دنوں بدنام ہے ہر ایک دیوانے کا نام

محتسب کی خیر، اونچا ہے اسی کے فیض سے
رند کا، ساقی کا، مے کا،خم کا، پیمانے کا نام

ہم سے کہتے ہیں چمن والے،غریبانِ چمن!
تم کوئی اچھا سا رکھ لو اپنے ویرانے کا نام

فیض اُن کو ہے تقاضائے وفا ہم سے جنہیں
آشنا کے نام سے پیارا ہے بیگانے کا نام

191

To the Iranian students
Who gave their lives for peace and freedom.

Who are they, these
Free givers whose blood-drops,
Jingling coins, go pouring
Into earth's ever-thirsty
Begging –bowl, pour and run,
Filling the bowl brim-full?
What are they, land of their birth, these young
Self-squanderers whose
Limbs' golden store
Of surging youth
Lies here in the dust, shattered –
Lies strewn about the street and alley?
Oh land of their birth, oh land of their birth!
How could those eyes that laughed tear out
And toss their sapphire gems away,
Those lip their coral?
Who gained, who turned to profit,
Those hands' quivering silver?

Oh questioning stranger –
These striplings, these young lives,
Are fresh-grown pearls of that light,
New-budded shoots of that flame,
From which amid tyranny's dense night sprang
The rosebed dawn of revolt
And dawn was in every nerve and soul.
Their argent and golden flesh,
Those coral and sapphire faces
That gleam and shine there and gleam –
Let the stranger who would see
Stand close, gaze long!
They are the jewellery of the queen of life,
They are the diadem of the goddess of peace.

Translation by Victor Kiernan

یہ کون سخی ہیں

جن کے لہو کی

اشرفیاں، چھن چھن، چھن چھن

دھرتی کے پیہم پیاسے

کشکول میں ڈھلتی جاتی ہیں

کشکول کو بھرتی جاتی ہیں

یہ کون جواں ہیں ارضِ عجم

یہ لکھ لٹ

جن کے جسموں کی

بھرپور جوانی کا کندن

یوں خاک میں ریزہ ریزہ ہے

یوں کوچہ کوچہ بکھرا ہے

اے ارضِ عجم، اے ارضِ عجم!

کیوں نوچ کے ہنس ہنس پھینک دیے

ان آنکھوں نے اپنے نیلم

ان ہونٹوں نے اپنے مرجاں

ان ہاتھوں کی ''بے کل چاندی

کس کام آئی، کس ہاتھ لگی؟''

''اے پوچھنے والے پردیسی!

یہ طفل و جواں

اس نور کے نورس موتی ہیں

اس آگ کی کچی کلیاں ہیں

جس میٹھے نور اور کچی آگ

سے ظلم کی اندھی رات میں پھوٹا

صبحِ بغاوت کا گلشن

اور صبح ہوئی من من، تن تن

ان جسموں کا چاندی سونا

ان چہروں کے نیلم، مرجاں

جگ مگ جگ مگ، رخشاں رخشاں

جو دیکھنا چاہے پردیسی

193

We'll keep on plying the pen

We'll keep on plying the pen
We'll keep on plying the pen on the page,
Record shall we the tale of our heart.
We'll keep providing the sorrows of love,
And fertilize the wastes of time.
The virulence of times is yet to grow,
The tyrants will stick to their tyrannous ways.
We welcome the virulence, accept the blows,
Life permitting, we'll redress our grief.
If the tavern stays, with the purple wine,
We'll deck the roofs and walls of the mosque.
While there is blood still in our veins,
Our tears will supply the tint to her cheeks.
A style of indifference will be her way,
A style of submission will be our creed.
Bring the flowers to bloom
Bring the flowers to bloom, let the spring breeze blow,
Come, my love, and rouse the garden from its sleep.
Gloom pervades the prison, say something to the breeze,
Someone, for God's sake, should talk about my love.
Sometime at least the sun should rise from the corner
of your lips,
Sometime at least the night should flow from your scented
locks.
Strong is the link of grief, no matter if the heart is poor,
Sorrowing hearts will flock, once they hear your name.
How I fared matters not, but O lonesome night,
My tears have ensured your peace, here and beyond.
My heart, Faiz, could not approve any place en route,
Forced out of my love's street, I made for the gallows straight.

Translation by Hamid Rahim Sheikh

لوحِ و قلم

ہم پرورشِ لوحِ و قلم کرتے رہیں گے
جو دل پہ گزرتی ہے ، رقم کرتے رہیں گے

اسبابِ غمِ عشق بہم کرتے رہیں گے
ویرانیِ دوراں پہ کرم کرتے رہیں گے

ہاں تلخیِ ایّام ابھی اور بڑھے گی
ہاں اہلِ ستم مشقِ ستم کرتے رہیں گے

منظور یہ تلخی ، یہ ستم ہم کو گوارا
دم ہے تو مداوائے الم کرتے رہیں گے

مے خانہ سلامت ہے تو ہم سرخیِ مے سے
تزئینِ درِ و بامِ حرم کرتے رہیں گے

باقی ہے لہُو دل میں تو ہر اشک سے پیدا
رنگِ لبِ و رخسارِ صنم کرتے رہیں گے

اک طرزِ تغافل ہے سو وہ ان کو مبارک
اک عرضِ تمنّا ہے سو ہم کرتے رہیں گے

195

Memory

In the desert of loneliness, my darling; quivers
The echo of your voice, the mirage of your lips.
In the desert of loneliness, beneath isolation's debris,
Are blooming jasmines and roses of your charming Self.

From somewhere close arises the warmth of your breath,
So gently it smoulders, drenched in its own scent.
Far away, across the horizon, shining like pearly drops,
Softly falls the dew from your blissful eyes.

With so much tenderness, my darling your memory has put,
Just now, its soothing hands on my turbulent heart,
It appears, although it is still the dawn of separation,
The day of parting is gone, and has come reunion's night.

Translation by Sain Sucha

196

یاد

دشت تنہائی میں، اے جان جہاں، لرزاں ہیں
تیری آواز کے سائے، تیرے ہونٹوں کے سراب
دشت تنہائی میں، دوری کے خس و خاک تلے
کھل رہے ہیں، تیرے پہلو کے سمن اور گلاب

اٹھ رہی ہے کہیں قربت سے تری سانس کی آنچ
اپنی خوشبو میں سلگتی ہوئی، مدھم مدھم
دور ___ افق پار، چمکتی ہوئی قطرہ قطرہ
گر رہی ہے تری دلدار نظر کی شبنم

اس قدر پیار سے، اے جان جہاں، رکھا ہے
دل کے رخسار پہ اس وقت تری یاد نے ہاتھ
یوں گماں ہوتا ہے، گرچہ ہے ابھی صبحِ فراق
ڈھل گیا ہجر کا دن، آ بھی گئی وصل کی رات

197

For a political leader

Years these chained hands scraped,
Like straw waging war on the sea,
At the hard black breast of the night,
Like moths assailing the rock:
Until in the stony dark breast of the night
So many wounds opened the light,
Wherever you looked, wove a pattern,
And pulse of morning, far off, started to beat.
Your stocks, your hopes, are these hands.
What else have you got but these hands?
You cannot accept victory of the dark,
But countenance the sword on these hands
And let the day laying wait in the east
Fall under the night's iron corpse.

Translation by Andrew McCord

سیاسی لیڈر کے نام

سالہا سال یہ بے آسرا جکڑے ہوئے ہاتھ
رات کے سخت و سیہ سینے میں پیوست رہے
جس طرح تنکا سمندر سے ہو سرگرمِ ستیز
جس طرح تیتری کہسار پہ یلغار کرے
اور اب رات کے سنگین و سیہ سینے میں
اتنے گھاؤ ہیں جس سمت نظر جاتی ہے
جا بجا نور نے اک جال سا بن رکھا ہے
دور سے صبح کی دھڑکن کی صدا آتی ہے
تیرا سرمایہ ، تری آس یہی ہاتھ تو ہیں
اور کچھ بھی تو نہیں پاس، یہی ہاتھ تو ہیں
تجھ کو منظور نہیں غلبہ ظلمت ، لیکن
تجھ کو منظور ہے یہ ہاتھ قلم ہو جائیں
اور مشرق کی کمیں گہ میں دھڑکتا ہوا دن
رات کی آہنی میّت کے تلے دب جائے!

199

The evening star has burnt out

The evening star has burnt out in dusk's ashes —
In the air wave the locks of the parting night.

Let someone proclaim life is running itself out,
The sky is held up the caravan of morning and evening.

This is their obduracy, these enemies of wine and cup —
Let there be no moon by night, no cloud by day.

The breeze has knocked at the prison door again:
Dawn is about to break, tell the heart not to feel so restive.

Translation by Shiv K. Kumar

شفق کی راکھ میں جل بجھ گیا ستارۂ شام
شبِ فراق کے گیسو ہوا میں لہرائے

کوئی پکارو کہ اک عمر ہونے آئی ہے
فلک کو قافلۂ روز و شام ٹھہرائے

یہ ضد ہے یادِ حریفانِ بادہ پیما کی
کہ شب کو چاند نہ نکلے، نہ دن کو ابر آئے

صبا نے پھر درِ زنداں پہ آ کے دی دستک
سحر قریب ہے، دل سے کہو نہ گھبرائے

The season of fetters and gallows

The same season of waiting haunts every day,
no season brings the season of spring,
heavy on the heart is the daily plain of survival;
now is the time by the lover's beauty.

Blessed is the moment when a friend's face appears,
blessed is the heart's repose in a season of turmoil,
without the custom of wine and Saqi, to what purpose
the season of cloud drifting over the mountain peak?
If friendly society is beyond us what good is there
inthis season where the shadows dance of cypress
and poplar?

Translation by Rafey Habib

طوقِ و دار کا موسم

روش روش ہے وہی انتظار کا موسم
نہیں ہے کوئی بھی موسم، بہار کا موسم

گراں ہے دل پہ غمِ روزگار کا موسم
ہے آزمائشِ حسنِ نگار کا موسم

خوشا نظارۂ رخسارِ یار کی ساعت
خوشا قرارِ دلِ بے قرار کا موسم

حدیثِ بادہ و ساقی نہیں تو کس مصرف
خرامِ ابر سرِ کہسار کا موسم

نصیبِ صحبتِ یاراں نہیں تو کیا کیجئے
یہ رقصِ سایۂ سرو و چنار کا موسم

یہ دل کے داغ تو دیکھتے تھے یوں بھی پر کم کم
کچھ اب کے اور ہے ہجرانِ یار کا موسم

یہی جنوں کا، یہی طوقِ و دار کا موسم
یہی ہے جبر، یہی اختیار کا موسم

قفس ہے بس میں تمہارے، تمہارے بس میں نہیں
چمن میں آتشِ گل کے نکھار کا موسم

صبا کی مست خرامی تہِ کمند نہیں
اسیرِ دام نہیں ہے بہار کا موسم

بلا سے ہم نے نہ دیکھا تو اور دیکھیں گے
فروغِ گلشن و صوتِ ہزار کا موسم

203

Messiah of crystals

Messiah of Crystals
Pearl, crystal, goblet
Once broken is broken
Tears cannot mend it,
It's lost if broken.
You gather the shards
Save them for naught
There is no Messiah of Crystals,
What good is your hope?
Perhaps these fragments hold
The chalice of your heart
That haughty angel's perch
The nectar of life's sweet agony
The world snatched your chalice away
Smashed it,
Scattered that nectar into dust
Cleaved the angel's wing
These colourful shards are perhaps
Fragments of those dazzling dreams
With whose brilliance you decorated
Your bed-chamber in ebullient youth
Beggary, toil, hunger, pain
Kept smashing at those dreams
Brutal was the rain of stones
What could these crystal skeletons do
Or perhaps, in these fragments
Is the jewel of your honour and your humility
The envy
Of the high-statured ones
The jewel was craved by many
Traders, robbers
In this land of thieves, the poor
Can save either life or honour
These goblets, crystals, these jewels
If whole, carry some value,
Broken, they merely
Prick, cut, evoke blood-tears
You gather the shards,

شیشوں کا مسیحا کوئی نہیں

موتی ہو کہ شیشہ، جام کہ دُر
جو ٹوٹ گیا، سو ٹوٹ گیا
کب اشکوں سے جڑ سکتا ہے
جو ٹوٹ گیا، سو ٹوٹ گیا

نادارى، دفتر، بھوک اور غم
اِن سپنوں سے ٹکراتے ہیں
بے رحم تھا چومکھ پتھراؤ
یہ کانچ کے ڈھانچے کیا کرتے

تم ناحق ٹکڑے چن چن کر
دامن میں چھپائے بیٹھے ہو
شیشوں کا مسیحا کوئی نہیں
کیا آس لگائے بیٹھے ہو

یا شاید اِن ذروں میں کہیں
موتی ہے تمہاری عزت کا
وہ جس سے تمہارے عجز پہ بھی
شمشاد قدوں نے رشک کیا

شاید کہ انہی ٹکڑوں میں کہیں
وہ ساغرِ دل ہے جس میں کبھی
صد ناز سے اترا کرتی تھی
صہبائے غمِ جاناں کی پری

اس مال کی دُھن میں پھرتے تھے
تاجر بھی بہت، رہزن بھی کئی
ہے چورنگر، یہاں مفلس کی
گر جان بچی تو آن گئی

پھر دنیا والوں نے تم سے
یہ ساغر لے کر پھوڑ دیا
جو مے تھی بہا دی مٹی میں
مہمان کا شہپر توڑ دیا

یہ ساغر، شیشے، لعل و گہر
سالم ہوں تو قیمت پاتے ہیں
یوں ٹکڑے ٹکڑے ہوں، تو فقط
چھتے ہیں، لہو رُلواتے ہیں

یہ رنگیں ریزے ہیں شاید
اُن شوخ بلوریں سپنوں کے
تم مست جوانی میں جن سے
خلوت کو سجایا کرتے تھے

تم ناحق شیشے چن چن کر
دامن میں چھپائے بیٹھے ہو
شیشوں کا مسیحا کوئی نہیں
کیا آس لگائے بیٹھے ہو

205

Save them for naught
There is no Messiah of Crystals,
What good is your hope?
On mended collars of memory
The heart does not linger
Unmasking, masking truths
How can life be spent like this?
In the workplace of Being
These goblets and crystals are forged
Everything is replaceable,
All wants can be fulfilled
Every hand that reaches is a helper
Every eye that looks, fortunate
There is no end to riches here
No matter the robbers who lie in wait
Looting, robbing cannot empty
The coffers of Being
Diamonds on every mountain
Pearls in every ocean
Some,
Wish to cordon off this wealth
Auction
Every mountain and ocean
Others fight
Break down those walls
Foil the schemes
Of the thieves of Being
They grapple, fight
In every village and vale
In every happy home
On every lane
There are those who blacken all around them
Others who light candles
Those who set fires and
Those who put them out
Every goblet, crystal, jewel
Is enjoined in the fight
Arise, all idle hands
Are summoned to the fight.

Translated by Ali Madeeh Hashmi

یادوں کے گریبانوں کے رفو
پر دل کی گزر کب ہوتی ہے
اک بخیا ادھیڑا ، اک سیا
یوں عمر بسر کب ہوتی ہے؟

کچھ وہ بھی ہیں جو لڑ بھڑ کر
یہ پردے نوچ گراتے ہیں
ہستی کے اٹھائی گیروں کی
ہر چال اُلجھائے جاتے ہیں

اس کارگہِ ہستی میں جہاں
یہ ساغر ، شیشے ڈھلتے ہیں
ہر شے کا بدل مل سکتا ہے
سب دامن پُر ہو سکتے ہیں

ان دونوں میں رن پڑتا ہے
ہِنت بستی بستی ، نگر نگر
ہر بستے گھر کے سینے میں
ہر چلتی راہ کے ماتھے پر

جو ہاتھ بڑھے ، یاور ہے یہاں
جو آنکھ اُٹھے ، وہ بختاور
یاں دھن دولت کا انت نہیں
ہوں گھات میں ڈاکو لاکھ ، مگر

یہ کالک بھرتے پھرتے ہیں
وہ جوت جگاتے رہتے ہیں
یہ آگ لگاتے پھرتے ہیں
وہ آگ بجھاتے رہتے ہیں

کب لُوٹ جھپٹ سے ہستی کی
دوکانیں خالی ہوتی ہیں
یاں پربت پربت ہیرے ہیں
یاں ساگر ساگر موتی ہیں

سب ساغر، شیشے ، لعل و گہر
اس بازی میں بد جاتے ہیں
اُٹھو سب خالی ہاتھوں کو
اس رن سے بلاوے آتے ہیں

کچھ لوگ ہیں جو اس دولت پر
پردے لٹکاتے پھرتے ہیں
ہر پربت کو ، ہر ساگر کو
نیلام چڑھاتے پھرتے ہیں

207

You haven't come, nor has the night of waiting gone

You haven't come, nor has the night of waiting gone.
Looking for you the morn has called again and again.

Time spent in madness was time well spent.
Though my heart suffered ravages untold.

I must have spent that night in the street of my love,
The night when the preacher with me did debate.

What did not even figure in the tale entire,
To that he has taken very grave offence.

No flowers no wine noi sight of my friend.
In what a queer way we've spent this spring.

What havoc in the garden has the flower-pluckier wrought?
Disturbed blew the breeze beside my cage to-day.

تم آئے ہو، نہ شبِ انتظار گزری ہے
تلاش میں ہے سحر، بار بار گزری ہے

جنوں میں جتنی بھی گزری، بکار گزری ہے
اگرچہ دل پہ خرابی ہزار گزری ہے

ہوئی ہے حضرتِ ناصح سے گفتگو جس شب
وہ شب ضرور سرِ کوئے یار گزری ہے

وہ بات سارے فسانے میں جس کا ذکر نہ تھا
وہ بات ان کو بہت ناگوار گزری ہے

نہ گل کھلے ہیں، نہ ان سے ملے، نہ مے پی ہے
عجیب رنگ میں اب کے بہار گزری ہے

چمن پہ غارتِ گلچیں سے جانے کیا گزری
قفس سے آج صبا بے قرار گزری ہے

209

Two loves

(1)
Oh rose-like Saqi, fresh yet in my memory
are those days whose bright mirror still vibrates with her;
those moments we met, like an opening flower,
the moments, like fluttering heartbeats, I waited for her—
Lo!—hope, roused by the sad heart's good luck;
Lo!—that love's night of heartache had come to end;
Lo!—that those sleepless stars of sorrow were sinking,
that promised joy so long dormant had awakened.
From this rooftop the sun of your beauty will rise,
from that corner its rays red as henna will dawn,
from this doorway your steps like quicksilver will flow,
by that pathway your twilit dress will blossom!
Fevered days too have I known, separation's pangs,
when lament was forgotten in the soul's sorrow,
each night's dark load so heavy, the heart was crushed,
each morning's flame piercing it like an arrow.
In solitude, how could I keep from thinking of you?
What refuges did my sad heart not seek?
Sometimes I felt the hand of the morning-breeze on my brow,
sometimes I put my arms around the moon's neck.

دو عشق

(۱)

تازہ ہیں ابھی یاد میں اے ساقیِ گلفام
وہ عکسِ رخِ یار سے لہکے ہوئے ایّام
وہ پھول سی کھلتی ہوئی دیدار کی ساعت
وہ دل سا دھڑکتا ہوا امید کا ہنگام

امید کہ لو جاگا غمِ دل کا نصیبہ
لو شوق کی ترسی ہوئی شب ہوگئی آخر
لو ڈوب گئے درد کے بےخواب ستارے
اب چمکے گا بےصبر نگاہوں کا مقدر

اِس بام سے نکلے گا ترے حسن کا خورشید
اُس کنج سے پھوٹے گی کرن رنگِ حنا کی
اِس در سے بہے گا تری رفتار کا سیماب
اُس راہ پہ پھولے گی شفق تیری قبا کی

پھر دیکھے ہیں وہ ہجر کے تپتے ہوئے دن بھی
جب فکرِ دل و جاں میں فغاں بھول گئی ہے
ہر شب وہ سیہ بوجھ کہ دل بیٹھ گیا ہے
ہر صبح کی لو تیر سی سینے میں لگی ہے

تنہائی میں کیا کیا نہ تجھے یاد کیا ہے
کیا کیا نہ دلِ زار نے ڈھونڈی ہیں پناہیں
آنکھوں سے لگایا ہے کبھی دستِ صبا کو
ڈالی ہیں کبھی گردنِ مہتاب میں باہیں

211

(2)

In this same way I have loved my darling country;
in this same way my heart has pounded with devotion to her;

in this same way my passion has sought the respite of a
resting-place,
in the curve of her cheek, in the curls of her hair.
In this same way, to that sweetheart world, my heart and eyes
have called out with laughter, cried out with tears.
All the demands of her summons I have fulfilled;
I made light every pain and calmed every fear.
No bidding toward ecstasy ever went unheeded,
never did the bell's echo return to the tower alone.
The heart's ease, creature comforts, a station in life,
all the connivers shrewd advice, forgotten.
What befalls all travellers on that road befell me,
a solitary prison cell, my name ridiculed in the market;
self-anointed holy men from their pulpits thundered,
dictators roared from their seats of power.
No treacherous arrows were spared me by strangers,
no scorn was omitted by those most esteemed,
but my heart feels shame neither for this love nor that love;
there is every scar on this heart but the scar of shame.

212

چاہا ہے اسی رنگ میں لیلائے وطن کو
تڑپا ہے اسی طور سے دل اس کی لگن میں
ڈھونڈی ہے یونہی شوق نے آسائشِ منزل
رخسار کے خم میں کبھی کاکل کی شکن میں

اس جانِ جہاں کو بھی یونہی قلب و نظر نے
ہنس ہنس کے صدا دی، کبھی رو رو کے پکارا
پورے کئے سب حرف تمنا کے تقاضے
ہر درد کو اجیالا، ہر اک غم کو سنوارا

واپس نہیں پھیرا کوئی فرمان جنوں کا
تنہا نہیں لوٹی کبھی آواز جرس کی
خیریتِ جاں ، راحتِ تن ، صحتِ داماں
سب بھول گئیں مصلحتیں اہلِ ہوس کی

اس راہ میں جو سب پہ گزرتی ہے وہ گزری
تنہا پسِ زنداں ، کبھی رسوا سرِ بازار
گرجے ہیں بہت شیخ سرِ گوشہء منبر
کڑکے ہیں بہت اہلِ حکم برسرِ دربار

چھوڑا نہیں غیروں نے کوئی ناوکِ دشنام
چھوٹی نہیں اپنوں سے کوئی طرزِ ملامت
اس عشق نہ اُس عشق پہ نادم ہے مگر دل
ہر داغ ہے اِس دل میں بجز داغِ ندامت

213

Elegy for a brother

This, my brother, I hold against you,
When you left, you also took away
The book of times past;
It had pictures I can never replace,
Pictures of my childhood, my youth.
And in their place you've left me
The red rose of grief,
A gift I cannot accept.
Take it all away,
I ask you one last time
You never were one to say no
Come back then and take away this glowing rose
Just give me back my book of times past.

Translation by Khalid Hasan

نوحہ

مجھ کو شکوہ ہے مرے بھائی کہ تم جاتے ہوئے

لے گئے ساتھ مری عمرِ گذشتہ کی کتاب

اس میں تو میری بہت قیمتی تصویریں تھیں

اس میں بچپن تھا مرا، اور مرا عہدِ شباب

اس کے بدلے تم مجھے دے گئے جاتے جاتے

اپنے غم کا یہ دمکتا ہوا خوں رنگ گلاب

کیا کروں بھائی ، یہ اعزاز میں کیونکر پہنوں

مجھ سے لے لو مری سب چاک قمیضوں کا حساب

آخری بار ہے، لو مان لو اک یہ بھی سوال

آج تک تم سے میں لوٹا نہیں مایوس جواب

آ کے لے جاؤ تم اپنا یہ دمکتا ہوا پھول

مجھ کو لوٹا دو مری عمرِ گذشتہ کی کتاب

215

We, who were slain in unlit pathways...
Inspired by the letters of Ethel and Julius Rosenberg

We, who were slain in unlit pathways,
Wishing for the roses of your lips,
we offered ourselves to a gallows' twig.
Longing for the radiance of your glowing hands,
we let ourselves be slain in unlit pathways.
On the gallows away from our face
darted the redness of your ruby lips,
waved the playfulness of your youthful locks,
shone the glow of the silver palms.
When the evening of suffering settled in your alleys
we came, as far as our steps could bring
Words of poetry on our lips, a lamp of anguish in our hearts
Our suffering was a testimony to your beauty
See, we were faithful to our pledge
We, who were slain in unlit pathways.
If failure was our destined end
your love was indeed our own doing.
Who is to blame if all the roads of passion
led to the killing grounds of separation.
Picking up our flags from these grounds
will march forth more caravans of your lovers
For whose journeys' sake, our footsteps
have shortened the lengths of the agonizing quest
For whose sake we have made universal
by losing our lives, the pledge to your faithfulness
We, who were slain in unlit pathways.
Ask me not, my love . . .
Ask me not, my love, for the love of the former days,

I had thought, with you around, life would be dazzling bright,
With your grief to fill my heart, other grieves would vaporize
Your beauty keeps the spring alive,
The world contains naught but your starry eyes,
To own you is to own the fortunes richest prize.
It wasn't so, I simply wished it could be so!
Besides the grieves of love, there're other grieves in life,
Besides the joy of union there're other delights.
The dark, devilish spells o'er several centuries cast,
Woven in silks and satins, in brocade finely wrought;
Human bodies for sale in every street and shop,
Bodies bathed in blood, splashed with gory spots,
I cannot help but see them all.
Your beauty still attracts the heart; but what to do?
There are other grieves in life,
Besides the joy of union, there are other delights

Translation by Hamid Rahim Shiekh

ہم جو تاریک راہوں میں مارے گئے

تیرے ہونٹوں کے پھولوں کی چاہت میں ہم

دار کی خشک ٹہنی پہ وارے گئے

تیرے ہاتوں کی شمعوں کی حسرت میں ہم

نیم تارک راہوں میں مارے گئے

سولیوں پر ہمارے لبوں سے پرے

تیرے ہونٹوں کی لالی لپکتی رہی

تیری زلفوں کی مستی برستی رہی

تیرے ہاتھوں کی چاندی دمکتی رہی

جب گھلی تیری راہوں میں شام ستم

ہم چلے آئے، لائے جہاں تک قدم

لب پہ حرف غزل، دل میں قندیل غم

اپنا غم تھا گواہی تیرے حسن کی

دیکھ قائم رہے اس گواہی پہ ہم

ہم جو تاریک راہوں میں مارے گئے

نارسائی اگر اپنی تقدیر تھی

تیری الفت تو اپنی ہی تدبیر تھی

کس کو شکوہ ہے گر شوق کے سلسلے

ہجر کی قتل گاہوں سے سب جا ملے

قتل گاہوں سے چن کر ہمارے علم

اور نکلیں گے عشاق کے قافلے

جن کی راہِ طلب سے ہمارے قدم

مختصر کر چلے درد کے فاصلے

کر چلے جن کی خاطر جہاں گیر ہم

جاں گنوا کر تیری دلبری کا بھرم

ہم جو تاریک راہوں میں مارے گئے

217

Crosses

There are so many crosses
planted by my window
each carrying its own Christ
each yearning to meet his God.
On some the spring is sacrificed
on some the moon lies crucified
on some the fruitful branch is blinded
on some the morning breeze is slaughtered.
Each passing day
these blood-laced visions
come into my mind.
Each passing day, in front of me
their martyred bodies are
resurrected.

Translation by Mahmood Jamal

دریچہ

گڑی ہیں کتنی صلیبیں میرے دریچے میں
ہر ایک اپنے مسیحا کے خوں کا رنگ لئے
ہر ایک وصلِ خداوند کی امنگ لئے

کسی پہ کرتے ہیں ابرِ بہار کو قربان
کسی پہ قتلِ مہِ تابناک کرتے ہیں
کسی پہ ہوتی ہے سرمست شاخسار دونیم
کسی پہ بادِ صبا کو ہلاک کرتے ہیں

ہر آئے دن یہ خداوندگان مہر و جمال
لہو میں غرق مرے نمکدے میں آتے ہیں
اور آئے دن میری نظروں کے سامنے ان کو
شہد جسم سلامت اٹھائے جاتے ہیں

219

Africa come back

Come Back, I've heard the surge of your drums
Come Back, my heart beats lasciviously

'Africa come back'

Come Back, I've raised my face out from the dust
Come Back, I've peeled off the pellicle of sorrow from
my eyes
Come Back, I've snatched away my arms from the grip
of pain
Come Back, I've wrenched apart the hasp of gloom

'Africa come back'

The shackle's clasps have made the mace too much to bear
So I've fashioned a mould by ripping the strap round
my neck

'Africa come back'

The bear's death-eyes blaze in every lair
Enemy blood has reddened the negritude of night

'Africa come back'

The ground is pirouetting with me Africa
Rivers throbbing to the rhythm pouring out of the woods
I am Africa, your stature mirrors mine
I am you, my gait is the gait of your lions
'Africa come back'
Come stride like your lions
'Africa come back'.

Translation by Rehan Qayoom

آ جاؤ افریقا

آجاؤ، میں نے سن لی ترے ڈھول کی ترنگ

آجاؤ، مست ہو گئی میرے لہو کی تال

‏''آ جاؤ افریقا''

آ جاؤ، میں نے ڈھول سے ماتھا اٹھا لیا

آ جاؤ، میں نے چھیل دی آنکھوں سے غم کی چھال

آ جاؤ، میں نے درد سے بازو چھڑا لیا

آ جاؤ، میں نے نوچ دیا بے کسی کا جال

‏''آ جاؤ افریقا''

پنجے میں ہتھکڑی کی کڑی بن گئی ہے گرز

گردن کا طوق توڑ کے ڈھالی ہے میں نے ڈھال

‏''آ جاؤ افریقا''

جلتے ہیں ہر کچھار میں بھالوں کے مرگ نین

دشمن لہو سے رات کی کالک ہوئی ہے لال

‏''آ جاؤ افریقا''

دھرتی دھڑک رہی ہے مرے ساتھ افریقا

دریا تھرک رہا ہے تو بن دے رہا ہے تال

میں افریقا ہوں، دھار لیا میں نے تیرا روپ

میں تو ہوں، میری چال ہے تیری ببر کی چال

‏''آ جاؤ افریقا''

آؤ ببر کی چال

‏''آ جاؤ افریقا''

221

City of lights

On each patch of green, from one shade to the next,
the noon is erasing itself by wiping out all colour,
becoming pale, desolation everywhere,
the poison of exile painted on the walls.
In the distance,
there are terrible sorrows, like tides:
they draw back, swell, become full, subside.
They've turned the horizon to mist.
And behind that mist is the city of lights,
my city of many lights.

How will I return to you, my city,
where is the road to your lights? My hopes
are in retreat, exhausted by these unlit, broken walls,
and my heart, their leader, is in terrible doubt.

But let all be well, my city, if under
cover of darkness, in a final attack,
my heart leads its reserves of longings
and storms you tonight. Just tell all your lovers
to turn the wicks of their lamps high
so that I may find you, Oh, city,
my city of many lights.

Translation by Agha Shahid Ali

اے روشنیوں کے شہر

سبزہ سبزہ ،سوکھ رہی ہے پھیکی ، زرد دوپہر

دیواروں کو چاٹ رہا ہے تنہائی   کا زہر

دور افق تک گھٹتی ،بڑھتی، اٹھتی،گرتی رہتی ہے

کہر کی صورت بے رونق دردوں کی گدلی لہر

بستا ہے اس کہر کے پیچھے روشنیوں کا شہر

اے روشنیوں کے شہر

کون کہے کس سمت ہے تیری روشنیوں کی راہ

ہر جانب بے نور کھڑی ہے ہجر کی شہر پناہ

تھک کر ہر سو بیٹھ رہی ہے شوق کی ماند سپاہ

آج مرا دل فکر میں ہے

اے روشنیوں   کے شہر

شب خوں سے منہ پھیر نہ جائے ارمانوں کی رو

خیر ہو تیری لیلاؤں کی، ان سب سے   کہہ دو

آج کی شب جب دیئے جلائیں ، اونچی رکھیں لو

223

A lover to his beloved

This path of memory,
On which you have walked for so long,
Will end, If your were to proceed a few steps more,
Where it diverts to oblivion's desolation
And from there onwards neither you nor I exist.
My eyes, still on you, wait that any instant,
You may return, pass on, or just look back.

Yet, I am aware,
That it is merely an illusion:
When I believe that if my eyes
ever embrace you somewhere,
A new path shall erupt there;
And a similar encounter shall resume;
Under the fall of your locks,
The journey of my arms.

Then, the other situation is just a false,
Because my heart knows:
There is no diversion, desolation or hiding,
Which may conceal my beloved from me.
So, while this path erupts under your feet,
Let it be so;
And if you never even look back,
It doesn't matter.

Translated by Sain Sucha

کوئی عاشق کسی محبوبہ سے!

یاد کی راہ گزر جس پہ اسی صورت سے
مدتیں بیت گئی ہیں تمہیں چلتے چلتے
ختم ہو جائے جو دو چار قدم اور چلو
موڑ پڑتا ہے جہاں دشتِ فراموشی کا
جس سے آگے نہ کوئی میں ہوں نہ کوئی تم ہو
سانس تھامے ہیں نگائیں کہ نہ جانے کس دم
تم پلٹ آؤ، گزر جاؤ، یا مُڑ کر دیکھو

گرچہ واقف ہیں نگائیں کہ یہ سب دھوکا ہے
گر کہیں تم سے ہم آغوش ہوئی پھر سے نظر
پھوٹ نکلے گی وہاں اور کوئی راہ گزر
پھر اُسی طرح جہاں ہوگا مقابل پیہم
سایۂ زُلف کا اور جنبشِ بازو کا سفر

دوسری بات بھی جھوٹی ہے کہ دل جانتا ہے
یاں کوئی موڑ کوئی دشت کوئی گھات نہیں
جس کے پردے میں مرا ماہِ رواں ڈوب سکے
تم سے چلتی رہے یہ راہ، یونہی اچھا ہے
تم نے مُڑ کر بھی نہ دیکھا تو کوئی بات نہیں

225

We all were killed

We all were killed
this our final
triumph
    for we did reach the destination
    we met your challenge
    and returned after dying
    Oh victory

Whether every flame
or minds lit by suns
or a solitary heart in ashes
    love
    each final fire
    emerged from your door
    shaped thus
    by your graced or disdain

As such I came away from the evening
every one still there with you
among the lights
    only the heart felt
    it's terrible defeat
    only it knows its desolation
    and it could speak
    only to itself

Each footstep mean death
and even the promise of life
    for I've returned from the lane
    where the executioner lives
    I've loitered there
    as if to get some air

Faiz
be grateful to autumn
    to its cold winds
    that are seasoned postmen
    carrying letters as mere habit
    from spring
    it's custom to announce thus
    that will surely come

Translation by Agha Shahid Ali

سب قتل ہوئے تیرے مقابل سے آئے ہیں
ہم لوگ سُرخرو ہیں کہ منزل سے آئے ہیں

شمعِ نظر ، خیال کے انجم ، جگر کے داغ
جتنے چراغ ہیں ، تری محفل سے آئے ہیں

اُٹھ کر تو آ گئے ہیں تری بزم سے مگر
کچھ دل ہی جانتا ہے کہ کس دل سے آئے ہیں

ہر اک قدم اجل تھا ، ہر اک گام زندگی ہیں
ہم گھوم پھر کے کوچۂ قاتل سے آئے ہیں

بادِ خزاں کا شکر کرو ، فیض ، جس کے ہاتھ
نامے کسی بہار شمائل سے آئے ہیں

227

I am being accused of loving you

I am being accused of loving you, that is all
It is not an insult, but a praise, that is all

My heart is pleased at the words of the accusers
O my dearest dear, they say your name, that is all

For what I am ridiculed, it is not a crime
My heart's useless playtime, a failed love, that is all

I haven't lost hope, but just a fight, that is all
The night of suffering lengthens, but just a night, that is all

In the hand of time is not the rolling of my fate
In the hand of time roll just the days, that is all

A day will come for sure when I will see the truth
My beautiful beloved is behind a veil, that is all

The night is young, Faiz start saying a Ghazal
A storm of emotions is raging inside, that is all

Translation by Hamid Rahim Shiekh

228

ہم پر تمہاری چاہ کا الزام ہی تو ہے
دشنام تو نہیں ہے، یہ اکرام ہی تو ہے

کرتے ہیں جس پہ طعن کوئی جرم تو نہیں
شوقِ فضول و اُلفتِ ناکام ہی تو ہے

دل مدعی کے حرفِ ملامت سے شاد ہے
اے جانِ جاں یہ حرف ترا نام ہی تو ہے

دل ناامید تو نہیں، ناکام ہی تو ہے
لمبی ہے غم کی شام، مگر شام ہی تو ہے

دستِ فلک میں گردشِ تقدیر تو نہیں
دستِ فلک میں گردشِ ایّام ہی تو ہے

آخر تو ایک روز کرے گی نظرِ وفا
وہ یارِ خوش خصال سرِ بام ہی تو ہے

بھیگی ہے رات فیض غزل ابتدا کرو
وقتِ سرود، دردِ کا ہنگام ہی تو ہے

229

Let the breeze pour colours

Let the breeze pour colours
    Into the waiting blossoms

    Unlock the warehouses
    Where those colours are stored

    Oh Love now return
    So the promised springtime may finally begin

There is weeping in the prisons
    Friends say some thing
    Just speak

    Today
    If only for the sake of God
    Let her name pass through a cage

From the corner of your lips
    Let the dawn begin
    At least for once

    And let it be fragrant
    The night which will descend
    When you open your hair

My heart is poor
    It needs no reminding
    But it holds all the wealth of longing

    On hearing your name
    I'll always return

    One again become the one
    To share your sorrow

Whatever the pain
    I endured its very moment but

    Oh Night of Sorrow you weren't diminished

    My tears made sure
    You would remain a legend
    Even in afterlife

She goes to the office of desires
    To see who's still listed
    In the ledger of lovers

    We are already there waiting
    Our shirts ripped to threads

    In our hands those threads
    (proof that we were faithful)
    Tied stubbornly into knot

After farewell Oh Faiz
    Nothing could hold you back
    Nothing at any stop was worthy of desire

    From her streets you walked
    Straight to the district of executions

    You climbed the steps to the gallows
    Lost yourself in the hangman's arm

Translation by Agha Shahid Ali

گلوں میں رنگ بھرے بادِ نوبہار چلے

چلے بھی آؤ کہ گلشن کا کاروبار چلے

قفس اُداس ہے یارو صبا سے کچھ تو کہو

کہیں تو بہرِ خدا آج ذکرِ یار چلے

کبھی تو صبح ترے کنجِ لب سے ہو آغاز

کبھی تو شب سرِ کاکل سے مشکبار چلے

بڑا ہے درد کا رشتہ ، یہ دل غریب سہی

تمہارے نام پہ آئیں گے غمگسار چلے

جو ہم پہ گزری سوگزری مگر شبِ ہجراں

ہمارے اشک تری عاقبت سنوار چلے

حضورِ یار ہوئی دفترِ جنوں کی طلب

گرہ میں لے گریباں کا تار تار چلے

مقام، فیض، کوئی راہ میں بچا ہی نہیں

جو کوئے یار سے نکلے تو سوئے دار چلے

231

Pain will creep in soft-footed

After a while, when my lonesome heart will once again,
be seized by angst, how shall I cure the loneliness?
Pain will then creep in soft-footed, carrying a red taper –
that pain which throbs beyond the heart's precincts.

As this flame will leap forth in the side,
on the heart's wall will be rekindled every mark –
somewhere a lock's whorl, somewhere a cheek's curve,
somewhere the wilderness of parting, the joy
of seeing the beloved, a kind word, or love's assent.

Then will I say, O my heart,
this thought, the beloved of your loneliness,
is only a visitant for a moment –
so how can your problem be solved?

After it's gone, will rise enraged
savage shadows, which will linger on
for me to battle with all through the night.

This is war, O my heart, not a frolic;
all your life's enemies, all your assassins –
this harsh night, these shadows, this loneliness.
There's nothing common between pain and war, O my heart.
Fetch m an ember of fierce passion and kindle it,
get me from somewhere the mighty flame of wrath
and that garden ablaze –
with it heat, its dynamism, it puissance.

Maybe a limb of our tribe is waiting
on the other side of the ramparts of darkness.
Let's alert our comrades of our presence
through fiery martial songs.
Well, even if they don't reach us, they'll call out to us
to intimate how far the dawn still is.

Translation by Shiv K. Kumar

232

درد آئے گا دبے پاؤں ...

اور کچھ دیر میں، جب مرے تنہا دل کو
فکر آ لے گی کہ تنہائی کا کیا چارہ کرے
درد آئے گا دبے پاؤں، لئے سرخ چراغ
وہ جو اک درد دھڑکتا ہے کہیں دل سے پرے

شعلۂ درد جو پہلو میں لپک اٹھے گا
دل کی دیوار پہ ہر نقش دمک اٹھے گا
حلقہ زلف کہیں، گوشہ رخسار کہیں
ہجر کا دشت کہیں گلشن دیدار کہیں
لطف کی بات کہیں، پیار کا اقرار کہیں

دل سے پھر ہوگی مری بات کہ اے دل اے دل
یہ جو محبوب بنا ہے تری تنہائی کا
یہ جو مہماں ہے گھڑی بھر کا، چلا جائے گا
اس کب تیری مصیبت کا مداوا ہو گا
مشتعل ہو کے ابھی اٹھیں گے وحشی سائے
یہ چلا جائے گا، رہ جائیں گے باقی سائے
رات بھر جن سے ترا خون خرابا ہوگا
جنگ ٹھہری ہے کوئی کھیل نہیں ہے اے دل
دشمن جاں ہیں سبھی، سارے کے سارے قاتل
یہ کڑی رات بھی، یہ سائے بھی، تنہائی بھی
درد اور جنگ میں کچھ میل نہیں ہے اے دل
لاؤ، سلگاؤ کوئی جوش غضب کا انگار
طیش کی آتش جرّار کہاں ہے لاؤ
وہ دمکتا ہوا گلزار کہاں ہے لاؤ
جس میں گرمی بھی ہے، حرکت بھی، توانائی بھی

ہو نہ ہو اپنے قبیلے کا بھی کوئی لشکر
منتظر ہو گا اندھیرے کی فصیلوں کے ادھر
ان کو شعلوں کے رجز اپنا پتہ تو دیں گے
خیر، ہم تک وہ نہ پہنچیں بھی، صدا تو دیں گے
دور کتنی ہے ابھی صبح، بتا تو دیں گے

233

This crop of hope

Cut them to the ground,
Cut all these wounded plants,
Do not leave them fighting for life,
Pull them out.
As for these listless flowers,
Do not leave them drooping from the branch.

This crop of our hopes,
Will once again be laid to waste;
All our work through night and day,
Will once again have turned out to be in vain.

Remake the flower beds,
Water the earth with your blood,
Make it wet with your tears
And wait for the next springtime.

Think of the next planting season,
For what we sow today will perish.
Keep planting till what we sow stands high.
Never give up, for that's what we must do.

Translation by Khalid Hasan

یہ فصل امیدوں کی ہمدم

سب کاٹ دو

بسمل پودوں کو

بے آب سسکتے مت چھوڑو

سب نوچ لو

بیکل پھولوں کو

شاخوں پہ بلکتے مت چھوڑو

یہ فصل امیدوں کی ہمدم

اِس بار بھی غارت جائے گی

سب محنت، صبحوں شاموں کی

اب کے بھی اکارت جائے گی

کھیتی کے کونوں، کھدروں میں

پھر اپنے لہُو کی کھاد بھرو

پھر مٹی سینچو اشکوں سے

پھر اگلی رُت کی فکر کرو

پھر اگلی رُت کی فکر کرو

جب پھر اک بار اُجڑنا ہے

اک فصل پکی تو بھر پایا

جب تک تو یہی کچھ کرنا ہے

235

Brief meeting

(1)
This night
Is the tree of a pain
That's of greater consequence than me or you.
Greater because myriad caravans of torch-bearing stars
were circled round and lost
in its branches. A thousand moons have wept away
all their luminance
in its shade.
This night
is the tree of a pain
That's of greater consequence than me or you.
Yet from the tree of this very night have fallen off
these pale leaves of a few moments,
Fallen off and caught in your tresses, they have become
red, like the pomegranate blossom.
From the cold dew of this very night
These few drops of silence have rained down
And have made a wreath of diamonds
on your forehead.
(2)
This night is dark, very dark. But from its very darkness
a river of blood shines out, the river of blood
that's my voice.
Light-creating, in the shadow of this night, a golden wave
That's your eye.
The grief that at this time smoulders
in the rose-garden
of your arms,
(the grief, which is the fruit of this night)
Let it burn some more in the fire
of our sighs.
For then this grief will itself become
a fire-spark.
All the arrows
Shot forth by the black bow of all the boughs
of this tree broke into our breast;
we pulled them out and moulded each of them
into mountain-cleaving axes.

236

(۱)

ملاقات

یہ رات اس درد کا شجر ہے
جو مجھ سے ، تجھ سے عظیم تر ہے
عظیم تر ہے کہ اس کی شاخوں
میں لاکھ مشعل بکف ستاروں
کے کارواں، گھر کے کھو گئے ہیں
ہزار مہتاب ، اس کے سائے
میں اپنا سب نور ، رو گئے ہیں
یہ رات اس درد کا شجر ہے
جو مجھ سے ، تجھ سے عظیم تر ہے
مگر اسی رات کے شجر سے
یہ چند لمحوں کے زرد پتے
گرے ہیں ، اور تیرے گیسوؤں میں
الجھ کے گلنار ہو گئے ہیں
اسی کی شبنم سے خامشی کے
یہ چند قطرے ، تری جبیں پر
برس کے ، ہیرے پرو گئے ہیں

(۲)

بہت سیہ ہے یہ رات لیکن
اسی سیاہی میں رونما ہے
وہ نہر خوں جو مری صدا ہے
اسی کے سائے میں نور گر ہے
وہ موج زر جو تری نظر ہے
وہ غم جو اس وقت تیری باہوں
کے گلستاں میں سلگ رہا ہے
(وہ غم ، جو اس رات کا ثمر ہے)
کچھ اور تپ جائے اپنی آہوں
کی آنچ میں تو یہی شرر ہے

ہر اک سیہ شاخ کی کماں سے
جگر میں ٹوٹے ہیں تیر جتنے
جگر سے نوچے ہیں ، اور ہر اک
کا ہم نے نیشتر بنا لیا ہے

(3)
The day of the broken-hearted, of those
whose portion is anguish, will not dawn
on the skies.
It's here, where we two stand,
Morning's bright horizon is just here.
It's here that the fire-sparks of pain have blossomed
to become the garden of the rosy dawn.
It's here that the shiny axes of murderous sorrows
Row after row have become
fiery garlands of the light
of the sun.
The sorrow bequeathed by this night--
The sorrow is transformed now, has become
our true belief for the morning.
True belief which gives more than what sorrow gives:
The morning which is of greater consequence
than the night.

Translation by Shamsur Rahman Faruqi

(۳)

الم نصیبوں ، جگر فگاروں
کی صبح ، افلاک پر نہیں ہے
جہاں پہ ہم تم کھڑے ہیں دونوں
سحر کا روشن افق یہیں ہے
یہیں پہ غم کے شرار کھِل کر
شفق کا گلزار بن گئے ہیں
یہیں پہ قاتل دھنوں کے تیشے
قطار اندر قطار کرنوں
کے آتشیں ہار بن گئے ہیں
یہ غم جو اس رات نے دیا ہے
یہ غم سحر کا یقیں بنا ہے
یقیں جو غم سے کریم تر ہے
سحر جو شب سے عظیم تر ہے

239

You say we're out of options

You say that the battle is over
Though the fighting hasn't even begun:
No one's stepped on the field, neither us nor the enemy,
No lines have formed, no flag
Has summoned scattered comrades
Or told of the enemy's location.
You say that the battle is over
Though we haven't even begun to fight.

You say we're out of options:
Our bodies are broken, our hands are weak,
We cannot bear the stone of injustice -
The stone of injustice, the mountain of grief -
One touch and we all stepped to one side
Matched words with words and were satisfied.

Friends, in the dust of the beloved's street
Shall our blood no longer shine?
Shall no gardens blossom crimson
In the dust at the beloved's feet?
Shall this mourning not be broken
by the returning cries of lovers
who demand their rights?
The slogans of those not afraid to die?

The tests that grief set us she set us,
The wounds we bore we bore.
There are more wounds owed yet,
More life and limb to be mourned,
More bitter tests to be borne.

240

تم یہ کہتے ہو اب کوئی چارہ نہیں!

تم یہ کہتے ہو وہ جنگ ہو بھی چکی!
جس میں رکھا نہیں ہے کسی نے قدم
کوئی اُترا نہ میداں میں، دشمن نہ ہم
کوئی صف بن نہ پائی، نہ کوئی علم

مُنتشر دوستوں کو صدا دے سکا
اجنبی دشمنوں کا پتہ دے سکا
تم یہ کہتے ہو وہ جنگ ہو بھی چکی!
جس میں رکھا نہیں ہم نے اب تک قدم
تم یہ کہتے ہو اب کوئی چارہ نہیں
جسم خستہ ہے، ہاتھوں میں یارا نہیں

اپنے بس کا نہیں بارِ سنگِ ستم
بارِ سنگِ ستم، بارِ کہسارِ غم
جس کو چھو کر سبھی اک طرف ہو گئے
بات کی بات میں ذی شرف ہو گئے

دوستو، کوئے جاناں کی نامہرباں
خاک پر اپنے روشن لہُو کی بہار
اب نہ آئے گی کیا؟ اب کھلے گا نہ کیا
اِس کفِ نازنیں پر کوئی لالہ زار؟
اِس حزیں خامشی میں نہ لوٹے گا کیا
شورِ آوازِ حق، نعرۂ گیر و دار

شوق کا امتحاں جو ہوا سو ہوا
جسم و جاں کا زیاں جو ہوا سو ہوا
سود سے پیشتر ہے زیاں اور بھی
دوستو، ماتمِ جسم و جاں اور بھی
اور بھی تلخ تر امتحاں اور بھی

241

Solitary confinement

Far away
A light flickered on the horizon –
In the domain of mind, arose the reign of pain;
In the world of fantasy, my restlessness increased;
In the realm of solitude, the dawn arrived.
After blending my day's venom with life's gall,
I filled the bowl of my heart with that drink.

Far away
A light flickered on the horizon –
Away from my sight, bearing the news of a dawn,
Some song, some scent or some pretty maid,
Passed by the way – incensing me with hope.

After blending my day's venom with life's gall,
I endorsed my longing for the day of reunion:
In the name of the friends of this libertine – home or afar,
In the name of Earth's beauty, the grace of a human face.

Translation by Sain Sucha

242

قیدِ تنہائی

دور آفاق پہ لہرائی کوئی نور کی لہر
خواب ہی خواب میں بیدار ہوا درد کا شہر
خواب ہی خواب میں بیتاب نظر ہونے لگی
عدم آبادِ جدائی میں سحر ہونے لگی
کاسئہ دل میں بھری اپنی صبوحی میں نے
گھول کر تلخیِ دیروز میں امروز کا زہر
دور آفاق پہ لہرائی کوئی نور کی لہر
آنکھ سے دور کسی صبح کی تمہید لئے
کوئی نغمہ، کوئی خوشبو، کوئی کافرصورت
بے خبر گزری، پریشانیِ امید لئے
گھول کر تلخیِ دیروز میں امروز کا زہر
حسرتِ روزِ ملاقات رقم کی میں نے
دیس پردیس کے یارانِ قدح خوار کے نام
حسنِ آفاق، جمالِ لب و رخسار کے نام

243

The evening

It appears as if every tree is a temple:
An abandoned, desolate, ancient temple,
Looking for some pretence to fall apart,
Its edifice torn, the doors hanging loose.

The sky looks like an ascetic priest:
Its body ashen, a streak of the red on the forehead,
Sitting with his had bowed, no one knows since when.

One feels the presence of a sorcerer somewhere:
He has cast his spell on the heavens around,
The time's lap stitched to the lap of the evening.

Now
Neither the dusk will fall,
Nor the darkness arrive.
Neither the night will end,
Nor the dawn arise.

The sky waits hopefully, for this spell to break –
The chain of silence may snap,
The lap of time may become free.
A trumpet would sound,
An anklet would clink
Some goddess might awake from her deep sleep,
Some damsel might lift the veil from her face.

Translation by Sain Sucha

244

شام

اس طرح ہے کہ ہر اک پیڑ کوئی مندر ہے
کوئی اُجڑا ہوا ،   بے نور پرانا   مندر
ڈھونڈتا ہے جو خرابی کے بہانے کب سے
چاک ہر بام، ہر اک در کا دمِ آخر ہے
آسماں کوئی پروہت ہے جو ہر بام تلے
جسم پر راکھ ملے ، ماتھے پہ سندُور ملے
سرنگوں بیٹھا ہے چپ چاپ نہ جانے کب سے
اس طرح ہے کہ پسِ پردہ کوئی ساحر ہے
جس نے آفاق پہ پھیلایا ہے یوں سحر کا دام
دامنِ وقت سے پیوست ہے یوں دامنِ شام
اب کبھی شام بجھے گی نہ اندھیرا ہوگا
اب کبھی رات ڈھلے گی نہ سویرا ہوگا

آسماں آس لئے ہے کہ یہ جادو ٹوٹے
چپ کی زنجیر کٹے ، وقت کا دامن چھوٹے
دے کوئی سنکھ دہائی ، کوئی پایل بولے
کوئی بُت جاگے ،کوئی سانولی گھونگھٹ کھولے

245

Let us walk in bazaar in shackles

Let us walk in bazaar in shackles
Wet eyes and restless soul is not enough
Being charged for nurturing concealed love is not enough
Let us walk in bazaar in shackles
Let us go with glitter in hand, in trance and dancing
Go with dust on head and blood on garb
Go as the city of my beloved is waiting
City's ruler and crowd of commoners
Arrow of false charge, stone of accusation
Morning of sorrow, day of failure
Who is their friend except me
Who is untainted in the city of beloved
Who deserve the killers or executioners hand
Get ready for the journey of heart, go wounded heart
Let me go to be executed.

Translation by Anis Zuberi

246

آج بازار میں پابجولاں چلو

چشمِ نم ، جانِ شوریدہ کافی نہیں
تہمتِ عشق پوشیدہ کافی نہیں
آج بازار میں پا بجولاں چلو

دستِ افشاں چلو، مست و رقصاں چلو
خاک بر سر چلو ، خوں بداماں چلو
راہ تکتا ہے سب شہرِ جاناں چلو

حاکمِ شہر بھی ، مجمعِ عام بھی
تیرِ الزام بھی ، سنگِ دشنام بھی
صبحِ ناشاد بھی ، روزِ ناکام بھی

ان کا دم ساز اپنے سوا کون ہے
شہرِ جاناں میں اب با صفا کون ہے
دستِ قاتل کے شایاں رہا کون ہے

رختِ دل باندھ لو دل فگارو چلو
پھر ہمیں قتل ہو آئیں یارو چلو

Pain

When will this pain stop, my dear heart,
when will this night end ?
I had heard she was to come,
the day will break !

When will this life have life
When will this tear become a pearl
When these misty eyes will be happy
When will the spring come
When will the wine flow
When will we be free to talk
When will we begin to see ?

No preacher, hermit, advisor or despot,
how will we survive in this place ?
How long shall I wait, my friend,
when is the Doomsday ?
You must have some idea...

Translation by unknown

کب ٹھہرے گا درد اے دل، کب رات بسر ہو گی
سنتے تھے وہ آئیں گے ، سنتے تھے سحر ہو گی

کب جان لہُو ہوگی ، کب اشک گہر ہو گا
کس دن تری شنوائی اے دیدۂ تر ہو گی

کب مہکے گی فصلِ گل ، کب بہکے گا میخانہ
کب صبحِ سخن ہو گی ، کب شام نظر ہو گی

واعظ ہے نہ زاہد ہے ، ناصح ہے نا قاتل ہے
اب شہر میں یاروں کی کس طرح بسر ہو گی

کب تک ابھی رہ دیکھیں اے قامتِ جانانہ
کب حشر معیّن ہے تجھ کو تو خبر ہو گی

249

Elegy – The rain of stones is finished

For Hassan Nasir, tortured to death in
the Lahore Fort in 1959

Today as I started, suddenly a string snapped,
and the moon and sun were smashed in the sky.
No darkness is left in any corner, and no light –
Behind me the road of fidelity lies broken,
its lights extinguished, like my heart;
and nothing remains ahead. Friends, what will happen now?

Conveys of pain bearing cargoes of love must keep moving,
but someone else must now wave them forward.
and other must tend the garden here ardour blooms –
I can't: the dew of my eyes has dried: I won't weep again.
All rapture, the pure madness fo passion, has ceased,
and no one's left to bear the rain of storm.

That road behind me: it was always the Beloved's street.
It is now the colour of her lips;
my blood, like a flag has been unfurled there.
I have nothing left to give.

And a glass is being filled gain.
Friends, let one of you now come forward,
For the cry has began: "Who'll dare to drink this wine of love"
that is blood and poison? Who?"
This is the cry in the tavern after I'm gone.

Translation by Agha Shahid Ali

250

ختم ہوئی بارش سنگ

ناگہاں آج مرے تارِ نظر سے کٹ کر
ٹکڑے ٹکڑے ہوئے آفاق پہ خورشید و قمر
اب کسی سمت اندھیرا نہ اُجالا ہوگا
بجھ گئی دل کی طرح راہِ وفا میرے بعد

دوستو! قافلۂ درد کا اب کیا ہوگا
اب کوئی اور کرے پرورشِ گلشنِ غم
دوستو ختم ہوئی دیدۂ تر کی شبنم
تھم گیا شورِ جنوں ختم ہوئی بارش سنگ

خاک رہ آج لئے ہے لبِ دلدار کا رنگ
کوئے جاناں میں کھلا میرے لہو کا پرچم
دیکھئے کس کس کو صدا دیتے ہیں میرے بعد
"کون ہوتا ہے حریفِ مئے مرد افگنِ عشق
ہے مکرر لبِ ساقی پہ صلا میرے بعد"

251

Wave on wave the grief is stilled the suffering soul becalmed.

Wave on wave the grief is stilled the suffering soul becalmed.

As if I breathe the breath of spring or hear the tidings of my love.

He stands by me in actual from whose desire I thought was but a dream.
My heart looks forward to the morrow I feel convinced of yesterdays.

Is it a would that burst, a flower bloomed a tear welled or a cloud surged?
The cups are brimming with the lovers blood.

Hearts simmer scars burn.
The session of pain bustles again the night of desire is all aglow.

Martyrdom acquires a novel style at the call of death to the site of gallows.
Some have arrived carrying the cross some with halters round their necks.
I know not Faiz why to-day I expect to hear the news.

The vendor softens to the drinkers the assassin loves the broken hearts.

Translation by unknown

آج یوں موج در موج غم تھم گیا اس طرح غم زدوں کو قرار آ گیا
جیسے خوشبوئے زلفِ بہار آ گئی جیسے پیغامِ دیدارِ یار آ گیا

جس کی دید و طلب وہم سمجھے تھے ہم روبرو پھر سرِ رہگزار آ گیا
صبحِ فردا کو پھر دل ترسنے لگے ، عمرِ رفتہ ترا اعتبار آ گیا

رُت بدلنے لگی رنگِ دل دیکھنا، رنگِ گلشن سے اب حال کھلتا نہیں
زخم چھلکا کہ کوئی یا کوئی گل کھلا، اشک اُمڈے کہ ابرِ بہار آ گیا

خونِ عشاق سے جام بھرنے لگے ، دل سلگنے لگے ، داغ جلنے لگے
محفلِ درد پھر رنگ پر آ گئی ، پھر شبِ آرزو پر نکھار آ گیا

سرفروشی کے انداز بدلے گئے ، دعوتِ قتل پر مقتلِ شہر میں
ڈال کر کوئی گردن میں طوق آ گیا، لاد کر کوئی کاندھے پہ دار آ گیا

فیض کیا جانئے یارکس آس پر، منتظر ہیں کہ لائے گا کوئی خبر
میکشوں پر ہوا محتسب مہرباں ، دلِ فگاروں پہ قاتل کو پیار آ گیا

253

So softly

Footpath, shadows, trees,
destination, entrance, and the gallery.
The moon bared its breast on the balcony – so softly.
As if some beauty disrobes – so softly.
Under the balcony – the sapphirine of shadows;
The lake – an expansion of the sapphirine.
In the lake floated a bubble's leaf;
Held a while, and then it burst – so softly.

So softly, lightly, the pale coloured wine,
It was filled in my goblet – so gently.
The glass, the carafe,
The roses formed by your hands:
As if a distant shadow, in some dream,
It arose and then faded – so gently.

The heart recalled a promise – so tenderly.
You said: "Tenderly".
The Moon bowed and murmured:
"Still more tenderly".

Translation by Sain Sucha

254

منظر

رہ گزر، سائے، شجر، منزل دور، حلقۂ بام

بام پر سینۂ مہتاب کھلا، آہستہ

جس طرح کھولے کوئی بند قبا، آہستہ

حلقۂ بام تلے، سایوں کا ٹھہرا ہوا نیل

نیل کی جھیل

جھیل میں چپکے سے تیرا، کسی پتّے کا حباب

ایک پل تیرا، چلا، پھوٹ گیا، آہستہ

بہت آہستہ، بہت ہلکا، خنک رنگِ شراب

میرے شیشے میں ڈھلا، آہستہ

شیشہ و جام، صراحی، تیرے ہاتھوں کے گلاب

جس طرح دور کسی خواب کا نقش

آپ ہی آپ بنا اور مٹا، آہستہ

دل نے دُہرایا کوئی حرفِ وفا، آہستہ

تم نے کہا،'' آہستہ''

چاند نے جھک کے کہا

''اور ذرا آہستہ''

Your half-drawn arrow

Do not waste your half drawn arrow; I have already lost
broken pieces of my heart.
Collect and save the left-over stones, my injured or
wounded body is already wasted.

Let my health giver know, let the procession of foes know
He whose soul was indebted, has settled his dues today.

Keep the burial shroud atilt on my forehead, lest my assassin
may have misgivings that Pride of self-importance or
arrogance of love, I forgot after death.

On that side there was one word 'kill', on my side there
were hundred thousand reasons to explain why I behaved
the way I did
What I said you heard, not paid attention; what I wrote you
you read and erased.

I am mountain when I stop; I am beyond life when I walk
I have, turned every step on the path of the beloved into
a memorial.

Translation by Anis Zuberi

نہ گنواؤ ناوکِ نیم کش دلِ ریزہ ریزہ گنوا دیا
جو بچے ہیں سنگ سمیٹ لو تنِ داغ داغ لٹا دیا

مرے چارہ گر کو نوید ہو صفِ دشمناں کو خبر کرو
وہ جو قرض رکھتے تھے جان پر وہ حساب آج چُکا دیا

کرو کج جبیں پہ سرِ کفن مرے قاتلوں کو گماں نہ ہو
کہ غرورِ عشق کا بانکپن پسِ مرگ ہم نے بھلا دیا

اُدھر ایک حرف کہ کشتنی یہاں لاکھ عُذر تھا گفتنی
جو کہا تو سن کے اُڑا دیا، جو لکھا تو پڑھ کے مٹا دیا

جو رُکے تو کوہِ گراں تھے، جو چلے تو جاں سے گزر گئے
رہِ یار ہم نے قدم قدم تجھے یاد گار بنا دیا

Be near me

Be near me now,

My tormentor, my love, be near me-

At this hour when the night comes down,

When we have drunk form the gash of sunset, darkness comes

With the balm of musk in its hands, its diamond lancets

When it comes with cries of lamentation, with laughter, with songs

Its blue –grey anklets of pain clinking every step

At this hour when the hearts, deep in their hiding places

Have begun to hope once more, when they start their vigil

For hands still enfolded in sleeves;

When wine being poured makes the sound of inconsolable children

Who, though you try with all your heart, cannot be soothed.

When whatever you want to do cannot be done

When nothing is of any use

At this hour when the night comes down,

When the night comes dragging its long face dressed in mourning

Be with me

My tormentor, my love, be near me.

Translation by Naomi Lazard

پاس رہو

تم مرے پاس رہو

میرے قاتل، مرے دلدار، مرے پاس رہو

جس گھڑی رات چلے

آسمانوں کا لہو پی کے سیہ رات چلے

مرہمِ مُشک لیے، نشترِ الماس لئے

بین کرتی ہوئی، ہنستی ہوئی، گاتی نکلے

درد کے کاسنی پازیب بجاتی نکلے

جس گھڑی سینوں میں ڈوبے ہوئے دل

آستینوں میں نہاں ہاتھوں کی رہ تکنے نکلیں

آس لئے

اور بچوں کے بلکنے کی طرح قلقلِ مئے

بہرِ ناسودگی مچلے تو منائے نہ منے

جب کوئی بات بنائے نہ بنے

جب نہ کوئی بات چلے

جس گھڑی رات چلے

جس گھڑی ماتمی، سنسان، سیہ رات چلے

پاس رہو

میرے قاتل، مرے دلدار مرے پاس رہو

259

It's the colour of my heart

When you didn't come,
things were they should be -
the sky was as far as I could see,
the road to travel by was a road,
the goblet was a glassful of wine.

And now, a glassful of wine,
the road to travel by,
and the colour of the sky,
are like the colours of my blood,
flowing from my heart to my liver.

Sometimes golden, like the
shine of your eyes when we meet.
Sometimes grey and saddening like
the sickening feelings of partings.

Other times like colours of old
leaves, of trash, of dry grass,
of red flowers in flower-beds,
of dark sky, of poison, of blood.

Now I see the sky, the road,
the glass full of wine, my wet
robe, my aching nerves in a mirror,
changing moment by moment.

Since you've come, please stay.
May the things - the colours, the seasons,
stay as if they were in one place.
May everything be as it used to be -

The sky, as far as I could see,
the road to travel by, a road,
the goblet, brimming with wine.

Translation by Ravi Kopra

260

رنگ ہے دل کا مرے

تم نہ آئے تھے تو ہر چیز وہی تھی کہ جو ہے
آسماں حدِ نظر، راہگزر، راہگزر شیشۂ مے شیشۂ مے
اور اب شیشۂ مے، راہگزر، رنگِ فلک
رنگ ہے دل کا مرے، ''خونِ جگر ہونے تک''
چمپئی رنگ کبھی راحتِ دیدار کا رنگ
سرمئی رنگ کہ ہے ساعتِ بیزار کا رنگ
زرد پتوں کا، خس و خار کا رنگ
سرخ پھولوں کا دمکتے ہوئے گلزار کا رنگ
زہر کا رنگ، لہو رنگ، شبِ تار کا رنگ
آسماں، راہگزر، شیشۂ مے
کوئی بھیگا ہوا دامن، کوئی دُکھتی ہوئی رگ
کوئی ہر لحظہ بدلتا ہوا آئینہ ہے

اب جو آئے ہو تو ٹھہرو کہ کوئی رنگ، کوئی رت، کوئی شے
ایک جگہ پر ٹھہرے،
پھر سے اک بار ہر اک چیز وہی ہو کہ جو ہے
آسماں، حدِ نظر، راہگزر، شیشۂ مے، شیشۂ مے

261

The smell of blood

The smell of blood
or the fragrance of a lover's lips?
I wonder what the breeze
will bring for me
today.

Has spring arrived in the garden? Or
have the prisons found new inhabitants?
Where will the music come from today.
the sound of singing?

Translation by Mahmood Jamal

یہ خوں کی مہک ہے کہ لبِ یار کی خوشبو

کس راہ کی جانب سے صبا آتی ہے دیکھو

گلشن میں بہار آئی کہ زنداں ہوا آباد

کس سمت سے نغموں کی صدا آتی ہے دیکھو

Your sorrow in search of someone

Your sorrow came, searching for life,
But those who would have died for you are gone,
Those who would have bowed their heads when you passed
Have all gone their own ways.

And the night is gone too,
Annoyed with you for keeping it waiting;
And those who came to console me have left,
Angry with me because I would not cry.

There is no question of love now,
I cannot complain, cannot say what grieves me,
I have no suggestions to make
In the tyranny of your love
My heart has lost all its rights.

I was the one
Whose shirt turned red with the blood from the streets;
These are the stains that I wore proudly
All the way to my beloved's house.

But passion is out of style now,
And this rope, these gallows, are no longer needed;
Those who were proud to be accused of love
Have all vanished like criminals.

Translation by unknown

تیرے غم کو جاں کی تلاش تھی ترے جاں نثار چلے گئے
تری رہ میں کرتے تھے سر طلب ، سرِ رہگزار چلے گئے

تری کج ادائی سے ہار کے شبِ انتظار چلی گئی
مرے ضبطِ حال سے روٹھ کر مرے غم گسار چلے گئے

نہ سوالِ وصل ، نہ عرضِ غم ، نہ حکایتیں نہ شکایتیں
ترے عہد میں دلِ زار کے سبھی اختیار چلے گئے

یہ ہمیں تھے جن کے لباس پر سرِ رہ سیاہی لکھی گئی
یہی داغ تھے جو سجا کے ہم سرِ بزمِ یار چلے گئے

نہ رہا جنونِ رخِ وفا ، یہ رسن یہ دار کرو گے کیا
جنہیں جرمِ عشق پہ ناز تھا وہ گناہ گار چلے گئے

265

When in your sea eyes

Edge of sunlight – nascent evening
Where the two polarities of time meet.
Neither day or not.
Neither today nor tomorrow.
At one moment, eternal.
At another, no more than mist.
The leap of lips.
The embrace of rhythmic arms.
This mingling of ours.
Is neither true nor false.
Why complain?
Why listen to what the other say?
Why delude ourselves?
When in your sear eyes
The sun of this evening sinks
Everyone in this house
Will sleep blissfully
And the traveller will go his way.

Translation by Daud Kamal

جب تیری سمندر آنکھوں میں

(گیت)

یہ دھوپ کنارا ،شام ڈھلے

ملتے ہیں دونوں وقت جہاں

جو رات نہ دن، جو آج نہ کل

پل بھر میں امر ، پل بھر میں دھواں

اس دھوپ کنارے، پل دو پل

ہونٹوں کی لپک

باہوں کی چھنک

یہ میل ہمارا ، جھوٹ نہ سچ

کیوں زار کرو، کیوں دوش دھرو

کس کارن جھوٹی بات کرو

جب تیری سمندر آنکھوں میں

اس شام کا سورج ڈوبے گا

شکھ سوئیں گے گھر در والے

اور راہی اپنی رہ لے گا

267

On my return from Dhaka

Will we who remain strangers after all kindnesses are over
Become familiar after all these meetings are over?

How many seasons of rain will have to fall over
Scarred leaves before their greenness comes unbloodied
to mind?

The instant when pain of love ceased brought only
numbness.
Mornings are merciless after the merciful nights are over.

How I wanted, but how my fractured heart did not allow,
Flirtatious complaints after the supplications were over.

And what you came so willing to give up all for, Faiz,
Was utterly unvoiced when all the talking was over.

Translation by Andrew McCord

ڈھاکہ سے واپسی پر

ہم کے ٹھہرے اجنبی اتنی ملاقاتوں کے بعد

پھر بنیں گے آشنا کتنی مداراتوں کے بعد

کب نظر میں آئے گی بے داغ سبزے کی بہار

خون کے دھبے دھلیں گے کتنی برساتوں کے بعد

تھے بہت بے درد لمحے ختمِ دردِ عشق کے

تھیں بہت بے درد صبحیں مہرباں راتوں کے بعد

دل تو چاہا پر شکستِ دل نے مہلت ہی نہ دی

کچھ گلے شکوے بھی کر لیتے مناجاتوں کے بعد

اُن سے جو کہنے گئے تھے فیض جاں صدقہ کئے

ان کہی ہی رہ گئی وہ بات سب باتوں کے بعد

269

The day death comes

How will it be, the day death comes?
Perhaps like the gift at the beginning of night,
the first kiss on the lips given unasked,
the kiss that opens the way to brilliant worlds
while, in the distance, an April of nameless flowers
agitates the moon's heart.

Perhaps in this way: when the morning,
green with unopened buds, begins to shimmer
in the bedroom of the beloved,
and the tinkle of stars as they rush to depart
can be heard on the silent windows.

What will it be like, the day death comes?
Perhaps like a vein screaming
with the premonition of pain
under the edge of a knife, while a shadow,
the assassin holding the knife,
spreads out with a wingspan
from one end of the world to the other.

No matter when death comes, or how,
even though in the guise of the disdainful beloved
who is always cold,
there will be the same words of farewell to the heart:
"thank God it is finished, the night of the broken-hearted.
Praise be to the meeting of lips,
the honeyed lips I have known."

Translation by Naomi Lazard

جس روز قضا آئے گی

کس طرح آئے گی جس روز قضا آئے گی
شاید اس طرح کہ جس طور کبھی اوّلِ شب
بے طلب پہلے پہل مرحمتِ بوسۂ لب
جس سے کھلنے لگیں ہر سمت طلسمات کے در
اور کہیں دور سے انجان گلابوں کی بہار
یک بیک سینۂ مہتاب کو تڑپانے لگے

شاید اس طرح کی جس طور کبھی آخرِ شب
نیم وا کلیوں سے سرسبز سحر
یک بیک ہجرہِ محبوب میں لہرانے لگے
اور خاموش دریچوں سے یہ ہنگامِ رحیل
جھنجھناتے ہوئے تاروں کی صدا آنے لگے

کس طرح آئے گی جس روز قضا آئے گی
شاید اس طرح کہ جس طور یہ نوکِ سناں
کوئی رگ واہمۂ درد سے چلانے لگے
اور قزاقِ سناں دست کا دھندلا سایہ
از کراں تا بہ کراں دہر پہ منڈلانے لگے

جس طرح آئے گی جس روز قضا آئے گی
خواہ قاتل کی طرح آئے کہ محبوب کی صفت
دل سے بس ہو گی یہی حرفِ ودع کی صورت
للّٰہ الحمد بانجامِ دلِ دل زدگاں
کلمۂ شکر بنامِ لبِ شیریں دہناں

271

O' True God

O' true God! You had decreed:
"My Man! You are the King if this world,
My bounties are now your riches,
You are my deputy and viceroy."

After sending me away on this pretence,
Have you ever asked?
"How have you endured life, my Man?"
Have you ever enquired, O' My Lord!
How this world has treated your viceroy?

On the one hand there is intimidation by the police,
On the other there is persecution by the stewards.
This skeleton of mine carries a heart which trembles,
The way a sparrow flutters when caught in a trap.

What a King have you made? O' My Lord!
A chain of sufferings, not a moment's peace for him.

I do not wish any kingship, O' My Creator!
A bit of dignity shall suffice for me.
These palaces and mansions are not my choice,
A corner in life's fabric is all what I ask.

If you listen to me, then I will listen to you,
I swear in you name: "I shall never go astray."
But if this demand of mine is not met by you,
Then I must also search, and find a new God.

Translation by Sain Sucha

272

ربّا سچّیا

ربّا سچّیا توں تے آکھیا سی
جا اوئے بندیا جگ دا شاہ ہیں توُں
ساڈیاں نعمتاں تیریاں دولتاں نیں
ساڈا نیب تے عالیجا ایں توُں
ایس لارے تے ٹور کد پُچھیا ای
کہ ایس نمانے تے بیتیاں نیں
کدی سار وی لئی اُو ربّ سائیاں
تیرے شاہ نال جگ کیہ کیتیاں نیں
کِتّے دھونس پولیس سرکار دی اے
کِتّے دھاندلی مال پٹوار دی اے
اینویں ہڈّاں وچ کلپے جان میری
جیویں پھاہی چ کونج کرلاوندی اے
چنگا شاہ بنایا ہی ربّ سائیاں
پولے کھاندیاں وار نہ آوندی اے

مینوں شاہی نئیں چاہیدی ربّ میرے
میں تے عزت دا ٹکر منگناں ہاں
مینوں تاہنگ نئیں محلاں ماہڑیاں دی
میں تے جیویں دی نگر منگناں ہاں
میری منہ تے تیریاں میں منّاں
تیری سونہہ جے اک وی گل موڑاں
جے اے مانگ نئیں پُجدی تیں ربّا
فیر میں جاواں تے ہور کوئی ربّ لوڑاں

A letter from prison

Translation from the Turkish poet Nazim Hikmet

My love let me share
this most delicate matter with you:
a man is altered by a new home.

Here I've begun to fall in love with my dreams:
for at night when sleep,
with her warm, compassionate hands, open the gate,
the prison walls collapse at my feet.
At that moment I'm drowned in my dream
the way a ray falls into still waters.
I walk out and roam free,
filled with relentless joy –
how freely I roam
in wide, lit up places
where no word id found for sorrow and pain,
no word for prison.

"Then how crushing it will be
for you to wake up?"

No, that isn't so – my love!
Let me tell you one more thing:
with sheer strength, with stubborn will,
I bestow only those dreams on my sleep
that has already claimed,
the ones that are its necessary share.

Translation by Agha Shahid Ali

274

مری جاں تجھ کو بتلاؤں، بہت نازک یہ نکتہ ہے

بدل جاتا ہے انساں جب مکاں اس کا بدلتا ہے!

مجھے زنداں میں پیار آنے لگا ہے اپنے خوابوں پر

جو شب کو نیند اپنے مہرباں ہاتھوں سے

وا کرتی ہے در اس کا

تو آ گرتی ہے ہر دیوار اس کی میرے قدموں پر

میں ایسے غرق ہو جاتا ہوں اس دم اپنے خوابوں میں

کہ جیسے اک کرن ٹھہرے ہوئے پانی پہ گرتی ہے

میں ان لمحوں میں کتنا سرخوش و دلشاد پھرتا ہوں

جہاں کی جگمگاتی وسعتوں میں کس قدر آزاد پھرتا ہوں

جہاں درد و الم کا نام ہے کوئی نہ زنداں ہے

''تو پھر بیدار ہونا کس قدر تم پر گراں ہوگا؟''

نہیں ایسا نہیں ہے میری جاں! میرا یہ قصہ ہے

میں اپنے عزم و ہمت سے

وہی کچھ بخشتا ہوں نیند کو جو اُس کا حصہ ہے

275

Do what you have to do

Why talk now
of the day
when the heart
will be broken
into pieces
and all sorrows
will be wiped out.
What has been found
will be lost
and what has not
been attained
willl be attained.

This is really
the first day of love
for which
we have always yearned
and of which
we were always afraid.
This day has been
hundreds of times.
planted and then uprooted –
plundered and the recompensed.

Why worry now
about that day
when the heart
will be broken
into pieces
and all sorrows
will be wiped out.
Throw away
on the rubbish heap
of oblivion
all our doubts
and fears.
If there is laughter
we will laugh.
If there is weeping
we will weep.
Do what you
have to do
and let the future
take care
of itself.

Translation by Daud Kamal

تم اپنی کرنی کر گزرو

اب کیوں اُس دن کا ذکر کرو
جب دل ٹکڑے ہو جائے گا
اور سارے غم مٹ جائیں گے
جو کچھ پایا کھو جائے گا
جو مل نہ سکا وہ پائیں گے
یہ دن تو وہی پہلا دن ہے
جو پہلا دن تھا چاہت کا
ہم جس کی تمنا کرتے رہے
اور جس سے ہر دم ڈرتے رہے
یہ دن تو کتنی بار آیا
سو بات بسے اور اُجڑ گئے
سو بار لٹے اور بھر پایا

اب کیوں اس دن کی فکر کرو
جب دل ٹکڑے ہو جائے گا
اور سارے غم مٹ جائیں گے
تم خوف و خطر سے درگزرو
جو ہونا ہے سو ہونا ہے
گر ہنسنا ہے تو ہنسنا ہے
گر رونا ہے تو رونا ہے
تم اپنی کرنی کر گزرو
جو ہوگا دیکھا جائے گا

277

If my suffering found a tongue

My suffering is a song unsung
My soul a speck without a seal
If my surfing found a tongue
My name and sign it would reveal
If of my soul I found the sign
I would perceive the world's design
If this secret were in my reach
My silence would acquire speech
Sway over all created things
And the empire of both worlds be mine.

مرے درد کو جو زباں ملے

مرا درد نغمۂ بے صدا
مری ذات ذرۂ بے نشاں
مرے درد کو جو زباں ملے
مجھے اپنا نام و نشاں ملے
مری ذات کا جو نشاں ملے
مجھے راز نظم جہاں ملے
جو مجھے یہ راز نہاں ملے
مری خامشی کو بیاں ملے
مجھے کائنات کی سروری
مجھے دولت دو جہاں ملے

Sajjad Zaheer, an elegy

Never again will we walk through rose-strewn gardens,
Nor step out to meet the executioner,
Nor confide in each our encounters with the fair ones,
Nor write our tales of lost loves with the blood of our
hearts,
Nor court the muse as we used to love,
Nor shed tears over our melancholy homeland.

Never again will we hear the rattling of our chains,
Nor clink our glasses as the night goes by,
Drinking to beloveds of passing delicacy,
Or in memory of doe-eyed sweethearts.
Never will we drink to the friends we had,
Nor recall our days in prison.

The breeze whispers as it blows,
The morning breaks and smiles,
Up there in space there is a light,
Which is where the great tavern-keeper sits,
So let the morning be dedicated to him, O cup-bearer!
Our drinking day is now done,
Take it all away,
Snuff out the candles,
Let's down just one last drink
And smash our goblets thereafter.

Translation by Khalid Hasan

سجاد ظہیر کے نام

نہ اب ہم ساتھ سیرِ گل کریں گے
نہ اب مل کر سرِ مقتل چلیں گے
حدیثِ دلبراں باہم کریں گے
نہ خونِ دل سے شرحِ غم کریں گے
نہ لیلائے سخن کی دوست داری
نہ غم ہائے وطن پر اشکباری
سنیں گے نغمۂ زنجیر مل کر
نہ شب بھر مل کے چھلکائیں گے ساغر

بنامِ شاہدِ نازک خیالاں
بیادِ مستیِ چشمِ غزالاں
بنامِ انبساطِ بزمِ رنداں
بیادِ کلفتِ ایّامِ زنداں

☆

صبا اور اس کا اندازِ تکلم
سحر اور اس کا آغازِ تبسم
فضا میں ایک ہالہ سا جہاں ہے
یہی تو مسندِ پیرِ مغاں ہے
سحر گہ اب اسی کے نام ساقی
کریں اِتمامِ دورِ جام ساقی
بساطِ بادہ و مینا اُٹھا لو
بڑھا دو شمعِ محفل بزم والو
پیو اب ایک جامِ الوداعی
پیو اور پی کے ساغر توڑ ڈالو

281

The Leningrad cemetery

On cold granite slabs
A sprinkling of flowers
Reminiscent of blood.
There are no names
On the headstones
But every petal is engraved
With its own parable.

The young heroes sleep
Transfigured to the roots
Of their hair.
Only Mother is awake –
Massive, with her rosary of stars.
The sky bows down with her.
She is the sky.

Translation by Daud Kamal

لینن گراڈ کا گورستان

سرد سلوں پر

زرد سلوں پر

تازہ گرم لہو کی صورت

گلدستوں کے چھینٹے ہیں

کتبے سب بے نام ہیں لیکن

غافل سونے والے کا

یاد میں رونے والے کا

اپنے فرض سے فارغ ہو کر

اپنے لہو کی تان کے چادر

سارے بیٹے خواب میں ہیں

اپنے غموں کا ہار پرو کر

اماں اکیلی جاگ رہی ہے

283

Love song

I look around, I look everywhere,
but I do not see you.
O you who've gone to another land,
birds of the air I ask you to carry my word to you,
good luck charms I lay out;
I beg the wandering wind;
then I think of you and my eyes go wet.
When I talk about you, I burst out laughing
but no more where I look
O my gone away Beloved.

My pain I keep it to myself,
my secret I share with no one,
I feel as I am dying a slow death.
Who can I show my stricken heart to?
From whom can I I beg a favour?
who can I call upon for help
O beloved who's gone to another land?

I wait through the evening,
I wait when the morning breaks,
I can wait my entire life, if you say so.
Every home in the neighbourhood is bright with lights,
but my light is fading.
O God! I alone am forlorn,
the world passes me by,
I look around and I do not see you,
I do not see you,
O my gone away beloved!

Translation by Khalid Hasan

گیت

کدھرے نہ پینڈیاں دساں
وے پردیسیا تیریاں
کاگ اُڈاواں ، شگن مناواں
وگدی وا دے ترلے پاواں
تیری یاد پوے تے رووِاں
تیرا ذِکر کراں تاں ہساں
وے پردیسیا تیریاں

درد نہ دساں گھلدی جاواں
راز نہ کھولاں مکلدی جاواں
کِس نوں دل دے داغ وکھاواں
کِس دے اگے جھولی ڈاہواں
وے میں کِس دا دامن کھساں
کدھرے نہ پینڈیاں دساں
وے پردیسا تیریاں

شام اُڈیکاں ، فجر اُڈیکاں
آکھیں تے ساری عمر اُڈیکاں
آہنڈ گوانڈی دیوے بلدے
ربّا ساڈا چانن گھلدے
جگ وسدائے میں وی وساں
کدھرے نہ پینڈیاں دساں
کدھرے نہ پینڈیاں دساں
وے پردیسا تیریاں

When spring came

With the arrival of spring,
Returned, also, from oblivion,
All those dreams, and youthful memories,
Which had died for your lips,
They had died, but were born again.

And all those roses have opened,
Witch are infused with the scent of your memory,
Imbrued with the blood of your lovers.

And all those torments have returned too –
Regrets and sufferings of the friends,
The drunkenness induced by the embrace of nymphs,
The pain recalled by the mind;
Your and mine.
And all the queries, the replies too,
With the arrival of spring have opened,
Once again all the accounts anew.

Translation by Sain Sucha

بہار آئی

بہار آئی تو جیسے یکبار

لوٹ آئے ہیں پھر عدم سے

وہ خواب سارے ، شباب سارے

جو تیرے ہونٹوں پہ مر مٹے تھے

جو مِٹ کے ہر بار پھر جیئے تھے

نِکھر گئے ہیں گلاب سارے

جو تیری یادوں سے مُشکبو ہیں

جو تیرے عشاق کا لہُو ہیں

اُبل پڑے ہیں عذاب سارے

ملالِ احوالِ دوستاں بھی

خُمارِ آغوشِ مہ وشاں بھی

غُبارِ خاطر کے باب سارے

ترے ہمارے

سوال سارے جواب سارے

بہار آئی تو کِھل گئے ہیں

نئے سرے سے حساب سارے

287

Wash the blood from your feet

Where should we go and what should we do
When every road is scattered
With the thorns of our fallen loves?
When the friendships of centuries
Have broken, one by one?
Whatever path we take, whatever direction we choose
Our feet come away bathed in blood.
And the onlookers say:
What is this ritual you have devised?
Why have you tattooed yourself with these wounds?
Who are you to question
The barrenness of faith?
Wash the blood from your feet.
When the night has passed
A hundred new roads will blossom.
You must steady your heart,
For it has to break many, many times.

Translation by Agha Shahid Ali

پاؤں سے لہُو کو دھو ڈالو

ہم کیا کرتے کس رہ چلتے

ہر راہ میں کانٹے بکھرے تھے

ان رشتوں کی جو چھوٹ گئے

ان صدیوں کے یارانوں کے

جو اک اک کرکے ٹوٹ گئے

جس راہ چلے ، جس سمت گئے

یوں پاؤں لہُو لہان ہوئے

سب دیکھنے والے کہتے تھے

یہ کیسی ریت رچائی ہے

یہ مہندی کیوں لگائی ہے

وہ کہتے تھے کیوں قطرۂ وفا

کا ناحق چرچا کرتے ہو

پاؤں سے لہُو کو دھو ڈالو

یہ راہیں جب اٹ جائیں گی

سو رستے ان سے پھوٹیں گے

تم دل کو سنبھالو جس میں ابھی

سو طرح کے نشتر ٹوٹیں گے

289

Evening, be gracious

O evening, be gracious –
O evening of the city of friends
be gracious to me.
The hellish noon of oppression,
senseless cruelties,
the noon of pain, rage and sorrow,
inarticulate pain, rage and sorrow,
the whiplashes of this demonic noon –
are all, like the rainbow, branded on my body
arc within arc.

All the wounds have come alive again
when even the scars had vanished.
Surely, there must be something
in your sack – a shawl
to cover up that part of the body
where the pain is most intense.
O evening, be gracious –
O evening of the city of friends,
be gracious to me.

The infernal wilderness of scorn,
callous scorn –
splinters of jealous eyes –
the litter of estrangements.
Such dreary highways
So many crowed abattoirs,
through which we have passed,
like blisters at every step.
This is how our feet have been bruised,
pathways have shrunken.
Spread out today your velvety clouds
under our feet;
be the alleviator of suffering wayfarers.

O evening, be gracious
O moon of the night of love,
O consoler of agonised hearts
commune with us this evening.
O evening, be gracious;
O evening of the city of friends,
be gracious to us.

Translation by Shiv K. Kumar

290

اے شام مہرباں ہو!

اے شام مہرباں ہو

اے شامِ شہریاراں

ہم پہ مہرباں ہو

دوزخی دوپہر ستم کی

بے سبب ستم کی

دوپہر درد و غیظ و غم کی

اس دوزخی دوپہر کے تازیانے

آج تن پر دھنک کی صورت

قوس در قوس بٹ گئے ہیں

زخم سب کھل گئے ہیں

داغ جانا تھا چھٹ گئے ہیں

تیرے توشے میں کچھ تو ہو گا

مرہمِ درد کا دوشالہ

تن کے اُس انگ پر اُڑھا دے

درد سب سے سوا جہاں ہو

اے شام مہرباں ہو

اے شامِ شہریاراں

ہم پہ مہرباں ہو

دوزخی دشت نفرتوں کے

بے درد نفرتوں کے

کرچیاں دیدۂ حسد کی

خس و خاشاک رنجشوں کے

اتنی سنسان شاہراہیں

اتنی گنجان قتل گاہیں

جن سے آئے ہم گزر کر

آبلہ بن کے ہر قدم پر

یوں پاؤں کٹ گئے ہیں

رستے سمٹ گئے ہیں

مخملیں اپنے بادلوں کی

آج پاؤں تلے بچھا دے

شفانیِ کربِ رہرواں ہو

اے شام مہرباں ہو

اے مہِ شب نگاراں

اے رفیقِ دلفگاراں

اس شام ہمزباں ہو

اے شام مہرباں ہو

اے شام مہرباں ہو

اے شامِ شہریاراں

ہم پہ مہرباں ہو

291

I search again for a word today

(1)
I search again for a word today
a soulful word, a hurtful word
a gentle word, an angry word
A word of love like a lover's glance
which meets me like a kiss,
so bright like a golden waves
like the advent of spring
upon a gathering of friends
A word of hatred, like an awesome sword
which destroys forever the tyrant's city,
so dark a word like blackest night
so black that when I speak it
my lips are blackened.

(2)
Every melody, every note dislocated
the singer's voice searches her being;
like the rent garment of Majnoon*
every string is broken with this pain.
The people beg the breeze to bring
some song, some voices
even an elegy would do
even a sad song would do
even the sound of judgement day
even the scream that heralds
the world's destruction.

*Majnoon literally means 'possessed' or 'mad' and refers to the powerful
Arabic story of Qais's love for Leila. Qais was obsessed to the point of
madness and sacrificed everything for his love. In both Persian and Urdu
poetry, the tale exalts the power and moral value of love.

Translation by Mahmood Jamal

آج اک حرف کو پھر ڈھونڈتا پھرتا ہے خیال

(۱)

آج اک حرف کو پھر ڈھونڈتا پھرتا ہے خیال

مدھ بھرا حرف کوئی ، زہر بھرا حرف کوئی

دل نشیں حرف کوئی ، قہر بھرا حرف کوئی

حرفِ اُلفت کوئی دلدارِ نظر ہو جیسے

جس سے ملتی ہے نظر بوسۂ لب کی صورت

اتنا روشن کہ سرِ موجۂ زر ہو جیسے

صحبتِ یار میں آغازِ طرب کی صورت

حرفِ نفرت کوئی شمشیرِ غضب ہو جیسے

تا ابد شہرِ ستم جس سے تبہ ہو جائیں

اتنا تاریک کہ شمشان کی شب ہو جیسے

لب پہ لاؤں تو مرے ہونٹ سیہ ہو جائیں

(۲)

آج ہر سُر سے ہر اک راگ کا ناتا ٹوٹا

ڈھونڈتی پھرتی ہے مطرب کو پر اس کی آواز

جوششِ درد سے مجنوں کے گریبان کی طرح

چاک در چاک ہوا آج ہر اک پردۂ ساز

آج ہر موجِ ہوا سے ہے سوالی خلقت

لا کوئی نغمہ ، کوئی صوت ، تری عمر دراز

نوحۂ غم ہی سہی ، شورِ شہادت ہی سہی

صورِ محشر ہی سہی ، بانگِ قیامت ہی سہی

Those people

Blessed were those that found work their true love
Those who spent their years courting careers
My life has been spent in but a hectic frenzy
torn between love and work, work and love
Work before love, love between work
Knarled together, knots for me to untie
Until one day at last I tired of both,
And walked away to leave them hanging

Translation by Kavita Khanna

کچھ عشق کیا، کچھ کام کیا

وہ لوگ بہت خوش قسمت تھے
جو عشق کو کام سمجھتے تھے
یا کام سے عاشقی کرتے تھے
ہم جیتے جی مصروف رہے
کچھ عشق کیا، کچھ کام کیا
کام عشق کے آڑے آتا رہا
اور عشق سے کام الجھتا رہا
پھر آخر تنگ آ کر ہم نے
دونوں کو ادھورا چھوڑ دیا

295

Prayer

Let us raise our hands in supplication,
we who do not remember the practice of prayer;

we who do not remember any idol, any god,
other than the burning passion of love.

Let us beseech that the beauty of the world
might substitute tomorrow's sweetness for
malevolent today.

Make light trials of those who carry their burdensome load.
Illuminate their night with lustrous shine,

whose eyes will face unfriendly dawn.
Bestow their footsteps with direction,

who lack strength to find the way.
Fit them with boldness to defy,

and courage to enquire;
who follow the religion of hypocrisy, and lies.

Give them, over whose heads hangs injustice's sword,
nerves to stay the assassin's hand.

May the mystery of the love which burns in the soul
stand declared; that its grief may be effaced.

May the word of truth
which anguishes the heart like a thorn,
be proclaimed;
and its torment forever be erased.

Translation by Estelle Dryland

دعا

آیئے ہاتھ اٹھائیں ہم بھی
ہم جنہیں رسمِ دعا یاد نہیں
ہم جنہیں سوزِ محبت کے سوا
کوئی بت ، کوئی خدا یاد نہیں

آیئے عرض گزاریں کہ نگارِ ہستی
زہرِ امروز میں شیرینیِ فردا بھر دے
وہ جنہیں تابِ گرانباریِ ایام نہیں
ان کی پلکوں پہ شب و روز کو ہلکا کر دے

جن کی آنکھوں کو رخِ صبح کا یارا بھی نہیں
ان کی راتوں میں کوئی شمع منور کر دے
جن کے قدموں کو کسی رہ کا سہارا بھی نہیں
ان کی نظروں میں کوئی راہ اجاگر کر دے

جن کا دیں پیرویِ کذب و ریا ہے ان کو
ہمتِ کفر ملے ، جراتِ تحقیق ملے
جن کے سر منتظرِ تیغِ جفا ہیں ان کو
دستِ قاتل کو جھٹک دینے کی توفیق ملے

عشق کا سرِ نہاں جان تپاں ہے جس سے
آج اقرار کریں اور تپش مٹ جائے
حرفِ حق دل میں کھٹکتا ہے جو کانٹے کی طرح
آج اظہار کریں اور خلش مٹ جائے

297

Lament for a soldier

Rise now from the dust
My darling young one. Wake.
Wake now. Wake now.
We've your life's bed to make.

Look how the dark night
Comes wrapped in a long blue shawl
Where these crying eyes
Have heaped up pearls—
So many pearls whose light
Casts on your wedding rite
A shimmering tonight
To brighten your name.

Rise now from the ground
My darling young one. Wake.
Wake now. Wake now
While in every house is gold new dawn
But at ours a pitch-dark yard.

Wanton, heroic, how long
Has your young bride to wait
Knowing your time is come?
Look, there is work to be done.
The enemy lords over the throne
And you lie in the dust, young one.
Rise from the ground. Wake.
Don't leave. Rise from the dust.
Wake, my darling young one.

Translation by Andrew McCord

سپاہی کا مرثیہ

اُٹھو اب ماٹی سے اُٹھو

جاگو میرے لال،

اب جاگو میرے لال

تمری تیج سجاون کارن

دیکھ وآئی رین اندھیارن

نیلے شال دوشالے لے کر

جن میں ان دُکھین اکھین نے

ڈھیر کئے ہیں اتنے موتی

اتنے موتی جن کی جیوتی

دان سے تمرا

جگ جگ لاگا

نام چمکنے

اٹھو اب ماٹی سے اٹھو

جاگو میرے لال

اب جاگو میرے لال

گھر گھر بکھرا بھورا کا کندن

گھور اندھیرا اپنا آنگن

جانے کب سے راہ تکے ہیں

بالی دلہنیا، بانکے ویرن

سونا تمرا راج پڑا ہے

دیکھو کتنا کاج پڑا ہے

بیری براجے راج سنگھاسن

تم ماٹی میں لال

اٹھو اب ماٹی سے اٹھو، جاگو میرے لال

ہٹ نہ کرو ماٹی سے اٹھو، جاگو میرے لال

اب جاگو میرے لال

299

Black out

Written during the India-Pakistan war of 1965

Even since the light failed,
I have been searching to see how I could see.
Where my eyes strayed in the dust?

You who know, give me proof.
Describe me to myself.

A bitter river rages in my vein.
And my heart, still longing for you,
flows on its poisonous waves.

Wait a little: perhaps from some other world
the hand of a prophet, carved in lighting,
is bringing me pearls for my lost eyes.

Wait till the river is stilled
And my submerged heart, annulled like a Sufi's,
Is washed up, cleansed, on a welcoming shore.

I will then begin a new translation of hope.
I will complete the texts of love.

Translation by Agha Shahid Ali

بلیک آؤٹ

جب سے بے نور ہوئی ہیں شمعیں

خاک میں ڈھونڈتا پھرتا ہوں نہ جانے کس کو

کھو گئی ہیں مری دونوں آنکھیں

تم جو واقف ہو بتاؤ کوئی پہچان مری

اس طرح ہے کہ ہر اک رگ میں اتر آیا ہے

موج در موج کسی زہر کا قاتل دریا

تیرا ارمان، تری یاد لئے جان مری

جانے کس موج میں غلطاں ہے کہاں دل میرا

ایک پل ٹھہرو کہ اس پار کسی دنیا سے

برق آئے مری جانب، یدِ بیضا لے کر

اور میری آنکھوں کے گم گشتہ گہر

جام ظلمت سے سیہ مست

نئی آنکھوں کے شب تاب گہر لوٹا دے

ایک پل ٹھہرو کہ دریا کا کہیں پاٹ لگے

اور نیا دل میرا

زہر میں دھل کے، فنا ہو کے کسی گھاٹ لگے

پھر چلے نظر نئے دیدہ و دل لے کے چلوں

حسن کی مدح کروں، شوق کا مضمون لکھوں

The heart gives up

Such was its pain that night·
the heart wanted to grip the veins
till the pore would open and its blood rush out.
It was as if somewhere far off,
as if in your courtyard,
each leaf, rinsed in my aching blood,
had wearied of the moon's lustre,
such beauty no longer sufferable.
Such was the heart's pain:
that the body seemed a desert
and the veins, those torn ropes, loosened,
were giving notice that life's caravan,
its cargo empting, was about to depart.
And when memory, for a moment, was a brief candle,
lighting up the consolation that you are,
it wasn't enough.
Something told me, "Linger, don't leave,"
but the heart didn't waver, it didn't wish to stay.

Translation by Agha Shahid Ali

302

ہارٹ اٹیک

درد اتنا تھا کہ اُس رات دلِ وحشی نے

ہر رگِ جاں سے الجھنا چاہا

ہر بُنِ مو سے ٹپکنا چاہا

اور کہیں دور ترے صحن میں گویا

پتّا پتّا مرے افسردہ لہو میں ڈھل کر

حسنِ مہتاب سے آزردہ نظر آنے لگا

میرے ویرانۂ تن میں گویا

سارے دکھتے ہوئے ریشوں کی طنابیں کھل کر

سلسلہ وار پتا دینے لگیں

رخصتِ فاصلۂ شوق کی تیاری کا

اور جب یاد کی بجھتی ہوئی شمعوں میں نظر آیا کہیں

ایک پل آخری لمحہ تری دلداری کا

درد اتنا تھا کہ اس سے بھی گزرنا چاہا

ہم نے چاہا بھی، مگر دل نہ ٹھہرنا چاہا

303

No trace of blood

Nowhere, there is any trace of blood!

Neither on the hands and nails of the slayer,
Nor any sign on the sleeve.
No redness in the dagger's edge,
Now any colour on the spear's head,
No stain in the earth's breast,
Or any smear on the ceiling.

Nowhere, there is any trace of blood!

It was
Not spent in service of kings,
To gin some bounty;
Nor offered in a religious rite,
To obtain absolution;
Nor spilled on the battlefield,
To attain fame – as inscription on a banner.

It cried for attention –
That unprotected, helpless blood.
Yet, none had time or the will –
To listen to that blood.
No accuser or any witness –
Just a "clean sheet".
That blood from the figures of clay –
The Earth consumed it.

Translation by Sain Sucha

لہو کا سراغ

کہیں نہیں ہے کہیں بھی نہیں لہو کا سراغ

نہ دستِ ناخنِ قاتل نہ آستیں پہ نشاں

نہ سرخیِ لبِ خنجر نہ رنگِ نوکِ سناں

نہ خاک پر کوئی دھبا نہ بام پر کوئی داغ

کہیں نہیں ہے کہیں بھی نہیں لہو کا سراغ

نہ صرفِ خدمتِ شاہاں کہ خوں بہا دیتے

نہ دیں کی نظر کہ بیعانہٴ جزا دیتے

نہ رزم گاہ میں برسا کہ معتبر ہوتا

کسی علم پہ رقم ہو کے مشتہر ہوتا

پکارتا رہا ، بے آسرا ، یتیم لہو

کسی کو بہرِ سماعت نہ وقت تھا نہ دماغ

نہ مدعی ، نہ شہادت ، حساب پاک ہوا

یہ خونِ خاک نشیناں تھا ، رزقِ خاک ہوا

305

Look at the town from here

If you
Look at the town from here:

In concentric circles
– like a jail –
There are walls all around.
Every path – some prisoner's footmarks;
But,
No milestone, destination,
Or a well-wisher's stand.

If someone moves too quickly,
Then one wonders:
Why has there not been
A warning shout to stop?
And,
If someone raises his hand,
Then one ponders:
Why no jingles been heard
From his manacled arms?

Look at the town from here:

In all that crowd –
No person with dignity.
No being with reason.
Every proud man
 – enchained as a criminal.
Every pretty maiden
 – proclaimed a slave.

Those shadows far away,
Dancing around the lamps!
It is hard to see from here
– an assembly of mourners,
        or a bunch of revellers?
Those colourful images,
Scattered on the walls!
One cannot tell from here
– are they blooming flowers,
  or someone's blood smears?

Translation by Sain Sucha

306

یہاں سے شہر کو دیکھو

یہاں سے شہر کو دیکھو تو حلقہ در حلقہ
کھنچی ہے جیل کی صورت ہر ایک سمت فصیل
ہر ایک راہ گزر گردشِ اسیراں ہے
نہ سنگِ میل، نہ منزل، نہ مخلصی کی سبیل

جو کوئی تیز چلے رہ تو پوچھتا ہے خیال
کہ ٹوکنے کوئی للکار کیوں نہیں آئی
جو کوئی ہاتھ ہلائے تو وہم کو ہے سوال
کوئی چھنک، کوئی جھنکار کیوں نہیں آئی؟

یہاں سے شہر کو دیکھو تو ساری خلقت میں
نہ کوئی صاحبِ تمکیں، نہ کوئی والی ہوش
ہر ایک مردِ جواں مجرمِ رسن بہ گلو
ہر اک حسینۂ رعنا، کنیز حلقہ بگوش

جو سائے دور چراغاں کے گرد لرزاں ہیں
نہ جانے محفلِ غم ہے کہ بزمِ جام و سبو
جو رنگ ہر در و دیوار پر پریشاں ہیں
یہاں سے کچھ نہیں کھلتا یہ پھول ہیں کہ لہو

307

Let me think

Let me think, just awhile –
in this garden
which at this moment is not even a wilderness,
on which bough sprouted the primal flowers
and which flower first blanched
with grief and fatigue?
And before this –
at which moment, and during which season
were we struck with the drought of blood
and the flower's jugular vein smarted
under time's harshness –
let me think.

Let me think a little.
This teeming city, now not even a desolate valley –
here, when and where
did the first fire break out;
in which one of its arrayed windows
was first born the arc of blood-drenched flames
and where did the first light flash –
let me think.

You ask me the whereabouts of that country
whose history and geography now elude my memory
and, if at all recalled somehow,
it's like a beloved of the past
encountering whom, face to face,
the heart feels unnerved.

but yes, as if someone
just to cheer up his lover,
shows up some time to spend the night.

I have now reached that point
when even if I go over to meet my beloved
it will be just for ritual's sake.

What's there to ask of my heart? –
let me think!

Translation by Shiv K. Kumar

سوچنے دو

اک ذرا سوچنے دو
اس خیاباں میں
جو اس لحظہ بیاباں بھی نہیں
کون سی شاخ میں پھول آئے تھے سب سے پہلے
کون بے رنگ ہوئی رنگ و تب سے پہلے
اور اب سے پہلے
کس گھڑی کونسے موسم میں یہاں
خون کا قحط پڑا
گل کی شہ رگ پہ کڑا
وقت پڑا
سوچنے دو

اک ذرا سوچنے دو
یہ بھرا شہر جو اب وادیِ ویراں بھی نہیں
اس میں کس وقت کہاں
آگ لگی تھی پہلے
اس کے صف بستہ دریچوں میں سے کس میں اول
زہ ہوئی سرخ شعاعوں کی کمال
کس جگہ جوت جگی تھی پہلے
سوچنے دو

ہم سے اس دیس کا تم نام و نشاں پوچھتے ہو
جس کی تاریخ نہ جغرافیہ اب یاد آئے
اور یاد آئے تو محبوبِ گزشتہ کی طرح
رو برو آنے سے جی گھبرائے
ہاں مگر جیسے کوئی
ایسے محبوب یا محبوبہ کا دل رکھنے کو
آنکلتا ہے کبھی رات بتانے کے لئے
ہم اب اس عمر کو آپہنچے ہیں جب بھی ہم یونہی
دل سے مل آتے ہیں بس رسم نبھانے کے لئے
دل کی کیا پوچھتے ہو
سوچنے دو

Stay away from me (Bangladesh I)

How can I embellish this carnival of slaughter,
    how to decorate this massacre?
Whose attention could my lamenting blood attract?
There's almost no blood in my rawboned body
and what's left
isn't enough to burn as oil in the lamp,
not enough to fill a wineglass.
It can feed no fire,
extinguish no thirst.
There's a poverty of blood in my ravaged body—
a terrible poison now runs in it.
If you pierce my veins, each drop will foam
    as venom at the cobra's fangs.
Each drop is the anguished longing of ages'
the burning seal of a rage hushed up for years.
Beware of me. My body is a river of poison.
Stay away from me. My body is a parched log in the desert.
If you burn it, you won't see the cypress or the jasmine,
but my bones blossoming like thorns in the cactus.
If you throw it in the forests,
instead of morning perfumes, you'll scatter
the dust of my seared soul.
So stay away from me.
Because I'm thirsting for blood.

Translation by Agha Shahid Ali

310

حذر کرو مرے تن سے

سجے تو کیسے سجے قتل عام کا میلہ
کسے لبھائے گا میرے لہو کا واویلا
مرے نزار بدن میں لہو ہی کتنا ہے
چراغ ہو کوئی روشن نہ کوئی جام بھرے
نہ اس سے آگ ہی بھڑکے نہ اس سے پیاس بجھے
مرے فگار بدن میں لہو ہی کتنا ہے
مگر وہ زہر ہلاہل بھرا ہے نس نس میں
جسے بھی چھیدو ہر اک بوند قہر اُفعی ہے
ہر اک کشید ہے صدیوں کے درد و حسرت کی
ہر اک میں مہر بلب غیظ و غم کی گرمی ہے

حذر کرو مرے تن سے یہ سم کا دریا ہے
حذر کرو کہ مرا تن وہ چوبِ صحرا ہے
جسے جلاؤ تو صحنِ چمن میں دیکھیں گے
بجائے سرو و سمن میری ہڈیوں کے ببول
اِسے بکھیرا تو دشت و دمن میں بکھرے گی
بجائے مُشکِ صبا، میری جانِ زار کی دھول
حذر کرو کہ مرا دل لہو کا پیاسا ہے

Stay away from me (Bangladesh II)

This is how my sorrow became visible:
its dust, pilling up for years in my heart,
finally reached my eyes,

the bitterness now so clear that
I had to listen when my friends
told me to wash my eyes with blood.

Everything at once was tangled in blood—
each face, each idol, red everywhere.
Blood swept over the sun, washing away its gold.

The moon erupted with blood, its silver extinguished.
The sky promised a morning of blood,
and the night wept only blood.

The trees hardened into crimson pillars.
All flowers filled their eyes with blood.
And every glance was an arrow,

each pierced image blood. This blood
--a river crying out for martyrs—
flows on its longing. And in sorrow, in rage, in love.

Let it flow. Should it be dammed up,
there will only be hatred cloaked in colors of death.
Don't let this happen, my friends,

bring all my tears back instead,
a flood to fill my dust-filled eyes,
to wash this blood forever from my eyes.

Translation by Agha Shahid Ali

312

تہ بہ تہ دل کی کدورت

تہ بہ تہ دل کی کدورت
میری آنکھوں میں اُمنڈ آئی تو کچھ چارہ نہ تھا
چارہ گر کی مان لی
اور میں نے گرد آلود آنکھوں کو لہُو سے دھو لیا
میں نے گرد آلود آنکھوں کو لہُو سے دھو لیا
اور اب ہر شکل و صورت
عالمِ موجود کی ہر شَے
میری آنکھوں کے لہُو سے اس طرح ہم رنگ ہے
خورشید کا کندن لہُو
مہتاب کی چاندی لہُو
صبحوں کا ہنسنا بھی لہُو
راتوں کا رونا بھی لہُو
ہر شجر مینارِ خوں، ہر پھول خونیں دیدہ ہے
ہر نظر اک تارِ خوں، ہر عکس خوں مالیدہ ہے
موجِ خوں جب تک رواں رہتی ہے اس کا سرخ رنگ
جذبۂ شوقِ شہادت، درد ، غیظ و غم کا رنگ
اور تھم جائے تو جلا کر
فقط نفرت کا، شب کا، موت کا،
ہر رنگ کے ماتم کا رنگ
چارہ گر ایسا نہ ہونے دے
کہیں سے لا کوئی سیلابِ اشک
آبِ وضو
جس میں دھل جائیں تو شاید دھل سکے
میری آنکھوں ، میری گرد آلود آنکھوں کا لہُو

313

Infatuation

When
It rains on the roof,
I dream of you.
It snows on the mountain,
I dream of you.
The dawn's fairy arises,
I dream of you.
The cuckoo sends her call
I dream of you.
Birds come and depart,
I dream of you.
Fragrance sweetens the garden,
I dream of you.
The dew glows like pearls,
I dream of you.
There is an illusion in this love:
You are not a woman, but someone else!
Why should I, tell me,
Always,
Just dream of you?

Translation by Sain Sucha

میں تیرے سپنے دیکھوں

برکھ برسے چھت پر ، میں تیرے سپنے دیکھوں

برف گرے پربت پر ، میں تیرے سپنے دیکھوں

صبح کی نیل پری ، میں تیرے سپنے دیکھوں

کوئل دھوم مچائے ، میں تیرے سپنے دیکھوں

آئے اور اُڑ جائے، میں تیرے سپنے دیکھوں

باغوں میں پتے مہکیں، میں تیرے سپنے دیکھوں

شبنم کے موتی دمکیں ، میں تیرے سپنے دیکھوں

اس پیار میں کوئی دھوکا ہے

تو نار نہیں کچھ اور ہے شے

ورنہ کیوں ہر ایک سے

میں تیرے سپنے دیکھوں

315

Day and night

Darkness a net, and light a spear;
day a hunter, and so Is the night.
This world is a sea in which, far from the shore,
live Adam's progeny, like the fish.
The world is a sea on whose shores stand the fishermen;
some holding net, other spears.
Who knows when my turn will come
to be hunted down by the day's spear,
or be caught in the night's net.

Translation by Shiv K. Kumar

316

تیرگی جال ہے

تیرگی جال ہے اور بھلا ہے نور
اک شکاری ہے دن، اک شکاری ہے رات
جگ سمندر ہے جس میں کنارے سے دور
مچھلیوں کی طرح ابنِ آدم کی ذات
جگ سمندر ہے ساحل پہ ہیں ماہی گیر
جال تھامے کوئی ، کوئی بھالا لئے
میری باری کب آئے گی کیا جانئے
دن کے بھالے سے مجھ کو کریں گے شکار
رات کے جال میں یا کریں گے اسیر؟

317

Do not grieve

Do not grieve
This pain will cease.
Friends will return
Wounds will heal
Do not grieve.
Do not grieve.
Day will dawn.
Night will end.
Clouds will burst.
Do not grieve.
Do not grieve.
Times will change.
Birds will sing.
Spring will come.
Do not grieve.
Do not grieve.

Translation by Daud Kamal

غم نہ کر، غم نہ کر

درد تھم جائے گا ، غم نہ کر ، غم نہ کر

یار لوٹ آئیں گے، دل ٹھہر جائے گا، غم نہ کر، غم نہ کر

زخم بھر جائے گا ، غم نہ کر ، غم نہ کر

دن نکل آئے گا ، غم نہ کر ، غم نہ کر

ابر کھل جائے گا، رات ڈھل جائے گی، غم نہ کر، غم نہ کر

رت بدل جائے گی ، غم نہ کر، غم نہ کر

319

O traveller! my heart

The decree was passed for us,
to leave this beloved land,
to cry and weep in distant lands.
Sitting in alien cities,
we search for the postman
to bring us letters from our land.
From every stranger we seek
the fate of our left over dwellings.
In this land of unknown people
we have been ordained to spend our days and nights.
O Heart! Pass this time by talking to this or that fellow.
Do not ask us the pangs and agony of
this terrible evening of sorrow.
Even this living was better Heart!
If only we were made to know for how many days more.
For us even death was not unwelcome
Should it visit once only?
O Traveller! My Heart!

Translation by A. K. Mota

دل من مسافر من

مرے دل ، مرے مسافر

ہوا پھر سے حکم صادر

کہ وطن بدر ہوں ہم تم

دیں گلی گلی صدائیں

کریں رخ نگر نگر کا

کہ سراغ کوئی پائیں

کسی یار نامہ بر کا

ہر اک اجنبی سے پوچھیں

جو پتہ تھا اپنے گھر کا

سرِ کوئے ناشنایاں ،

ہمیں دن سے رات کرنا

کبھی اِس سے بات کرنا

کبھی اُس سے بات کرنا

تمہیں کیا کہوں کہ کیا ہے

شب غم بری بلا ہے

ہمیں یہ بھی تھا غنیمت

جو کوئی شمار ہوتا ،

ہمیں کیا برا تھا مرنا

اگر ایک بار ہوتا !

321

All the flowers have wilted

All the flowers are wilted
The sky's tears will not stop;
The candles have gone dark,
The mirrors lie shattered;
No more music do instruments make,
The anklets that sang once are now asleep.

And behind those clouds,
Far far in the distance,
Twinkles a star,
The star of pain,
But it makes music,
It smiles.

Translation by Khalid Hassan

پھول مرجھا گئے ہیں سارے

پھول مرجھا گئے ہیں سارے
تھمتے نہیں ہیں آسماں کے آنسو
شمعیں بے نور ہو گئی ہیں
آئینے پُور ہو گئے ہیں
ساز سب بُج کے کھو گئے ہیں
پایلیں بُجھ کے سو گئی ہیں
اور ان بادلوں کے پیچھے
دور اس رات کا دلارا
درد کا ستارا
ٹمٹما رہا ہے
جھنجھنا رہا ہے

323

The moment to lament time's death

The blue waters – Sky – stand still.
On the horizon has anchored,
Moon's pale coloured barque.
At the shore have landed,
All the sailors – every star.

The breath of leaves is choked,
The wind has fallen into a lull,
The gong demanding silence reverberates.
Then, stillness absorbed all the voices.
From the breast of dawn's nymph,
Fell the veil of darkness.
Instead,
Dark shadows of despair and loneliness
Have covered her whole being.
Yet, she is not aware of it.
No one is any longer aware, that at dusk,
When he left the town,
In which direction he proceeded;
There was no path, nor any goal.
No traveller, now,
Feels up to the journey.
This is a broken link of duration,
From the chain called as Day & Night –
This is the moment to lament Time's death.

On such occasion, quite subconsciously,
After removing the cloak of myself,
I too, sometimes, look at –
Those spots of rebuke,
And these blooms of affection.
Lines etched by running tears,
Stains left by the bleeding heart.
This rip scratched by the enemy's claw,
This image impressed by a friend's hand.
These jewels bestowed by tender lips,
These slashes gored by some evil tongue.

Still, this cloak,
My covering for day and night,
This torn mantle,
Is what I despise; yet, love.
At times frenzy demands:
"Rip it off, throw it away."
And sometimes love whispers:
"Cherish it; hold it close to your heart."

Translation by Sain Sucha

یہ ماتمِ وقت کی گھڑی ہے

ٹھہر گئی آسمان کی ندیا

وہ جاگی ہے افق کنارے

اداس رنگوں کی چاند نیا

اُتر گئے ساحلِ زمیں پر

سبھی کھویا

تمام تارے

اُکھڑ گئی سانس پتیوں کی

چلی گئیں اونگھ میں ہوائیں

گجر بجا حکمِ خامشی کا

تو چپ میں گم ہو گئیں صدائیں

سحر کی گوری کی چھاتیوں سے

ڈھلک گئی تیرگی کی چادر

اور اس بجائے

بکھر گئے اس کے تن بدن پر

نراس تنہائیوں کے سائے

اور اس کو کچھ بھی خبر نہیں ہے

کسی کو کچھ بھی خبر نہیں ہے

کہ دن ڈھلے شہر سے نکل کر

کدھر کو جانے کا رُخ کیا تھا

نہ کوئی جادہ، نہ کوئی منزل

کسی مسافر کو

اب دماغِ سفر نہیں ہے

یہ وقت زنجیر روز و شب کی

کہیں سے ٹوٹی ہوئی کڑی ہے

یہ ماتمِ وقت کی گھڑی ہے

یہ وقت آئے تو بے ارادہ

کبھی کبھی میں بھی دیکھتا ہوں

اُتار کر ذات کا لبادہ

کہیں سیاہی ملامتوں کی

کہیں پہ گل بُوٹے اُلفتوں کے

کہیں لکیریں ہیں آنسوؤں کی

کہیں پہ خونِ جگر کے دھبے

یہ چاک ہے پنجۂ عدو کا

یہ مُہر ہے یارِ مہرباں کی

یہ لعل لب ہائے مہوشاں کے

یہ مرحمتِ شیخِ بد زباں کی

یہ جامۂ روز و شب گزیدہ

مجھے یہ پیراہنِ دریدہ

عزیز بھی، ناپسند بھی ہے

کبھی یہ فرمانِ جوشِ وحشت

کہ نوچ کر اس کو پھینک ڈالو

کبھی یہ اسرارِ حرفِ اُلفت

کہ چوم کر پھر گلے لگا لو

325

Three voices

Tyrant

Come, let us rejoice!
Today is the festival
Of the death of hope.
Humanity is buried
Once and for all.
Compassion has fled
To the dark hills.
The graveyards are full.
I have freed you
From the bondage of night and day.
The splendour of dawn
Is not for you.
Sleep will bring you no comfort/
I have subjugated
All freedom-loving eyes
With my sword.
I have strangled every aspiration.
No more will the bough bend
With flowers.
Spring will in future bring
Only of fire of Nimrod.
Never will the pearly rain fall
During the monsoons.
Clouds will henceforth be made
Of thorns and straw.
I owe allegiance to a new creed.
My laws are different.
My code is unique.
Now the pious will bow
Before abominable idols
And the tall
Kiss the feet of clay pygmies.
On earth
The doors of devotion have been close
And in heaven
The gates of benediction have been sealed.

326

تین آوازیں

ظالم

جشن ہے ماتمِ اُمید کا آؤ لوگو
مرگِ انبوہ کا تہوار مناؤ لوگو
عدم آباد کو آباد کیا ہے میں نے
تم کو دن رات سے آزاد کیا ہے میں نے
جلوۂ صبح سے کیا مانگتے ہو
بسترِ خواب سے کیا چاہتے ہو
ساری آنکھوں کو تہِ تیغ کیا ہے میں نے
سارے خوابوں کا گلا گھونٹ دیا ہے میں نے

اب نہ مہکے گی کسی شاخ پہ پھولوں کی حنا
فصلِ گل آئے گی نمرود کے انگار لئے
اب نہ برسات میں برسے گی گہر کی برکھا
ابر آئے گا خس و خار کے انبار لئے
میرا مسلک بھی نیا راہِ طریقت بھی نئی
میرے قانوں بھی نئے راہِ شریعت بھی نئی
اب فقیہانِ حرم دستِ صنم چومیں گے
سروِ قدمٹی کے بونوں کے قدم چومیں گے
فرش پر آج درِ صدق و صفا بند ہوا
عرش پر آج ہر اک بابِ دعا بند ہوا

Victim

Night is the harbinger
Of pain
And the dawning day
Its maturity.
At noon
Every vein burst with agony
And at sunset
Appears the demon of fear.
O God!
This cyclic horror of night and day.
This never-ending
Restless journey of my life.
Was this what you destined for me?
Not even an iota of happiness?
They say
That cruelty pleases you
And that injustice
Is not possible
Without your consent.
If this is true
Should I deny your benevolence?
Should I listen to them
Or should I believe in you?

Voice from the Unknown

Warm the minions of authority
To hold fast
To their book of deeds.
When the masses
Surge into the streets
Crying for vengeance
All appeals for mercy
All blubbering excuses
Will be contemptuously spurned.
Patrons and powerful friends
Will be of no use.
Reward and punishment
Will be dispensed here.
Here will be hell and paradise.
Here and now
Will be the day of judgement.

Translation by Daud Kamal

مظلوم

رات چھائی تو ہر اک درد کے دھارے چھوٹے

صبح پھوٹی تو ہر اک زخم کے ٹانکے ٹوٹے

دوپہر آئی تو ہر اک رگ نے لہُو برسایا

دن ڈھلا، خوف کا عفریت مقابل آیا

یا خدا یہ میری گردانِ شب و روز و سحر

یہ مری عمر کا بے منزل و آرام سفر

کیا یہی کچھ مری قسمت میں لکھا ہے تو نے

ہر مسرت سے مجھے عاق کیا ہے تو نے

وہ یہ کہتے ہیں تُو خوشنود ہر اک ظلم سے ہے

وہ یہ کہتے ہیں ہر اک ظلم ترے حُکم سے ہے

گر یہ سچ ہے تو ترے عدل سے انکار کروں؟

اِن کی مانوں کہ تری ذات کا اقرار کروں؟

ندائے غیب

ہر اک اولیِ الامر کو صدا دو

کہ اپنی فردِ عمل سنبھالے

اُٹھے گا جب جمعِ سرفروشاں

پڑیں گے دار و رسن کے لالے

کوئی نہ ہوگا کہ جو بچالے

جزا سزا سب یہیں پہ ہو گی

یہیں عذاب و ثواب ہو گا

یہیں سے اُٹھے گا شورِ محشر

یہیں پہ روزِ حساب ہو گا

329

What should we do?

Countless yearnings,
Petrified
In your eyes and mind –
Lacerated hearts
Writhing
In your body and mine.
Numb fingers.
Paralysed pens.
And the minds
Frost-bitten.
Entombed in every street
Of our beloved city
Your footprints and mine.
The stars of our night
Are open wounds
And our morning roses
Torn petals –
Ruptured retinas –
Buffeted by a dark wind.
All our afflictions
Are incurable.
All our gashes
Beyond repair.

Translation by Daud Kamal

کیا کریں

مری نگاہ میں

جو لاکھ انتظار ہیں

جو میرے تیرے تن بدن میں

لاکھ دل فگار ہیں

جو میری تیری انگلیوں کی بے حسی سے

سب قلم نزار ہیں

جو میرے تیرے شہر کی

ہر اک گلی میں

میرے تیرے نقشِ پا کے بے نشاں مزار ہیں

جو میری تیری رات کے

ستارے زخم زخم ہیں

جو میری تیری صبح کے

گلاب چاک چاک ہیں

یہ زخم سارے بے دوا

یہ چاک سارے بے رفو

کسی پہ راکھ چاند کی

کسی پہ اوس کا لہو

یہ ہے بھی یا نہیں، بتا

یہ ہے کہ محض جال ہے

مرے تمہارے عنکبوتِ وہم کا بُنا ہوا

جو ہے تو اس کا کیا کریں

نہیں ہے تو بھی کیا کریں

بتا ، بتا

بتا ، بتا

331

We poets

We were there – in every age, in every clime,

drinking poison, singing songs;

we kept sacrificing ourselves for life's sake –

for the moment of rapture at love's union.

We kept squandering away our treasure of spirit and matter,

holding on to our provision of deprivation and hunger.

Whatever path we chose, we stuck to it

even while the affluent kept staring at us disdainfully,

reproachfully, rubbing their palms.

On them we hurled the stone of the word of truth

whose dread kept the world reeling

And for those who'd none to shed tears over,

our eyes rained tears for their sorrows.

At the ruler's command, we went out of sight,

endured prisons, suffered flogging.

As people listened to the strained of our heart's cries,

our song kept filtering through the prison bars.

We are the blood-stained mirrors of this blood-stained
world,

we are the sorrowful heart of anguished humankind.

A poet's temper is to battle against injustice and tyranny;

we are the arbiters of good and evil, right and wrong.

Translation by Shiv K. Kumar

شاعر لوگ

ہر اک دور میں ہم ، ہر زمانے میں ہم

زہر پیتے رہے ، گیت گاتے رہے

جان دیتے رہے ، زندگی کے لئے

ساعتِ وصل کی سرخوشی کے لئے

دین و دنیا کی دولت لٹاتے رہے

فقر و فاقہ کا توشہ سنبھالے ہوئے

جو بھی رستہ چنا اس پہ چلتے رہے

مال والے حقارت سے تکتے رہے

طعن کرتے رہے ، ہاتھ ملتے رہے

ہم نے اُن پر کیا حرفِ حق سنگ زن

جن کی ہیبت سے دنیا لرزتی رہی

جن پہ آنسو بہانے کو کوئی نہ تھا

اپنی آنکھ ان کے غم میں برستی رہی

سب سے اوجھل ہوئے حکمِ حاکم پہ ہم

قید خانے سہے ، تازیانے سہے

لوگ سنتے رہے سازِ دل کی صدا

اپنے نغمے سلاخوں سے چھنتے رہے

خونچکاں دہر کا خونچکاں آئینہ

دکھ بھری خلق کا دکھ بھرا دل ہیں ہم

طبعِ شاعر ہے جنگاہِ عدل و ستم

منصفِ خیر و شر، حق و باطل ہیں ہم

333

The order of my execution

The crowd gathers to listen on judgement day
As I am accused of loving you;
The spirit of drunkards sets the tavern aflame
Though no alcohol lights the fire.

Having laid a Silent City all around
what does the tyrant's sword seek now?
His game of swords and daggers
finds its resolution in my blood.

Bring me the order for my execution; I too want to see
whose seals does the head of my death-warrant bear?

لاؤ تو قتل نامہ مرا

سننے کو بھیڑ ہے سرِ محشر لگی ہوئی
تہمت تمہارے عشق کی ہم پر لگی ہوئی

رندوں کے دم سے آتشِ مے کے بغیر بھی
ہے میکدے میں آگ برابر لگی ہوئی

آباد کر کے شہرِ خموشاں ہر ایک سُو
کس کھوج میں ہے تیغِ ستمگر لگی ہوئی

آخر کو آج اپنے لہو پر ہوئی تمام
بازی میانِ قاتل و خنجر لگی ہوئی

'لاؤ تو قتل نامہ مرا میں بھی دیکھ لوں
کس کس کی مُہر ہے سرِ محضر لگی ہوئی'

335

All that I have

All that I have is what you gave me,
Good things and bad,
Moments of togetherness, times of separation,
Distances and nearness.
The verse that I wrote
Was in your longing,
Reliving a moment of union
Or evenings of separation.
What will I be left with
Were I to follow what the moralist says?
I will have neither enemy nor friend.
Let me show you what is left of this city,
There stand the graves of the pure,
And there lie those who are truthful.
But, my love, let not the sorrow of the day get you down,
For who knows what joys He who writes the future
Has placed in store for us?

Translated by Khalid Hassan

سبھی کچھ ہے تیرا دیا ہوا

سبھی کچھ ہے تیرا دیا ہوا، سبھی راحتیں، سبھی کلفتیں
کبھی صحبتیں، کبھی فرقتیں، کبھی دوریاں، کبھی قربتیں

یہ سخن جو ہم نے رقم کئے، یہ ہیں سب ورق تری یاد کے
کوئی لمحہ صبح وصال کا، کئی شام ہجر کی مدتیں

جو تمہاری مان لیں ناصح، تو رہے گا دامنِ دل میں کیا
نہ کسی عدو کی عداوتیں، نہ کسی صنم کی مروتیں

چلو آؤ تم کو دکھائیں ہم جو بچا ہے مقتلِ شہر میں
یہ مزارِ اہلِ صفا کے ہیں، یہ ہیں اہلِ صدق کی تربتیں

مری جان آج کا غم نہ کر کہ نہ جانے کاتبِ وقت نے
کسی اپنے کل میں بھی بھول کر، کہیں لکھ رکھی ہوں مسرتیں

337

My Guests

The door opens
on my sadness;
there they come, my guests.
There she is, the evening
to lay a carpet of despair.
There goes the night
to speak of pain to the stars.
Here comes the morning
with its shining scalpel
to open the wound of memory.
Then there is afternoon
hiding whips of flame in its sleeve.
All these are my guests
who come to see my day and night.
But when they come
and when they go,
I do not know.
My thoughts are always
drifting homeward,
holding doubts ad suspicions,
asking many questions.

Translation by Mahmood Jamal

میرے ملنے والے

وہ در کھلا میرے غمکدے کا
وہ آ گئے میرے ملنے والے
وہ آ گئی شام، اپنی راہوں میں
فرشِ افسردگی بچھانے
وہ آ گئی رات چاند تاروں کو
اپنی آزردگی سنانے
وہ صبح آئی دمکتے نشتر سے
یاد کے زخم کو مٹانے
وہ دوپہر آئی، آستیں میں
چھپائے شعلوں کے تازیانے
یہ آئے سب میرے ملنے والے
کہ جن سے دن رات واسطہ ہے
یہ کون کب آیا، کب گیا ہے
نگاہ و دل کی خبر کہاں ہے
خیال سوئے وطن رواں ہے
سمندروں کی ایال تھامے
ہزار وہم و گماں سنبھالے
کئی طرح کے سوال تھامے

339

To those Palestinians martyred in foreign lands

Sweet earth of Palestine,
Wherever I went
carrying the burning scars of your humiliation,
nursing in my heart the longing
to make you proud,
your love, your memories went with me,
the fragrance of your orange groves went with me.

A crowd of unseen friends stood by me
and so many hands clasped by mine.
In distant lands, on dark lanes,
in alien cities, on nameless streets,
wherever the banner of my blood unfurled,
I've left a Palestinian flag.
Your enemies destroyed one Palestine;
my wounds created many more.

Translation by Mahmood Jamal

فلسطینی شہداء جو پردیس میں کام آئے

میں جہاں پر بھی گیا ارضِ وطن
تیری تذلیل کے داغوں کی جلن دل میں لئے
تری حُرمت کے چراغوں کی لگن دل میں لئے
تیری اُلفت، تری یادوں کی کسک ساتھ گئی
تیرے نارنج شگوفوں کی مہک ساتھ گئی

سارے ان دیکھے رفیقوں کا جلو ساتھ رہا
کتنے ہاتھوں سے ہم آغوش مرا ہاتھ رہا
دور پردیس کی بے مہر گزر گاہوں میں
اجنبی شہر کی بے نام و نشاں راہوں میں
جس زمیں پر بھی کھلا میرے لہو کا پرچم
لہراتا ہے وہاں ارضِ فلسطیں کا علم
تیرے اعدا نے کیا ایک فلسطیں برباد
میرے زخموں نے کئے کتنے فلسطیں آباد

341

For today's massacre at Gaza!

Don't cry little one...
your mother
just slept weeping..

Don't cry little one...
your father
moments ago..
bid his sorrows adieu!

Don't cry little one..
your brother
chased the butterfly of his dreams
to some far away distant worlds...

Don't cry little one...
your sisters coffin
had been send
to some mysterious land

Don't cry little one...
in your garden
dead sun had been given funeral bath
and few hopes buried along with that!

Don't cry little one...
mother, father, sister, brother
the moon and the sun
will make you cry more; if you cried!
may one day come back disguised,
to play with you; if you smiled!

فلسطینی بچے کے لئے لوری

مت رو بچے
رو رو کے ابھی
تیری امی کی آنکھ لگی ہے
مت رو بچے
کچھ ہی پہلے
تیرے ابا نے
اپنے غم سے رخصت لی ہے
مت رو بچے
تیرا بھائی
اپنے خواب کی تتلی پیچھے
دور کہیں پردیس گیا ہے
مت رو بچے
تیری باجی کا
ڈولا پرائے دیس گیا ہے
مت رو بچے
تیرے آنگن میں
مردہ سورج نہلا کے گئے ہیں
چند رما دفنا کے گئے ہیں
مت رو بچے
امی، ابا، باجی، بھائی
چاندا اور سورج
تو گر روئے گا تو یہ سب
اور بھی تجھ کو رلوائیں گے
تو مسکائے گا تو شاید
سارے اک دن بھیس بدل کر
تجھ سے کھیلنے لوٹ آئیں گے

343

We shall see

We shall see
It is necessary that we shall also see
That day which has been promised
Which is written with God's ink
We shall see

When the mountains of cruelty and torture
Will fly like pieces of cotton
Under the feet of the governed
This earth will quake
And over the head of the ruler
When lightening will thunder
We shall see

When from God's Mecca
All the idols will be shattered
Us people standing in the mosque
Will be elevated to a higher platform
All the crowns will be tossed
All the thrones will be toppled

Then only God's name will remain
Who is both absent and present
Who is both the observer and the view itself
When the anthem of truth will be raised
Who I am and you are as well

And the people of God will reign
Who I am and you are as well
We shall see
It is necessary that we shall also see
We shall see

Translation by Ayesha Kaljuvee

ہم دیکھیں گے

ہم دیکھیں گے
لازم ہے کہ ہم بھی دیکھیں گے
ہم دیکھیں گے
وہ دن کہ جس کا وعدہ ہے
جو لوحِ ازل میں لکھا ہے
ہم دیکھیں گے

جب ظلم و ستم کے کوہِ گراں
روئی کی طرح اڑ جائیں گے
ہم محکوموں کے پاؤں تلے
یہ دھرتی دھڑ دھڑ دھڑکے گی
اور اہلِ حکم کے سر اوپر
جب بجلی کڑ کڑ کڑکے گی
ہم دیکھیں گے

جب ارضِ خدا کے کعبے سے
سب بت اٹھوائے جائیں گے
ہم اہلِ صفا، مردودِ حرم
مسند پہ بٹھائے جائیں گے
سب تاج اچھالے جائیں گے
سب تخت گرائے جائیں گے
بس نام رہے گا اللہ کا
جو غائب بھی ہے، حاضر بھی
جو منظر بھی ہے، ناظر بھی
اٹھے گا انا الحق کا نعرہ
جو میں بھی ہوں اور تم بھی ہو
اور راج کرے گی خلقِ خدا
جو میں بھی ہوں اور تم بھی ہو
ہم دیکھیں گے
لازم ہے کہ ہم بھی دیکھیں گے

345

We are committed to loyalty

The blood of how many do you need, O my motherland,
so that your lustreless cheek may turn crimson?
How many sighs will soothe your heart
and how many tears make your deserts bloom?

How many pledges lie splintered down your hallways
and how many promises that were never honoured?
How many eyes were cursed by the evil eye
and how many dreams were stoned to death on your
highways?

It matters little what suffering was the lot of love –
Don't tell her how much I endured – it's all over now.
Lest the blood be washed off your hem –
what's done is done.

We're indeed committed to loyalty but, O my love,
should lovers be treated so coldly?
Let God keep your assembly going till eternity:
we're only guests for a moment, we don't really matters.

Translation by Shiv K. Kumar

346

ہم تو مجبورِ وفا ہیں

تجھ کو کتنوں کا لہو چاہئے اے ارضِ وطن
جو ترے عارض بے رنگ کو گلنار کریں
کتنی آہوں سے کلیجہ ترا ٹھنڈا ہو گا
کتنے آنسو ترے صحراؤں کو گلزار کریں

تیرے ایوانوں میں پرزے ہوئے پیماں کتنے
کتنے وعدے جو نہ آسودہ اقرار ہوئے
کتنی آنکھوں کو نظر کھا گئی بدخواہوں کی
خواب کتنے تری شہ راہوں میں سنگسار ہوئے

بلاکشانِ محبت پہ جو ہوا سو ہوا
جو مجھ پہ گزری مت اس سے کہو، ہوا سو ہوا
مبادا ہو کوئی ظالم ترا گریباں گیر
لہو کے داغ تو دامن سے دھو، ہوا سو ہوا

ہم تو مجبورِ وفا ہیں مگر اے جانِ جہاں
اپنے عشاق سے ایسے بھی کوئی کرتا ہے
تیری محفل کو خدا رکھے ابد تک قائم
ہم تو مہماں ہیں گھڑی بھر کے، ہمارا کیا ہے

347

You think...

You think
Cruelty will teach
The custom of faithfulness
And idols point out
The path to God.

No, it does not happen like this.

You think
By counting the corpses
Of murdered aspirations
You will calculate
The blood-money.

No, it does not happen like this.

Neither viles
Nor punishment
Are of any use
To bring about
Love and acceptance

No, it does not happen like this.

True sometimes
Every night
Every moment seems like Doomsday
But every morning does not heralds
The Day of Judgement.

No, it does not happen like this.

Feel the pulse
Of the present and look
At all those revolving skies
You think
All is over
And there's nothing to be done

No, it does not happen like this.

Translation by Daud Kamal

348

ستم سکھلائے گا رسمِ وفا

ستم سکھلائے گا رسمِ وفا   ایسے نہیں ہوتا
صنم دکھلائیں گے راہِ خدا   ایسے نہیں ہوتا

گنو سب حسرتیں جو خوں ہوئی ہیں تن کے مقتل میں
مرے قاتل! حسابِ   خوں بہا ایسے نہیں ہوتا

جہانِ دل میں کام آتی ہیں تدبیریں ،نہ تعزیریں
یہاں پیمانِ تسلیم و رضا   ایسے نہیں ہوتا

ہر اک شب ہر گھڑی گزرے قیامت یوں تو ہوتا ہے
مگر ہر صبح ہو روزِ جزا ایسے نہیں ہوتا

رواں ہے نبضِ دوراں،گردشوں میں آسماں سارے
جو تم کہتے ہو سب کچھ ہو چکا، ایسے نہیں ہوتا

Enchained by love

With the hangman's rope around the neck,
The singers continued to sing each day.
On the jingles resounding from their fetters,
The dancers revelled in their own way.
We neither belonged to one row nor the other.
Standing there on the pathway –
We looked at them,
And, silently shed the tears.
On returning home we looked at the flowers,
Only the paleness remained, where once it was red.
On feeling at our breast we discovered,
Only the pain pulsated, where once beat the heart.
Sometimes an imagined collar around the neck,
At times feet felt the dance of the chains.
And, then, one day Love, just like them,
With the bond of "Rope around the neck",
Dragged us along with their caravan.

Translation by Sain Sucha

عشق اپنے مجرموں کو پابجولاں لے چلا

دار کی رسّیوں کے گلو بند گردن میں پہنے ہوئے
گانے والے ہر اک روز گاتے رہے
پایلیں بیڑیوں کی بجاتے رہے
ناچنے والے دھوم میں مچاتے رہے
ہم نہ اِس صف میں تھے اور نہ نہ اُس صف میں تھے
راستے میں کھڑے اُن کو تکتے رہے
رشک کرتے رہے
اور چپ چاپ آنسو بہاتے رہے

لوٹ کر آ کے دیکھا تو پھولوں کا رنگ
جو کبھی سُرخ تھا زرد ہی زرد ہے
اپنا پہلو ٹٹولا تو ایسا لگا
دل جہاں تھا وہاں درد ہی درد ہے
گلو میں کبھی طوق کا واہمہ
کبھی پاؤں میں رقصِ زنجیر
اور پھر ایک دن عشق انہی کی طرح
رسن در گلو، پابجولاں ہمیں
اسی قافلے میں کشاں لے چلا

351

A song for the battle-field of Beirut

Beirut, adornment of this assembled world.
Beirut, exquisite as the gardens of Paradise.
Shattered mirrors
of the smiling eyes of children,
now star-lit
illuminate this city at night
and luminous is the land of Lebanon.
Beirut, adornment of this assembled world!
Those faces, [on them] blood as rouge
resplendent beyond beauty,
now their elegant splendour
glitter the lanes of this city
and radiant is the land of Lebanon.
Beirut, adornment of this assembled world.
Every deserted home, each one of the ruins
is equal in dignity to the citadels of Darius
[and] every warrior makes Alexander envious
[and] every daughter is same as Laila.
This city is standing since the beginning of time
This city would exist till the end of time.
Beirut, adornment of this assembled world.
Beirut, exquisite as the gardens of Paradise.

Translation by T. Beeth

ایک نغمہ کربلائے بیروت کے لئے

بیروت نگارِ بزمِ جہاں

بیروت بدیلِ باغِ جناں

بچوں کی ہنستی آنکھوں کے

جو آئینے چکنا چور ہوئے

اب اُن کے ستاروں کی لو سے

اس شہر کی راتیں روشن ہیں

اور رُخشاں ہے ارضِ لبناں

بیروت نگارِ بزمِ جہاں

جو چہرے لہُو کے غازے کی

زینت سے سوا پُرنُور ہوئے

اب اُن کے رنگیں پرتو سے

اس شہر کی گلیاں روشن ہیں

اور تاباں ہے ارضِ لبناں

بیروت نگارِ بزمِ جہاں

ہر ویراں گھر ، ہر ایک کھنڈر

ہم پایہ قصر دارا ہے

ہر غازی رشکِ اسکندر

ہر دختر ہمسرِ لیلیٰ ہے

یہ شہر ازل سے قائم ہے

یہ شہر ابد تک دائم ہے

بیروت نگارِ بزمِ جہاں

بیروت بدیلِ باغِ جناں

353

You tell us what to do

When we launched life
on the river of grief,
how vital were our arms, how ruby our blood.
With a few strokes, it seemed,
we would cross all pain,
we would soon disembark.
That didn't happen.
In the stillness of each wave we found invisible currents.
The boatmen, too, were unskilled,
their oars untested.
Investigate the matter as you will,
blame whomever, as much as you want,
but the river hasn't changed,
the raft is still the same.
Now you suggest what's to be done,
you tell us how to come ashore.

When we saw the wounds of our country
appear on our skins,
we believed each word of the healers.
Besides, we remembered so many cures,
it seemed at any moment
all troubles would end, each wound would heal completely.
That didn't happen: our ailments
were so many, so deep within us
that all diagnoses proved false, each remedy useless.
Now do whatever, follow each clue,
accuse whomever, as much as you will,
our bodies are still the same,
our wounds still open.
Now tell us what we should do,
you tell us how to heal these wounds.

Translation by Agha Shahid Ali

تم ہی کہو کیا کرنا ہے

جب دکھ کی ندیا میں ہم نے
جیون کی ناؤ ڈالی تھی
تھا کتنا کس بل بانہوں میں
لوہو میں کتنی لائی تھی
یوں لگتا تھا دو ہاتھ لگے
اور ناؤ پورم پار لگی
ایسا نہ ہوا، ہر دھارے میں
کچھ ان دیکھی منجدھاریں تھیں
کچھ مانجی تھے انجان بہت
کچھ بے پرکھی پتواریں تھیں
اب جو بھی چاہو چھان کرو
اب جتنے چاہو دوش دھرو
ندیا تو وہی ہے ناؤ وہی
اب تم ہی کہو کیا کرنا ہے
اب کیسے پار اترنا ہے
جب اپنی چھاتی میں ہم نے
اس دیس کے گھاؤ دیکھے تھے
تھا ویدوں پر وشواش بہت
اور یاد بہت سے نسخے تھے
یوں لگتا تھا بس کچھ دن میں
ساری پیتا کٹ جائے گی
اور سب گھاؤ بھر جائیں گے
ایسا نہ ہوا کہ روگ اپنے
کچھ اتنے ڈھیر پرانے تھے

کچھ مانجی تھے انجان بہت
کچھ بے پرکھی پتواریں تھیں
اب جو بھی چاہو چھان کرو
اب جتنے چاہو دوش دھرو
ندیا تو وہی ہے ناؤ وہی
اب تم ہی کہو کیا کرنا ہے
اب کیسے پار اترنا ہے
جب اپنی چھاتی میں ہم نے
اس دیس کے گھاؤ دیکھے تھے
تھا ویدوں پر وشواش بہت
اور یاد بہت سے نسخے تھے
یوں لگتا تھا بس کچھ دن میں
ساری پیتا کٹ جائے گی
اور سب گھاؤ بھر جائیں گے
ایسا نہ ہوا کہ روگ اپنے
کچھ اتنے ڈھیر پرانے تھے
ویدان کی ٹوہ کو پا نہ سکے
اور ٹوٹکے سب بیکار گئے
اب جو بھی چاہو چھان کرو
اب جتنے چاہو دوش دھرو
چھاتی تو وہی ہے گھاؤ وہی
اب تم ہی کہو کیا کرنا ہے
یہ گھاؤ کیسے بھرنا ہے

355

Painting of Faiz Ahmed Faiz by Hasan Mehdi, Karachi, 2011

356

Section Five

Life of Faiz Ahmed Faiz
A chronology

Faiz at Government College, Lahore, late 1960s

Faiz after doing his M.A.
from Government
College, Lahore, 1933

Life of Faiz Ahmed Faiz – A brief chronology

1911

- Faiz Ahmed was born on February 12th in a village, Kala Qadir near Sialkot in the province of Punjab. Faiz's mother was Sultan Fatima and father, Chaudhry Sultan Muhammed Khan, was an educated person who studied in London to become a barrister. Previously he worked in the court of Amir Abdul Rehman, the ruler of Afghanistan. While in London, he acted as the ambassador of Afghanistan in London. He also wrote the biography of Amir Abdul Rehman.

1915

- Faiz started memorizing the Holy Quran at the age of four.

1916

- Faiz started his formal education in the famous school of Moulvi Ibrahim Sialkoti, and learned Urdu, Persian and Arabic.

1921

- Faiz was admitted to the Scotch Mission High School in class IV.

1927

- Passed his Matriculation Examination in the 1st Division from Murray College, Sialkot and during this period learnt Persian and Arabic from Allama Iqbal's teacher, Shamsul Ullama Moulvi Syed Meer Hasan and Professor Yousuf Saleem Chishti, who taught Urdu.

1928

- Faiz penned his first poem.

1929

- Start writing poetry in Urdu language which was published in the college magazine.
- His lecturers included Patras Bukhari and Sufi Ghulam Mustafa Tabbasum.

1931

- Faiz's father died.
- Faiz passed his B.A. (Honours) in Arabic from the Government College, Lahore.

1932

- Faiz passed M.A. in English from the Government College, Lahore.

1934

- Faiz passed his M.A. in Arabic in the 1st Division, from Oriental College, Lahore.
- He wrote his first article.

1935

- Progressive Writers Association (PWA) was established in London by Sajjad Zaheer, Dr. Taseer and Dr. Mulk Raj Anand. PWA commenced its existence at a time when the world was experiencing a severe economic crisis which had a major impact on India.
- Faiz was appointed lecturer in English at M. A. O. College in Amritsar. Faiz remained in this post till 1940.
- At MAO College he met two leading activists of Progressive Writers Association (PWA) – Sahibzada Mahmoodul Zafar and Rasheeda Jehan. They introduce him to the Communist Manifesto. Under their influence, Faiz became an active member of PWA.
- Faiz became involved in the trade union movement and become a member of Amritsar Labour Federation.

358

Faiz in his army uniform,
Delhi, 1942

1936
- Faiz started a branch of Progressive Writers' Movement in Punjab.
- Faiz attended the All India conference of Progressive Writers Association held in Lucknow.

1937
- PWA held its first annual conference in Amritsar. This conference took place at the same time as the national conference of Kissan (Peasant) Movement.

1938
- Alys Catherine George went to India to visit her sister who was married to Faiz's friend Dr Taseer and met and fell in love with Faiz Ahmed Faiz. While in Britain, Alys was a member of the Communist Party of Great Britain.
- Faiz becomes the editor of a literary journal 'Adab-e-Lateef'; he remained in this position till 1942.

1940
- Faiz joined the Hailey College of Commerce in Lahore and stayed at the college till 1942.

1941
- In October Faiz married Alys and the ceremony was performed by Sheikh Abdullah, the Lion of Kashmir. Those who attended the ceremony included Dr MD Taseer.
- First collection of verses Naqsh-e Farayaadi (Sorrowful Imprints) was published.

1942
- Under the instruction from the Communist Party of India (CPI) Faiz joined the British Army as Captain and worked in the section of Morale Directorate in the department of Public Relations in Delhi. He remained in the army till December, 1946. He left the army as the attitude of the British government became increasingly hostile to Soviet Union.

1943
- Faiz was promoted to the rank of Major.
- Faiz was awarded the Member of British Empire (MBE) for his innovative strategies to promote propaganda against fascism within the Indian British Army.
- His first daughter Salima was born in Delhi.

1944
- Faiz was promoted to the rank of Lieutenant Colonel.

1945
- Second daughter, Maneeza was born in Shimla.

1946
- Resigned from the army and returned to Lahore.
- Faiz became the founding member and the secretary of the Punjab branch of the Progressive Writers' Association.

1947
- On February 4, the newspaper: Pakistan Times began regular publication with eight pages. The Quaid-i-Azam's name appeared under the masthead as founder, while the printline bore the names of Mian Iftikharuddin as publisher and printer and Faiz Ahmed Faiz as acting editor. Faiz also headed the editorial board of its sister publications, the Urdu daily Imroze and the literary and political weekly Lail-o-Nahar. Faiz was then only 37 years old. As the editor of the Pakistan Times, the English-language left-leaning newspaper from Lahore, he wrote on an array of issues from 1947 until his arrest in the Rawalpindi Conspiracy Case in 1951. All these publications were part of the Progressive Papers Limited.

Faiz with his family,
Lahore, 1951

- First issue of Pakistan Times was published on February 4 from Lahore.
- August 14, British India was divided into India and Pakistan. The partition led to massacre of millions of people on both sides of the borders. Millions became refugees and one of the greatest migrations, never witnessed in history, took place.
- Became the convenor of Labour Advisory Committee and remained in this capacity till 1951.
- In addition to becoming active in the Journalist Union; Faiz became the Vice President of Railway Trade Union as well the President of Postal Union Workers.

1948

- Became the editor of monthly magazine: 'Adb-e-Latif' and remained in this capacity till 1958.
- First issue of daily Imroze published on March 4 from Lahore and Karachi.
- Faiz became active in the newly formed Pakistan Trade Union Federation (PTUF). The PTUF was affiliated with the Communist Party of Pakistan (CPP), and he worked closely with other stalwarts like CR Aslam.
- Faiz visited the USA for the first time to attend the International Labour Conference held at San Francisco.
- Faiz became the Office Secretary of the Railway Workers Union which was established by Mirza Ibrahim.
- Daily Imroze was launched. Maulana Charagh Hassan Hasrat and Faiz Ahmed Faiz were its editors.
- Faiz became a member of the Executive Council of the World Peace Council and continued till 1970.
- In November PWA held its first annual conference in Lahore.

1949

- Attended World Labour Organisation conference held in Geneva as the representative of Pakistani trade union movement.

1950

- Progressive Writers Association was declared a political party by the government thus denying facilities accorded to cultural and literary organisations. Faiz participated in organising a petition against this decision.

1951

- Faiz became the Vice President of Pakistan Trade Union Confederation.
- USA increases its influence in Pakistan through military and bureaucracy to oppose the spread of Communist movement in Pakistan.
- On March 9th, in a radio speech, Liaqat Ali Khan, the prime minister of Pakistan announced the existence of a 'conspiracy' to overthrow the government by force. Faiz was arrested for seditious activities under Safety Act and charged in the Rawalpindi Conspiracy case, and having borne the hardships of imprisonment for four years and one month in the jails of Sargodha, Montgomery (now Sahiwal), Hyderabad and Karachi, was released on April 2nd, 1955. Others arrested with him included Syed Sajjad Zaheer (General Secretary of Communist Party of Pakistan) and about a dozen officers (ranking from major general to captain) and three civilians.

1952

- Faiz's elder brother, Tufail Ahmed died on July 12, while Faiz was in prison.
- The second volume of poems *Dast-e Saba* (Hand of the Zephyr) was published.

Faiz with Dr.
Radhakrishnan, President
of India, Delhi, 1955

1953

- While in prison, the Communist Part of Pakistan was banned.
- Faiz was hospitalised for treatment while still in prison.

1954

- Progressive Writers Association was also banned by the Pakistani government as a subversive organisation.

1955

- Faiz was released from prison on bail April and was acquitted on appeal in September.
- People's Publishing House published Victor Kiernan's first translation of a selection from Faiz. The book, Poems by Faiz, had the Urdu text, prepared by Kiernan's closest collaborator, Nazir Ahmed, the well-known teacher in Lahore. It also had the Urdu transliterated into English, and then two translations, one literal and the other with flourishes.
- After his release from prison, Faiz attended a mushiara in Delhi on the insistence of Pakistani ambassador in India, Raja Ghanzafar Ali Khan
- Faiz moved to London for a year.

1956

- Faiz attended the first Conference of Asian Writers in Delhi.
- Faiz headed a delegation of journalist to visit People Republic of China on the invitation of Chinese Journalist Association.
- Third volume of poems *Zindan Nama* (Prison Diary) was published.

1957

- Influential left-leaning weekly journal, *Lail-o-Nihar* started on January 20 from Lahore.
- Faiz became President of Associated Press of Pakistan.
- The political situation in the country deteriorated rapidly. Sandhurst-trained army officer and a pro-British bureaucrat, Iskandar Mirza, with support of the army destabilised the political and democratic institutions paving way for full-bloodied intervention of the army next year.

1958

- Faiz attended the inaugural conference of Asian and African Writers Association in Tashkent.
- Faiz penned few songs for films made by progressive film-makers in Pakistan.
- Military, under General Ayub Khan and with the tacit support of the USA, takes over the administration of the country. Hundreds of progressive activists, students, peasant leaders, trade unionists and writers, were arrested. Faiz was still in Soviet Union when the army coup-d'état took place in October.
- Faiz was watching these developments from abroad. From Soviet Union he went to London. He was arrested after his return in December under the notorious Public Safety Act, enacted by British to quell any dissent. Others who were arrested with him included Sibte Hasan, Dada Ferozuddin Mansur, Fazal Ilahi Qurban and Dada Amir Haider. Faiz, for a long time was kept in solitary confinement at the Lahore Fort.
- Faiz resigns as the chief Editor of Progressive Papers limited.

1959

- Dada Ferozuddin Mansur, the veteran communist leader, was already a sick man when placed in detention at the notorious Lahore Fort, died in February. Faiz was greatly affected by this loss.
- Faiz was released in April from illegal detention by the military regime. Appointed as Secretary, Pakistan Arts Council and worked in that capacity till 1962.

Faiz welcomed on his return from England, Lahore, 1964

- The military regime, through an ordinance, takes over the control of Progressive Papers Limited and all the associated publication.
- *Jago Hua Savera* (Day Shall Dawn), a film directed by A.J. Kardar and script and lyrics penned by Faiz released. The film was adopted by Faiz from 1936 novel of Manik Bannerji: Padma Nadir Majhi (Boatman of the Padma). The film was shot in East Bengal. The film attracted international appreciation and acknowledgement. Faiz made some documentaries. His documentary on poet Mohammad Iqbal attracted large audiences in Pakistan. However, another film: 'Door Hai Sukh Ka Gaon' (Far is the Village of Peace) was never released. He also had vital participation in films like *Sukh Ka Sapna* and *Qasam Uss Waqt Kee.*

1962

- Faiz was awarded the Lenin Peace Prize, the Soviet Union equivalent of the Nobel Prize. Despite the warnings of the pro-American military government not to accept the award, Faiz proceeded to Moscow to receive the award. Faiz was the first Asian poet, others awarded with Lenin Peace Award included WEB Du Bois, Fidel Castro, Pablo Picasso, Bertold Brecht, Pablo Neruda, Mahmoud Darwish, Salvador Allende, Kwame Nkrumah and Angela Davis. In accepting the Lenin Prize, Faiz said: "Every foundation you see is defective, except the foundation of love, which is faultless… It takes moral courage to love even when you see the ugly face of tyranny'.
- After receiving the award, Faiz visited Britain, Hungary, Cuba and Lebanon. Faiz to remain in Britain till 1964, it was the first period of exile faced by the poet. During this period he visited Lebanon, Syria, Iraq, Egypt and Algeria. The decision to leave Pakistan was taken with heavy heart.

1963

- *Meezan* (Scales), a collection of critical articles on literature published.

1964

- Returned from London and settled down in Karachi and was appointed as Principal of Abdullah Haroon College in a under-privileged part of Karachi. He also joined Haji Abdullah Haroon Education Trust as the Vice President.
- Became Vice President of Pakistan Arts Council, Karachi and remained in this position till 1972.

1965

- General Ayub Khan wins another term in office through rigged elections. Faiz wrote a poem in response to murderous spree of military-backed thugs to punish those in Karachi who dare to vote against the military.
- In the 1965 war between India and Pakistan, he worked in an honorary capacity in the Department of Information.
- Faiz refused to join the group of poets who obliged the military regime by penning patriotic and chauvinist songs for whipping emotion against India. Instead, he wrote his famous poems: Sepahi ka Murssia (Eulogy to a Soldier).
- *Harf harf* (Word, word) a volume base on Faiz's articles was published.
- A major literary journal: *Aafkar* comes out with a special issue on Faiz Ahmed Faiz.
- Fourth volume of verses *Dast-e Teh-e Sang* (The Hand Under the Stone) was published.

1968

- Established *Idara-e-Yadgar-e-Ghalib*, an institute to promote the work on one of the leading nineteenth century Urdu poets, Mirza Ghalib in Karachi.
- Faiz undertook an extensive tour of Soviet Union.

Faiz with friend Sajjad
Zaheer, Moscow, 1970

1969

• Faiz organised the centenary celebrations of Mirza Ghalib in Karachi.

1970

• Lail-o-Nihar, the fortnightly journal commenced its publication after the crackdown of the regime against the press. Faiz was appointed the Chief Editor, the journal lasted another 18 months.

1971

• *Sar-e Wadi-e Sina* (Summit of the Valley of Sinai) the fifth volume of verses was published.

• *Saleeben Meray Dureecha Par* (Crosses on My Windows), a collection of articles was published.

• The brutal military crackdown carried by the Pakistani army in East Bengal had a major impact on Faiz. Thousands were massacred and millions were forced to become refugees in neighbouring India to avoid death. Faiz penned a number of poems to oppose the genocide which resulted in Indian armed intervention and the independence of Bangladesh.

1972

• Faiz wanted to leave the country after the 1971 war with India. However, he was convinced by Zulfiqar Ali Bhutto to become the Director of the Arts Council of Pakistan, Islamabad. He has to remain in this post for five years, seen as the most literary barren years. He managed to produce very little poetic output during this period.

• He visited India and Soviet Union.

1973

• Faiz attended the Asian and African Writers conference in Alma-ta.

• Faiz visited Philippines and Indonesia.

• A collection of essays, interviews, plays and speeches: *Mutah-e-Loh-o-Qalam* was published.

1974

• Faiz visited Bangladesh, as part of an official delegation as an advisor on culture. This visit prompted him to write '*Hum ke thehre ajnabi*' (We who have been rendered strangers).

1975

• Faiz awarded the Afro-Asian Literary prize.

• *Rat di rat* was published

1976

• Faiz received the Afro-Asian Literary Lotus prize.

1977

• General Zia-ul-Haq came to power in a military coup. And imposed martial law. He unleashed reactionary and fascistic terror in the name of Nizam-e-Mustafa (Islamic system). The lives of many progressive individual became unbearable in Pakistan.

• The elected Prime Minister, Zulfiqar Ali Bhutto, was arrested, tried and hanged in the prison in Lahore.

• Faiz went to India at the invitation of Jawaharlal Nehru University where he was accorded an honorary doctorate. He was offered visiting professorship by the university. Faiz was also offered the position of Iqbal Chair at the University of Kolkata. However, Faiz opted to become the Editor-in-Chief of Lotus, journal of Afro-Asian Writers' Association.

• Faiz hosted a major international Conference on Mohammad Iqbal in Lahore.

Faiz with writer of Abdullah Malik and singer Nayyara Noor on his last birthday party, Lahore, 1984

1978

- In February went into self-imposed exile for a period of five years. Faiz went to war-torn Beirut and worked with Yasser Arafat of the Palestine Liberation Organisation (PLO) while in charge of editing the International literary Journal, Lotus. He remained in Beirut till 1982. Lotus was published in Arabic and English and in German by the Journalist Association of Democratic Republic of Germany.

- Alys Faiz said that 'It was an opportunity for Faiz to write and to work away from the cramping conditions of Pakistan, which under general Zia's dictatorship had become impossible. So instead of separation we choose a pleasant exile'. Faiz confirmed this by saying that 'It is not that our struggle has ended. Only thing is that I am not as young as before, it is difficult to endure physical punishment in the old age. My spirit is still prepared to face physical punishment but body is reluctant'.

- Sixth volume of verses *Sham-e-shahr-e-Yaran* (Evening of Lover's City) was published

1979

- Faiz penned one of his most famous poems: *Dua* (Prayer) directly challenging Zia's military regime.

1980

- *Mere Dil, Mere Musaafir* (My Heart, My Traveller), seventh volume of verses was published. Faiz dedicated this book to the Palestinian leader, Yasser Arafat.

- Reminisce of his travels in Soviet Union: *Mah-o-sal-i ashnai – Yadoon ka majmoa* (Months and Years of Acquaintance) was published.

1981

- Faiz attended a literary event in Toronto, Canada.

1982

- Left Beirut after Israeli invasion of Lebanon. Faiz came back to Lahore, Pakistan.

1984

- *Nuskha-Hai-Wafa*, was published.
- Faiz died in Lahore on 20th November.

1985

- Faiz Amman Mela was initiated as an annual event to pay homage to Faiz.

1987

- 'The True Subject: Selected Poems of Faiz Ahmed Faiz', translated Naomi Lazard was published.
- Eight volume of verses: *Ghabar-e-Ayam* (Dust of Days) was published posthumously.

1991

- Agha Shahid Ali translation of Faiz's poems 'The Rebel's Silhouette' was published.

1995

- Revised edition of 'The Rebel's Silhouette: Selected Poems', translated by Agha Shahid Ali was published.

1988

- 'Poems of Faiz Ahmad Faiz: A Poet of the Third World', translated by Mohammed Zakir, and M.N. Menai was published.

2002

- 'Selected poems of Faiz Ahmad Faiz: With original Urdu text, Roman and Hindi transliteration and poetical translation into English' was published.
- '100 Poems by Faiz Ahmed Faiz, 1911-1984', edited by Sarvat Rahman was published.

Faiz Centeneary logo
produced by Progressive
Writers' Association,
Pakistan, 2011

2011

- The year was officially declared the Faiz Ahmed Faiz Century Year by the governments of India and Pakistan.
- Progressive Writer Association in Pakistan issued the Centenary Declaration.
- Hundred of celebratory events were organised in more than thirty countries around the world.
- In Britain more than fifty political, literary, and cultural events were organised to pay homage to one of the greatest poets of twentieth century.

Painting of Faiz Ahmed Faiz by Hasan Mehdi, Karachi, 2011

Section Six
Bibliography

iz receiving a warm welcome at Hyderabad, 1978

Bibliography on Faiz Ahmed Faiz

Naqhsh-e-Faryaadi, Faiz's first collection of poems was published in 1941 when Faiz was 30 years old. At the time of publication, he was already established as one of the leading poet as his poems were appearing in many literary journals and newspapers. Faiz participation in Mushiaras (poetry gatherings) throughout India also made him a familiar name. There are eight poetry books published over four decades. His last collection of poems was published after his death in 1987. In 2008 his collective poetry volume was published from London.

Faiz is the one of the most translated South Asian poet in English. Faiz Ahmed Faiz received the Lenin Peace Prize in 1962 and was a nominee for the Nobel Prize. Over the last fifty years, a number of his translations have been published. The most celebrated one was produced in 1962 by his friend and fellow communist from Scotland, Victor Kiernan.

The universality of Faiz's poetry spurred many other excellent translations. In addition to the publications mentioned below, his poems have been translated by many individuals. Faiz poems have been included in several anthologies, too numerous to mention here. In addition to English, Faiz's work has been translated in many other languages including Arabic, Baluchi, Bengali, Chinese, Czech, Farsi, French, German, Hindi, Italian, Japanese, Kazakh, Nepali, Russian, Polish, Punjabi, Sindhi, Singhalese, Tajik, Turkmen, Swahili and Uzbek. Recently some of his poems have been translated in Danish.

Poetry in Urdu

Naqhsh-e Faryaadi (1941) Muktaba-e-Karvan, Lahore, 112pp.

Dast-e Saba (1952) Azad Kitab Ghar, Delhi, 94pp.

Zindan Nama (1956) Maktabah-e-Karvan, Lahore, 100pp.

Dast-e-Teh-e Sang (1965) Maktabah-e-Karvan, Lahore, 79pp.

Sar-e Wadi-e Sina (1971) Muktaba-e-Danyal, Karachi, 128pp.

Shaam-e Shehr-e Yaaran (1978) Maktabah-e-Karvan, Lahore, 114pp.

Meray Dil, Meray Musafir (1981) Maktaba-e-Danyal, Karachi, 93pp.

Ghubaar-e Ayyaam (1987) 35pp. (incorpoatd in Nuskha hai Wafa)

Nuskha Hai Wafa (Collected Works) (2005) Educational Publishing House, London, 703pp.

Translations in English

Poems by Faiz (1962) Translated by Victor Kiernan, George Allen & Unwin (London) 288pp. Reprints: (1971) Oxford University Press (New Delhi); (1973) Oxford University Press (Karachi); (1987) Vanguard Books (Lahore) and (2010) Oxford University Press (Karachi)

Faiz Ahmed Faiz – Eleven Poems and Introduction (1971) Translated by C. M. Naim and Carlo Coppola, Dialogue, Calcutta (English)

Poems by Faiz (1982) Translated by Ikram Azam, Nairang-e-Khayal Publications (Rawalpindi), 59pp.

Selected Poems of Faiz Ahmed Faiz (1984) Translated by Daud Kamal, Pakistan Publishing House (Karachi), 79pp.

The Unicorn and the Dancing Girl (1984) Translated by Daud Kamal & Edited by Khalid Hasan, Publishing House (Karachi) 79pp. Reprint: (1988) Independent Publishing Co. (London) 113pp and (1988) Allied Publications (Ahmadabad), 113pp.

An Elusive Dawn: Selection from the Poetry of Faiz Ahmed Faiz (1985) Translated by Mahbub-ul-Haq, Pakistan National Commission for UNESCO (Islamabad), 87pp.

Memory (1987) Translated by Sain Sucha, Vudya Kitaban Forlag (Sollentuna, Sweden), 67pp.

Poemes: Faiz Ahmed Faiz (1979) Translated by Laiq Babree, Seghers, Paris, 119pp.

Yaqub's Selection and Translation of Poems by Faiz Ahmed Faiz (1987) Translated by M. Yaqub, Jacobs Newsagents (Nottingham), 139pp.

The True Subject: Selected Poems of Faiz Ahmed Faiz (1988) Translated by Naomi Lazard, Princeton University Press (Princeton), 133pp. Reprint: (1988) Vanguard Books (Lahore), 133pp.

The Rebel's Silhouette (1991) Translated by Agha Shahid Ali, University of Massachusetts Press, Amherst, 102pp. Reprint: (1991) Oxford University Press, New Delhi, 101pp. and (1995) University of Massachusetts Press, Amherst, 101pp.

Bulleh Shah's devotionals and Faiz Ahmed Faiz's Dast-e Saba (1992) Translation by Muhammad Sadiq Khan Satti, National Book Foundation, Islamabad, 105pp.

Faiz Ahmed Faiz 1911-1984: Urdu Poet of Social Realism (1993) Translated by Estelle Dryland, Vanguard Books, Lahore, pp306

Selected Poems of Faiz Ahmed Faiz (1995) Translated by Shiv K. Kumar, Viking Penguin Books India, New Delhi, 205pp.

Faiz Ahmed Faiz – Selected Poems (1996) Translated by Safdar Rasheed, Umair Publishers, Lahore, 72pp.

Poems of Faiz Ahmed Faiz: A Poet of the Third World (1995) Translated by Mu ammad Zakir & M. N. Menai, M.D. Publications Limited, New Delhi, 83pp.

100 Poems of Faiz Ahmed Faiz (2002) Translated by Sarvat Rahman, Abhinav Publications, New Delhi, 349pp.

Poetry of Faiz Ahmed Faiz: Urdu Text, Roman and Hindi Translation, and English Poetic Translation (2002) Translated by Khawaja Tariq Mahmood, Abhinav Publications, New Delhi, 344pp.

In English, Faiz Ahmed Faiz: A Renowned Urdu Poet (2008) Translated by Riz Rahim, Xlibris Corporation, New Delhi, 474pp.

O City of Lights: Faiz Ahmed Faiz – Selected Poetry and Biographical Notes (2006) Edited by: Khalid Hasan, Open University Press, Karachi, 291pp.

The Best of Faiz Ahmed Faiz (2010) Selection and Translation by Kuldip Salil, Rajpal & Sons, New Delhi, 173pp.

Other publications by Faiz Ahmed Faiz

Meezan: Tanqeedi Mazamine (1963) Urdu Academy Sind, Karachi – a collection of critical essays (Urdu)

Saleeben Meray Darechey Mein (1971) Muktaba-e-Danyal, Karachi, pp114 – 135 letters from prison (Urdu)

Humari Qoumi Saqafat (1972) Ghalib Library, Karachi – a collection of articles on Pakistani culture (Urdu)

Mutah-e-Loh-o-Qalam (1973) Muktaba-e-Danyal (Karachi) 360pp – a collection of speeches, articles, letters, broadcasts, reviews and interviews, 360pp. (Urdu)

Safarnama-e-Cuba (1973) National Publishing House, Lahore, 82pp. (Urdu)

Mah-o-Saal-e-Ashnaee: Yadoon ka Mujama (1980) Muktaba-e-Danyal, Karachi, 136pp – a collection of articles (Urdu)

Pakistani Culture aur Qaumi Tushuks ki Talash (1988) Edited by Sheema Majeed, Ferozsons, Lahore, 114pp. – a collection of articles on culture and identity (Urdu)

Culture and Identity: Selected English Writings of Faiz (2005) Edited by Sheema Majeed, Oxford University Press, Karachi, 261pp. (English)

Faiz Ahmed Faiz aur Pakistani Saqafat: Thairain aur Taqreerein (2006), Edited by Sheema Majeed, Pakistan Studies Centre, University of Karachi, Karachi (Urdu)

Song for This Day: 52 Poems by Faiz Ahmed Faiz (2009), Edited by Saleema Hashmi & Shoib Hashmi, Sang-e-Meel Publications, 2009 (English)

Who Jab Aye Hain Maail-e-ba Karam Aye hain: Faiz kay interviews, Peoples Publishing House, Lahore (Urdu)

Two Loves: Faiz's Letters from Jail (2011) Edited by Kyla Pasha & Salima Hashmi, Sang-e-Meel Publications, Lahore (English)

Publications on Faiz Ahmed Faiz – Selected Bibliography

The centenary year provided an impetus for writers to critical examine the role played by Faiz Ahmed Faiz on the contemporary political scene. A number of new publications emerged in the last few years. The re-interpretation of Faiz's poetry in the current context is essential to understand the politics and the world view of one of the most important radical South Asian poets in the twentieth century. Faiz's writings, particularly his poetry, transcend generations and geographic boundaries and it is as relevant today as it was in twentieth century.

The selected biography lists some of the key publications on Faiz. There are numerous articles on various aspects of Faiz's life and work. Edward Said, the Palestinian scholar and the famous Chilean poet and Nobel Laureate, Pablo Neruda have paid rich tributes to Faiz. Many of his contemporaries such as Sajjad Zaheer, Sibte Hasan, Ahmad Nadeem Qasmi, Ayub Mirza, Habib Jalib, Ahmad Faraz, Amin Mughal, Ralph Russell, Abdullah Malik, Victor Kreinan, have penned a number of articles on Faiz. A number of journals have produced specialist issues on Faiz; many broadcast channels including BBC have produced documentaries on the poet, the most celebrated was produced by Faris Kermani, a known British-based film director. We have decided to provide information on small selection of books; a more detailed research is required to assemble a detailed bibliography on the poet. The Faiz Ghar, a Lahore-based organisation, dedicated to Faiz Ahmed Faiz, has been preserving a range of material, including letters, photographs, films and articles relating to Faiz, for future generations of researchers.

ABBASSI, Nasim (Editor) (1978) *Naqad-e-Faiz*, Book Service, New Delhi (Urdu)

ABEDI, Syed Taqi (2011) *Faiz Fehmi: Tehqiq o Tanqeed,* Multimedia Affairs, Lahore, 1,043pp. (Urdu)

AFKAAR (1973) *Special Issue on Faiz Ahmed Faiz,* Muktaba-e-Afkaar, Karachi (Urdu)

AMDAD, Ateeq (1991) *Faiz Ahad aur Saheary,* Muktaba-e-Aalia, Lahore (Urdu)

AHMAD, Aftab (1999) *Faiz Ahmed Faiz: Shair aur Shaksh,* Muktaba-e-Danyal, Karachi, 152pp. (Urdu)

AHMAD, Khalil, *Mukalmat-e-Faiz,* Sang-e-Meel Publications (Urdu)

AHMAD, Ishtiaq (2010) *Faiz Ahmed ki Shayeri,* Kitab Sirai, Lahore (Urdu)

AHMAD, Vasi (1977) *Inqilabi Shair – Faiz Ahmed Faiz,* Vasi Ahmad, Lucknow, 110pp. (Urdu)

AHMAD, Sayyid Vasif (1990) *Kisht-i Faiz: Tanqeedi Mazamin ka Majmuah,* Book Emporium, Patna, 200pp. (Urdu)

ANJUM, Khaleeq (1985) *Faiz Ahmed Faiz – Tanqeedi Jiaza,* Anjuman Taraqi-e-Urdu, New Delhi (Urdu)

ARAF, Muhammad (2010) *Faiz Ahmed Faiz: Rooman aur Shayeri,* Writers Publications, Lahore (Urdu)

ARIF, Ifthikar (2011) *Kalam-e-Faiz ba khat-e-Faiz,* Sang-e-Meel Publications, Lahore, 239pp. (Urdu)

ASHRAFI, Shafiq (1993) *Faiz, afkar o iqdar,* Nusrat Publishers, Lucknow, 264pp. (Urdu)

ASHRAFI, Shafiq (1993) *Faiz ba aisyat naqqad,* Nusrat Publishers, Lucknow, 104pp. (Urdu)

BANO, Syeda Birjees (2000) *Faiz Ahmed Faiz ki Urdu sahafat,* Pakistan Studies Centre, University of Karachi, Karachi, 158pp. (Urdu)

CHOUDARY, Nusrat (1987) *Faiz ki Shairi: Ek Muttala,* Nigarshat, Lahore, 220pp

CHOUDARY, Nusrat (1995*) Faiz Ahmed Faiz, rivayat aur infiradiyat,* Simant Parkashan, New Delhi, 352pp (Urdu)

CHUGTAI, Mirza Saeeduzzafar (2008) *Faiz ka sarmayah-yi sukhan,* Ejukeshani Publising House, New Delhi, 142pp. (Urdu)

DILHLAVI, Murattib Amar (1984) *Faiz Ahmed Faiz ki shairi Urdu-Hindi men yakja,* Star Publications, New Delhi, 153pp. (Urdu)

FAIZ, Alys (1985) *Dear Heart:To Faiz in Prison (1951-1955),* Ferozsons, Lahore (English)

FAIZ, Alys (1993) *Over My Shoulder,* The Frontier Post Publications, Lahore (English)

FIRDAUSI, Amirah (1995) *Rivayati qadron ka jadid shair: Faiz Ahmed Faiz,* Muktabah-e-Firdausiyeh, Bihar, 96pp. (Urdu)

HAIDAR, Salah-ud-Din, *Jinhain jurm-e-ishq par naaz tha: Faiz Ahmed Faiz – Shaksiat-o-fun,* Sang Meel Publications, Lahore (Urdu)

HAMID, Ajmal (2008) *Ahang-i kalam-i Faiz,* Anis Kitab Ghar, Tonk, 176pp. (Urdu)

HASAN, Sibte (1987) *Sukhn dar Sukhn,* Maktaba-e-Danyal, Karachi, 109pp. (Urdu)

HASAN, Mirza Zafarul (1983) *Khoon-e-dil ki Kusheed,* Muktaba-e-Usloob, Karachi (Urdu)

HASHMI, A. A. (2009) *Jadid Urdu shairi par Faiz Ahmed Faizz ke asarat,* Nargis Publications, Kolkata, 448pp. (Urdu)

HUSSAIN, Ashfaq (1992) *Faiz kay Mughrabi Hawaley,* Jang Publishers, Lahore (Urdu)

HUSSAIN, Ashfaq (1992) *Faiz Habib-e-Umber Dast,* SMP Publications, Lahore (Urdu)

HUSSAIN, Imdad (1989) *An Introduction to the poetry of Faiz Ahmed Faiz,* Vanguard Books, Lahore (English)

HUSSAIN, Yousuf & NADEEM, Rawish (2011) *Faiz Ahmed Faiz – Faiz Sadi: Muntakhab Mazameen,* Muqtadira Qoumi Zaban, Islamabad, 475pp. (Urdu)

IQBAL, Sarfraz (1989) *Faiz Ahmad Faiz ke khutut Begam Sarfaraz Iqbal ke nam,* Mavara Publishers, Lahore, 126pp (Urdu)

KALSASI, Surajita (2003) *Romamsa tom yatharatha taka de do kawi Mohana Singha ate Faiza Ahimada Faiza - kawika samanantara adhiaina,* Taralocana Pabalisharaza, Chandigarh, 111pp. (Punjabi)

KAZAKOVA, Rimma (1986) *Faiz Memorial Lecture,* Urdu Markaz, London (English)

KULLAR, K. K. (1985) *Faiz Ahmed Faiz, Idarah Fakr-i-Jadid,* New Delhi, 166pp. (Urdu)

LODHI, Yousuf (1987) *Faiz, Vanguard books,* Lahore, 176pp (Urdu)

MADNI, Aziz Ahmad (1988) *Aj bazar men pa bah jaulan chalo: Faiz Ahmed Faiz, ek mutalah,* Urdu Academy, Karachi, 136pp. (Urdu)

MAHALI, Shahid (Editor) (1988) *Faiz Ahmed Faiz: Uks aur Jahateen,* Marava Publishers, Lahore, 416pp. (Urdu)

MAJEED, Sheema (Editor) *Bateen Faiz Say,* Rothas Books, Lahore, 215pp. (Urdu)

MALIK, Abdul Raoof (1988) *Faiz ki shairi ka naya dour,* Peoples Publishing House, Lahore, 143pp. (Urdu)

MALIK, Abdullah (1985) *Lao tu Qatal Nama: Ek Tujzia Ek Nazrana,* Kausar Publishers, Lahore, 224pp. (Urdu)

MALIK, Fateh Mohammed (1988) *Faiz, Sang Meel* Publications, Lahore (Urdu)

MIRZA, Ayub (2003) *Faiz Nama, Classic,* Lahore (Urdu)

MIRZA, Ayub (1977) *Hum Kay Tehrey Ajnabi,* Al-Kitab Printers, Lahore, 380pp. (Urdu)

NASIR, Agha, *Hum Jeetay Ji Musroof Rahey: Faiz Ahmed Faiz ki Shaiari,* KhaliSang-e-Meel Publications, (Urdu)

QUERSHI, Abu Saeed (1986) *Faizan-e-Faiz,* Muktaba-e-Usloob, Karachi, 184pp. (Urdu)

RAZMI, Saqib (1986) *Faiz: Mohabbat-o-Inquilab ka Shair,* Aieena-e-Adab, Lahore, 319pp. (Urdu)

SADAF, Sughra (2005) *Faiz ka Imrani Falsafa,* Multi media Publications, Lahore (Urdu)

SALIM, Ahmad (Editor) (1990) *Mauj-e-Zar: Faiz Ahmad ke idariyon aur nadir tahriron ka majmua,* Nigarashat, Lahore, 312pp. (Urdu)

SALIM, Ahmad (2011) *Faiz: Yadain, Battain: Kab Yaad mein tera saath nahin,* Sang-e-Meel Publications, 112pp. (Urdu)

SHAKIR, Shakir Hussain, *Teri Yadoon kay Naqoosh: Articles on Faiz Ahmed Faiz,* Sang-e-Meel Publications, (Urdu)

SOHAIL, Khalid & HUSSAIN, Ashfaq (2011) *Faiz – A Poet of Peace from Pakistan: His Poetry, Personality and Philosophy,* Pakistan Study Centre, University of Karachi, Karachi, 496pp. (English)

TUNSAVI, Tahir (1989) *Faiz ki Takhliqee Shakhsiat,* Sang-e-Meel Publications, Lahore (Urdu)

VASILIEVA, Ludmila (2007) *Faiz Ahmed Faiz, Translated by Asama Farooqi,* Open University Press, Karachi, 296pp. (Urdu)

ZAHOOR, Tanvir (2011) *Faiz aur Punjabi,* Jamoohri Publications, Lahore, 200pp. (Urdu)

ZIA, Abdulqavi (2001) *Faiz Shinasi,* Miyar Publications, New Delhi, 80pp. (Urdu)

ZIA, Sajid (2010) *Faiz Ahmed Faiz,* Alim, Lahore (English)

ZULFI, Tasleem Elahi (2011) *Faiz Ahmed Faiz Beruit Mein – Jalawatni ka Doosra Parao: Yaddashteen,* Pakistan Academy of Letters, Islamabad, 83pp. (Urdu)